Praise for *Poetics of Value*

"*Poetics of Value* is a riveting disquisition on the disruptive temporalities of proscribed social life lived in defiant survival of capitalist subsumption. Staging an important, necessary theoretical-political debate between value-critical Marxisms and critical theories of racial capitalism (in Black, feminist, queer, and postcolonial studies), Mason offers shimmering literary and philosophical readings that illuminate the insurgent presence of ante-capitalist sociality pressing against and beyond the power of value. Erudite, innovative, and sociable, Mason gives us a compelling, inspired performance of radical theory, commitment, and poetic praxis, so vital in today's fight against these brutal, late capitalist times."

NEFERTI X.M. TADIAR, author of *Remaindered Life*

"Through original readings of both poetry and theoretical texts, Mason reveals some of the exciting ways in which contemporary Marxisms and Black studies coincide or resonate when each draws on the principle that resistance is prior to power."

MICHAEL HARDT, author of *The Subversive Seventies*

"Elliot C. Mason's book charts a new and important path through some of the most pressing theoretical and poetic debates of our time, bringing together a novel mix of Marxism, insurgent Black social theory, and contemporary US poetry."

ASHLEY J. BOHRER, author of *Marxism and Intersectionality*

"A groundbreaking intervention at the intersection of Marxist value-form theory, poetry and poetics, and Black studies, *Poetics of Value* makes the compelling case that poetry might not only reveal but actually enact forms of life irreducible to capital, opening the possibility of revolutionary thought and practice in the ruins of the value-form."

DANIEL KANE, Uppsala University

Historical Materialism Book Series

The Historical Materialism Book Series is a major publishing initiative of the radical left. The capitalist crisis of the twenty-first century has been met by a resurgence of interest in critical Marxist theory. At the same time, the publishing institutions committed to Marxism have contracted markedly since the high point of the 1970s. The Historical Materialism Book Series is dedicated to addressing this situation by making available important works of Marxist theory. The aim of the series is to publish important theoretical contributions as the basis for vigorous intellectual debate and exchange on the left.

The peer-reviewed series publishes original monographs, translated texts, and reprints of classics across the bounds of academic disciplinary agendas and across the divisions of the left. The series is particularly concerned to encourage the internationalization of Marxist debate and aims to translate significant studies from beyond the English-speaking world.

For a full list of titles in the Historical Materialism Book Series available in paperback from Haymarket Books, visit: www.haymarketbooks.org/series_collections/1-historical-materialism.

Poetics of Value

The Primacy of Insurgency as Marxist Methodology

Elliot C. Mason

Haymarket Books
Chicago, IL

First published in 2025 by Brill Academic Publishers, The Netherlands

Published in paperback in 2026 by
Haymarket Books
P.O. Box 180165
Chicago, IL 60618
773-583-7884
www.haymarketbooks.org

ISBN: 979-8-88890-896-9

Distributed to the trade in the US through Consortium Book Sales and Distribution (www.cbsd.com) and internationally through Ingram Publisher Services International (www.ingramcontent.com).

This book was published with the generous support of Lannan Foundation, Wallace Action Fund, and the Marguerite Casey Foundation.

Special discounts are available for bulk purchases by organizations and institutions. Please call 773-583-7884 or email info@haymarketbooks.org for more information.

Cover art and design by David Mabb. Cover art developed from *Dialectical Proposition 9, Vavara Stepanova 'Textile Design in Black and White' on 'Kelmscott Manor' tea towel*, fabric mounted on plywood (2020).

Printed in the United States.

Library of Congress Cataloging-in-Publication data is available.

Contents

Acknowledgments

I lovingly give thanks to all my friends who have shared their survival with this project. They have formed the life of *Poetics of Value*. Those friends are: Eugenia Lapteva, Judith Kiros, Alessandro Coletti, Maria Wallstam, Mikael Omstedt, Leonard Driscoll, Julia Lindblom, Greg Darwin, Valentina Moro, Gustav Almestad, Samuel Girma, Daniel Kane, Cecília Tümler, Anton Ösgård, Jens Eriksson, Carlos Lozano, Saleh Abdelaziz, Ruben Hordijk, Fanny Söderbäck, Jorge Alvar, Pepe Chozas, Klara Kaliger, Bruno Vilhar, Brendan Sibley, Max Alletzhauser, Gabriel Cabral, Vanessa Noack, Fanny Wendt Höjer, Sarah Philipson Isaac, Sara Edenheim, and everyone who attended the reading group I hosted with Centrum för Marxistiska Samhällsstudier in Stockholm (special thanks to those who always attended and gave me endless opportunities for reflection: Lovisa Kasström, Camilla Bouchet, Anna Remmets, and, again, Gustav, Maria, and Max). All these people have made my life full of revolutionary love.

I also thank all the contributors to the volume of essays and the journal special issue I edited while writing this book. What I have learnt from them is uncountable and certainly exceeds the meagre gesture of an acknowledgement. They are: Sara Edenheim, Viola Bao, John Hörnquist, Sarah Philipson Isaac, Moya Lloyd, Alfred Sköld, Peter Clement Lund, Marina Vishmidt, Elena Loizidou, Bruno Monfort, Zona Zaric, and, again, Fanny Söderbäck and Valentina Moro. Thanks also to Michael Hardt for all his help in putting together the special issue. Also, by editing a review I wrote, Morteza Samanpour provided some remarkable insights into the temporalities of value, which helped me hugely in working out these tangled forms.

Dave Beech and Marina Vishmidt gave invaluable feedback on early drafts of this book. Dave came to Sweden to offer his help and critical engagement, which I am very grateful for. The same was planned for Marina, but the trip was cancelled, and shortly afterwards she passed away. The grief of her loss echoes everywhere in these pages. Rest in peace, comrade.

To all the organisers and activists at Academics for Palestine, Workers and Students in Swedish Academia for Palestine (WASSAP), and the Free University of Gaza, Uppsala Campus – the encampment at Uppsala University demanding the institution cuts ties with Israeli universities that develop the weaponry of genocide, and that it offers invitations and practical support to Palestinian students and academics – you are my heroes. When I grow up, I want to be you. Because of the brutal, reactionary prohibitions on protest the university and its departments and staff have resorted to in order to defend genocide, I will leave all these activists anonymous.

It is always surprising where revelations come from. In the acknowledgements of his brilliant poetry collection *Soho*, Richard Scott thanks all the queer poets and writers who have occasioned in him the poetic sensibility he writes with – Shakespeare, Foucault, Whitman, Sedgwick, Genet, Traub, Bersani, etc. – but I'm not sure knowledge is formed from texts directly. I don't feel like this project is for Marx, or the Marxist ghosts that animate all my comrades. It's not even for Fred Moten or Judith Butler, whose critical works are the foundation of my thinking here. It's for my friends, who live and share their survival with me. Again and again, at the pub after a conference or a chance encounter on a train, all my presuppositions and assured structures of belief are collapsed by a passing remark. Without that spontaneous emergence of primary sociality, the following pages would be a trite exercise in repeating institutional tropes, reordering the expected order of exclusive neologisms.

Some of the greatest of these chance encounters for me – which have broken this project open to a constitutive incompletion – have happened in conversations with Melody Howse, Delarys Ramos Estrada, Nicholas Thoburn, Javier Moreno Zacarés, Pedro Rey-Araújo, and Duncan M. Yoon.

I give particular thanks to Daniel Kane, Eugenia Lapteva, David Watson, Gustav Almestad, Judith Kiros, Dave Beech, Marina Vishmidt, Jesper Olson, Greg Darwin, Mikael Omstedt, Keston Sutherland, Seb Franklin, Elin Käck, and Roberto del Valle Alcalá, who have all read significant parts of *Poetics of Value* and provided invaluable feedback.

INTRODUCTION

The Poetics and Politics of Survival

1 The Primacy of Insurgency

In response to my reading of Fred Moten's claim that *insurgency is primary*, an anonymous peer reviewer underlined their point emphatically: 'what does this practically mean *at the level of what motherfuckers do*?'[1] My point in the article to which this reviewer is responding is that sociality is not a political assembly of subjects, formed in response to an oppressive authority that has overstepped the line. Instead, before the determination of subjects as named individuals and their subordination to the public setting of politics, there is a sociality that pervades and generates the possibility of life, and that sociality is constitutively insurgent, in that the fact of its survival antagonises the totalising production of subjects and value. Before the political life of subjects, sociality has created the conditions for survival. This sociality is not erased by individuation and subjection; instead, it survives in another temporality, which Moten calls *fugitivity*.[2] The insurgency of this temporality is its disjunctive survival in and despite the present.

Moten and his collaborator Stefano Harney give numerous examples of how the primacy of insurgency might be exposed. This practice

> may entail forming a band, hosting a barbeque, a dance and a drink. It may be a farm and a daycare, an experimental writing collective, or a mechanics shop. Any form of detoxification from the interpersonal. There will be no allies, no citations, no counter-portraiture. Every aggression will be massive. And when we win, blackness will rain in sun showers while the time disappears.[3]

1 The anonymous reviewer is to some extent citing Moten here, who proposes that we think of the 'sharing of a general pain ... not in terms of the bullshit rhetorical *expression* of solidarity, but the actual *practice* of solidarity, which manifests itself at the level of what motherfuckers do.' Moten and Harney 2020a, minutes 33–4.

2 Moten describes fugitivity as 'a desire for and a spirit of escape and transgression of the proper and the proposed. It's a desire for the outside, for a playing or being outside, an outlaw edge proper to the now always already improper voice or instrument. That is to say that it moves outside the intentions of the one who speaks and writes, moving outside their own adherence to the law and to propriety.' Moten 2018a, p. 131.

3 Harney and Moten 2021, p. 121.

At first, these examples seem impossibly quotidian, appealing to a poetic imaginary that has no practical application. But, for Moten, the removal of the appearance of interpersonality is always radical, in that it exposes what capital and its temporal order cannot bear: the survival of black sociality despite its racialisation by white supremacist ontology. In *Poetics of Value*, I attempt to show how this temporality of survival applies differentially to all sociality, not only in the case of racialisation but in all social determinations: social life persists antagonistically despite its determination by and subsumption in the production and expansion of value.

The fugitive black survival that Moten celebrates is not merely the revelation that brutalised lives survive within the frame of their eradication, but that they are held in a sociality that exceeds the temporality of their racialisation. In the excess of slavery and its afterlife in contemporary carceral capitalism, black sociality mobilises certain lives as surviving fugitively. 'Blackness,' as Moten says in his endlessly complex idiolect, 'is consent not to be one: not just to be more + less than one but the mobilization of that indiscretion and incompleteness against or "otherwise than being".'[4] Temporally as well as logically, insurgent sociality survives in a form that precedes and exceeds the individuation of social life as subjects.

The risk of the proposition of insurgency's primacy, as the reviewer above points out, is that the aim and impulse of radical political action is made pointless, since insurgency *already is*. Why assemble in struggle if sociality is already insurgency *per se*?

These criticisms of possible counterinsurgent passivity have recently been levelled at Moten.[5] The temporality of insurgent primacy, however, is not unique to his corpus. Peter D. Thomas argues against a similar temporality that he finds in the work of Carl Schmitt and Jacques Rancière, who, in Thomas's reading, posit a metaphysical social life, summarised as 'the Political', before the emergence of politics. For Thomas, the problem with this approach is that it necessarily relies on being accessed by philosophical criticism, reducing politics to academic discourse:

> The claim [that politics, or social life, precedes the police, or institutional authority], however, is tautological: insofar as such a concept of the Political is itself already a "metaphysical" construction ..., a certain type of metaphysical philosophy ... cannot but have privileged access to it, in

---

4 Moten 2018a, p. 242, citing Levinas.

5 See: Okoth 2023, p. 34f. I discuss this further in chapter one.

> a relationship of mutual confirmation. What remains unthought in this approach is both the material forms in which the Political achieves its dominance over politics and the way in which the production of the conceptual space of the Political is itself preeminently philosophical.[6]

For Thomas, those who posit a primacy of insurgent social life are unable and unwilling to situate this temporality in the practicalities of struggle. Whether or not Thomas's criticism of this temporality in Schmitt and Rancière is accurate, the 'unthought' philosophical specificity of temporalities of insurgent primacy becomes difficult to justify when read in relation to Moten's formulation of primacy, since so much of his corpus is focused specifically on a refusal of privileged academic access to criticism.[7] For Moten, the theory of primary insurgency is built necessarily and fully out of the practice of survival; it is the social practice of being and remaining together, in fugitive flight from full individuation, that opens the possibility of studying insurgency as logically primary.[8]

It remains nonetheless true that Moten to some extent takes this temporality for granted in his works, celebrating it as the basis for radical black struggles, animated by the survival of black social life. At no point does Moten provide a critical history of the precise material form in which insurgency survives, nor explain what exactly insurgency is. At stake in the primacy of insurgency, for Moten, 'is not so much what constitutes political experience but what ante-political forces remain in the wake of political reduction and regulation.'[9] A disruption of the political is awakened and actualised in turning to the ante-political force of insurgency, but the practical mechanics of that turning, as well as what to look for in the forms of sociality that precede the political, are as yet unclear.

My intention in *Poetics of Value* is to stage a debate between Moten's primacy of insurgency and a tradition that may seem impossibly distant from Moten's poetic project in black studies: the broad tendencies in Marxist scholarship grouped under the name of value-form theory, which I call value-critical Marxisms. While these tendencies are far from having a unified political project of any kind, their central concern is Marx's writings on value. Close attention to these writings and interpretations of their continued importance in understanding capitalism are what unifies the range of value-critical Marxisms. Recent developments in these traditions have centred the temporality of form-

---

6 Thomas 2023, p. 101.
7 See: Harney and Moten 2013.
8 Moten and Russell 2024.
9 Moten 2018b, p. 107.

determined subject-production, which has been of increasing interest lately to cultural, art, and literary studies. I aim to contribute to the current interest in value-critical cultural studies by drawing on the poetic temporalities exposed in contemporary poetry, which I read as an antagonism in the temporal requirements of value. In the following chapter I explain these terms and their political and theoretical significance, alongside an overview of recent developments in these traditions.

While I employ postcolonial literary theory, feminism, queer studies, and psychoanalytic theory throughout this book, my principal aim is to contribute to literary Marxist studies by disrupting the temporal understanding of value through the insurgent temporalities of black studies, which I locate in contemporary American poetry.

This is not to suggest, though, that black studies is the only critical tradition concerned with the temporality of primary insurgency. Similar temporalities have been studied, for example, by Massimiliano Tomba in political theory,[10] Neferti X.M. Tadiar in postcolonial studies,[11] Marco Checchi and Ruben Hordijk in philosophy,[12] Alia Al-Saji in phenomenology,[13] Rahul Rao in queer theory,[14] Harry Harootunian and Dipesh Chakrabarty in history,[15] Samo Tomšič in psychoanalytic theory,[16] Michael Hardt and Antonio Negri in autonomist Marxism,[17] and AbdouMaliq Simone in urban studies.[18] No work has yet focused specifically on the possibility of introducing poetic temporalities of insurgency to value's temporal mode. I argue that black studies is particularly dedicated to a poetic temporality of insurgent survival, which I will define at length in the coming pages. 'Poetic' here has a dual meaning. Firstly, this temporality is speculative and involves creative and unexpected associations that disrupt the order of signification, forming new imaginative possibilities by speculatively linking the survival of blackness in the present with the dedicated erasure of blackness in the modern history of racialisation; in its unexpected creation of new meanings for objects and signifiers that already exist, this temporality is poetic. Secondly, I attempt to draw out these speculative temporalities through

10 Tomba 2019; Tomba 2013a.
11 Tadiar 2022.
12 Checchi 2021; Hordijk 2024.
13 Al-Saji 2018.
14 Rao 2020.
15 Harootunian 2015; Chakrabarty 2008.
16 Tomšič 2021. See: p. 108.
17 Hardt and Negri 2017. See: p. 78.
18 Simone 2022, See: p. 24.

poetry, by way of close of readings of four contemporary poets. They are: Alli Warren, Rob Halpern, Rowan Ricardo Phillips, and Fred Moten.

2 Marxist Temporalities

In *Poetics of Value*, I draw out a temporal imaginary from value-critical Marxisms. These diverse traditions, generally named 'value-form theory' but linked by very little other than their Marxist criticism of value, rarely posit a precise temporality of value: although time is crucial to understanding value, in that value is a relation that determines time, there is nonetheless no coherent proposition for value's temporality in value-critical Marxisms. To account for this absence, I attempt to locate a temporal proposition through the works of numerous value-critical theorists, who – as I explore at length in chapter one – understand the present as an expansive, homogeneous temporality in which the commodified time of capital determines all human activity according to its relation to the production of value.

Labour-power is the only commodity that is productive of value, adding a surplus to commodities and services produced by labour that is purchased and consumed as a commodity by capitalists. The specific mode of productive consumption of labour by capitalists renders *concrete* labour as *abstract* labour, which represents a homogeneous and universal potential for production. 'Abstract labor,' as I.I. Rubin writes, '"creates" value, it is the "content" or "substance" of value.'[19] Abstract labour homogenises the differential expenditure of time, creating the necessary social equality that allows capitalists to consume labour in its abstract form.[20] Abstract labour allows capitalists to consume time as an equal form; the capitalist mode of production equalises every differential global temporality, subsuming it into the possibility of value-production. This results, for some value-critical theorists, in a normative temporality that structures all experiences of time: all time must become determined as potentially value-productive in order for value to expand.

Dipesh Chakrabarty's canonical study *Provincializing Europe* criticises Marxism's theoretical immersion in this homogeneous temporality of abstract labour at the expense of a dedication to the differential temporalities that persist in the Global South.[21] Following this crucial precedent, I argue that the

19 Rubin 2020, p. 221.
20 Ibid., p, 224.
21 Chakrabarty 2008, p. 65f. Rao has a similar critique, but from the perspective of queer postcolonial temporalities: Rao 2020.

implicit temporality of value-critical Marxisms, which centres the expansion of homogeneous commodified time, makes it impossible to open radical emancipatory practices to the fugitive, antagonistic temporalities that survive within the present. These temporalities exceed the form of value-production; the systematic expansion of value is reliant on the persistence of an excess, and that excess can be actualised as an insurgent disruption in the continuity of homogeneous expansion. It is this excess that I seek to access here by way of poetry.

Marx's own reflections on the temporalities of struggle appear in different forms throughout his corpus. In his early writings, there are some oblique references to what could be defined as the primacy of insurgency, but without a precise focus on temporality. In his 1843 letters from the *Franco-German Yearbooks*, Marx describes the intentions of communism:

> we shall develop for the world new principles from the existing principles of the world. We shall not say: Abandon your struggles, they are mere folly; let us provide you with the true campaign slogans. Instead we shall simply show the world why it is struggling, and consciousness of this is a thing it *must* acquire whether it wishes or not.[22]

Here, while neither a strictly logical nor temporal argument, the struggle is certainly prior to its specifically communist deployment against the power of capital. The struggle *per se* comes before consciousness of communist class struggle.

In *On the Jewish Question*, meanwhile, Marx distinguishes between *gaining freedom* as a political tactic of liberal subjection and *being free from* this freedom as the radical strategy of communism. The aim of this strategy is to return to a condition in which humanity is free from subjection in numerous forms, a return that is not nostalgic but rather abolitionist: 'only when man has recognized and organized his [own forces] as *social forces* so that social force is no longer separated from him in the form of *political* force, only then will human emancipation be complete.'[23] Again, the collective struggle of workers precedes the imposition of individuation as the illusory 'freedom to engage in trade'.[24] Importantly, however, the specific revolutionary program of communism is not necessarily based on this historical primacy of social forces.

22 Marx 1992b, pp. 208–9. Original emphasis.

23 Ibid., p. 234. Original emphasis. I have translated the words in brackets from their original French.

24 Ibid., p. 233.

Where a temporality of struggle (in Marx's terms) or insurgency[25] (in mine, following Moten) can be found, it is usually in relation to the production of subjects. Marx's concern with 'subjects' as the political form of human lives largely falls by the wayside after the 1848 *Manifesto*, turning instead to *capital* as the archetypal and operative subject.[26] In the *Grundrisse*, however, Marx ruminates on the disjunctive relation between human subjects and capital as subject. Marx argues that money, which 'is originally the representative of all values', is inverted in capitalism, 'and all real products and labours become the representatives of money'. With this universalisation of money, social relations are determined by the requirement of exchange. One can only exchange one's labour for 'the general capacity to exchange' which spans all interactions.[27] In this twisted temporality, social life is determined by the result of the process of exchange.

In *Capital*, Volume 1, Marx is concerned with the assembly of concrete labour and its conversion into abstract labour through the production process. The goal of this process is not so much the production of commodities but the commodification of labour-power, which is ultimately the sole condition for the expansion of surplus-value. The production process is always also the production of subjectivity, which operates through the commodification of time. This determines not only *exchange-value* as the symbolic form of each commodity that represents a certain quantity of money, but also *use-value* as the commodity's material and singular form. The use of commodities and commodified services is determined by the eventual and necessary expansion of value.

In production, then, numerous processes occur in tandem. At the primary economic level is the production and circulation of goods for consumption. The use of these goods, however, is of no concern to the market itself, embodied as capitalists. It is only their accumulation of value that matters. Through this, commodities are standardised and regarded only as potential carriers of value, rather than as useful and concrete objects. This totalising representation by value is then applied retroactively to the producers of these commodities, determining them only as potential carriers of value. The commodity-form and the subject-form are determined as abstract carriers of value by the production process, which constitutes the form-determination of subjectivity by capital.

25 On the distinction between these terms, see: Tomba 2019, pp. 1–10.

26 Thomas 2023, p. 213.

27 Marx 1993, pp. 149–50.

'Free competition', as Marx writes in the *Grundrisse*, is the fundamental condition for the universalisation of capital; capital's aim is 'the free development of its conditions and of itself as the process which constantly reproduces these conditions.'[28] The condition for the reproduction of capital by capital is the establishment of free competition, in which all barriers to the process of capital's self-reproduction are taken down and ideologically rendered as capital's own conditions of existence. Whatever appeared external – the time in which workers reproduce their own conditions of survival, for example – is retroactively turned into a condition of capital, requiring workers' 'freedom' to enter the contractual obligation of exploitation.

Crucially, Marx clarifies this illusory freedom: 'It is not the individuals who are set free by free competition; it is, rather, capital which is set free.'[29] This distinction shows the duplicity of the formation of subjects: it is not the individual human form through which subjection operates, but rather through capital, which subordinates social life as individual, competitive units operating in the service of capital's own expansion. The production of subjects is the subjection of social life.

In Volumes II and III of *Capital*, Marx turns to circulation and the totality of the system respectively, focusing, among many other topics, on the forms of productive activity not directly mediated by the production of surplus-value.[30] Credit money, for example, is not involved in the production of any commodity or service, but rather functions to maintain the circulation of capital, pursuing ways of making circulation productive of value, establishing – as Marina Vishmidt studies – speculation as a mode of production.[31] Credit functions both to maintain competition between capitalists, with those invested in production, finance, and logistics respectively pursuing antagonistic accumulations of capital,[32] and to produce subjects permanently tied to the promised return of expanded capital from the speculative future in which debt and credit accumulate.

As Rebecca Carson writes, the suspended temporality of credit produces subjects permanently tied to the promised future of expansion and the return

28 Ibid., p. 650. Original emphasis.

29 Ibid., p. 650.

30 One of the other main focuses of Volume III, which this project does not have the space to study, is competition between capitalists and intra-class struggle. For a clear overview of the three volumes, see: Mandel 1991, pp. 9–13.

31 Vishmidt 2018a.

32 Marx 1992a, pp. 409–10. Competition between capitalists is explained throughout Marx 1992a, pp. 394–424. For Marx's concise summary, see: ibid., p. 422.

of credit: 'A crucial part of the legitimation of fictitious capital relies on the constitution of a corresponding subject who lives a life pathologically driven towards the ability to repay, and pay for, what has been credited to them.'[33] However, insofar as subjects are required to survive and reproduce their social life in conditions that exceed the strict temporality of credit money, their existence is never fully subsumed by capital. Although value is productive of the relations of production – it determines the labour posited in the valorisation process as abstract labour – it nonetheless leaves an undetermined residue, which Carson reads as social reproduction, and which I read as the primary insurgency of sociality.[34]

Highlighted throughout *Capital* is the complexity of the determination of subjects in capitalism. Suspended between a future of promised and obligatory expansion, a past marked by differential conditions of survival and arrival at the scene of production, and a present of commodified labour which each subject can only experience in a universalised and abstract form, the subject is an intricate network of constitutive temporalities whose primary function is the maintenance of value-productive order. The temporalities of social life are locked in this repetitive cycle of appropriation and accumulation, keeping dedication to the production of surplus-value constant.

The temporal present of value-production, then, is a necessarily standardised and homogeneous form; it functions as the expansive imposition of units of productive labour-time onto the vastly differential and multiform experience of time in human social life. In many of the value-theoretical texts I study at length in subsequent chapters, this homogeneous present is understood as primary; it assumes primacy over other temporalities, which are gradually eradicated by capital through subsumption. As Frederick Harry Pitts writes, the German value-theoretical tradition of *Neue Marx-Lektüre* (the New Reading of Marx, hereafter NML) assumes a fundamental 'impossibility of unmediated life, whether within or beyond the rule of value', since 'working-class subjectivity is *socially determined* itself by the value form and its constitution.'[35] There is, for NML theorists as for Moten in black studies, no stable ontology that precedes or exceeds capital. However, while Moten understands this as precisely the radical excess exposed by sociality, in that the persistence of social life is not reducible to the form of potential value-productivity,[36] for NML theorists this means that

33 Carson 2023, p. 27. I have written more fully about this elsewhere: Mason 2024.
34 Carson 2023, pp. 73–4.
35 Pitts 2021, pp. 116–17. See also: ibid., p. 101.
36 Moten 2008, p. 187.

> the resistance of the worker against the duress of the labour process is not a manifestation of an antagonistic will or subjectivity external to the logic of the capitalist mode of production, but rather fully part and parcel of it.[37]

Given the absence of an ontological grounding to which human sociality can return in the absence of value, for many NML theorists all interactions are not only mediated but produced by the form of value. Accordingly, they reject class struggle and situate their revolutionary desire instead in the crisis of value itself, relying on value to instantiate its own collapse, which would give rise to a total temporal break, opening a future unknowable from the vantage of the present.[38]

Peter Osborne takes a more cautious route into the homogeneity of the present, arguing that contemporaneity is produced as

> a new temporal form, bringing together in disjunctive conjunction a multiplicity of temporalities that are forced into relations with one another as a result of the increased social dependencies of globalizing capital.[39]

The homogeneous time of the present is not a permanent order imposed on multiplicious temporalities by capital, for Osborne as well as for Søren Mau in *Mute Compulsion*, but rather part of capitalism's continuous project of expansion, which requires it to struggle against the differential temporalities that survive within and despite the homogeneous present.[40] Here, while value's temporality is still totalising, its process of totalisation is understood as a constant struggle against the persistence of social difference. There is, here, a gesture approximating recognition of differential temporalities that persist within the present, but these remain ultimately subordinate to the primary temporality of capital and its requirement of a value-productive, homogeneous present.

A similar pessimism regarding the survival of insurgency dominates the other principal tradition in German value-criticism, *Wertkritik*, which pub-

37 Pitts 2021, p. 117.

38 See: Larsen et al., eds. 2014.

39 Osborne 2022, p. 118.

40 With a disappointing absence of any reference to black studies and its many criticisms of logistics, as I study further in chapter one, Mau posits logistics as the temporal and spatial modality that 'carv[es] the logic of capital into the crust of the earth.' Mau 2023, p. 289. Emphasis removed.

lishes the journal *Exit!* and gathers under the name of the Krisis Group. One of the group's theorists, Anselm Jappe, begins with what appears as a rare moment of hope, theorising an existent revolutionary opening in the present. He argues that

> even within contemporary society, there are many aspects of life, and aspects without which life would be impossible, which do not take place in the form of an exchange of equivalents, which are not measurable as quantities of abstract labour, and which do not immediately serve the material interests of their creators. Value can only 'function' because of the existence of non-value.[41]

This, however, is quickly folded back into fatalist pessimism as the temporality of this 'non-commodified sphere only exists as a subordinated and mutilated sphere.'[42] Ultimately, for Jappe's value-critical tendency, there is no way out of value's form-determination of subjectivity, resulting in the necessity of a total break with the expansive homogeneity of the present, which forecloses the radical possibility of actualising the differential and antagonistic temporalities that persist *within* the present, *despite* the form-determining totality of value. All revolutionary possibility, in *Wertkritik*'s understanding, becomes suspended in the future.

While there is no cohesive project of 'value-form theory' *per se*, what I am attempting to show here is that there is nonetheless a general trend throughout value-critical Marxisms of seeing the present as a temporal form that expands through the commodification of labour, consuming difference and turning it into a standardised abstraction. The German traditions that follow Adorno's late lectures but disagree on crisis (as I study in chapter three) and the Anglophone traditions that apply critiques of value – with varying degrees of proximity to Marx – to aesthetic theory diverge on many theoretical and political issues, but their understanding of the temporal function of the present is quietly unified. My intention, though, is not to so much to *criticise* these value-theoretical tendencies, but to *contribute* to the general project of Marxist value-criticism by introducing the irreducible survival of insurgent temporalities, which I find in the practice of poetry.

For Pitts, NML is necessarily 'pessimistic and [offers] no easy answers' because it understands abstract labour as an expansive totality that produces

41 Jappe 2017, p. 94.
42 Ibid., p. 95.

history itself, forming subjects as productive units of potential value-expansion.[43] What this misses is the persistence of that which value determines. The survival of black life despite its adamant erasure by centuries of slavery reveals the antagonism of survival, in that the object that must be mutely appropriated for the expansion of commodified labour-time always finds fugitive ways of maintaining social life, of living together in and as fugitivity. 'The history of blackness is testament to the fact that objects can and do resist,' as Moten writes.[44] This is, for Moten, 'the magic of objects', in that the surplus produced by objects (either commodities or enslaved people) exposes the surplus of those objects.[45]

Value accumulates the social life that resists individuation; that continued resistance is the constant activity of sociality that provides the conditions both for social survival despite individuation and for value-productive individuals. The primacy afforded by value-critical tendencies to value's form-determining present is here exposed to the irreducible persistence of insurgent sociality. The temporality of value-production and its attendant production of individuated, competitive subjects is always split by a primary temporality of resistance that persists in the practice of social gathering. As Harney and Moten write, 'Prior resistance to individuation is both the primary mode of our perversion as well as the structure and activity of persistence that is most essentially productive of value.'[46]

3 The Excess of Subjects

For both Marx and the contemporary traditions I focus on here, the modern political subject as an autonomous and independently conscious actor with a certain pregiven capacity for civic action, who accumulates the rights of the state and redeploys them as democratic will, is certainly obsolete. While many value-critical Marxisms understand this obsoletion as evidence of the increasing crisis of value, which will eventually implode and leave an undetermined temporality in which communism can be constructed,[47] black studies attempts to locate the internally differentiated multiplicity of temporalities as, in, and despite which subjects exist. What black radical scholars attempt to expose, as

43 Pitts 2021, p. 133.
44 Moten 2003, p. 1.
45 Moten 2017b, p. 38.
46 Harney and Moten 2021, p. 63.
47 Pitts 2021, pp. 132–3.

I show in chapter one, is not a pure and prior subject, but the unruly sociality appropriated into individual subjection, a sociality that persists in the practice of social life.

In order to arrive at the excess of subjects, at an opening into the primacy of insurgent sociality, it is first necessary to understand how and why subjects are produced in their current form. Anglophone literary traditions of value criticism, following Marx, generally understand the production of subjectivity as a process of 'form-determination', which is not a single procedure but a vast ideological, political, and ontological process. This process occurs both *within* subjects and *as* subjects; it is their generator and their content. Analysing the profound reach of this production of subjectivity is what makes Marx's criticism so persistent; he never stops at a certain level of determination, favouring *good* or *free* subjects over *bad* or *exploited* subjects. Instead, he dialectically criticises the form of subjectivity itself. As Moishe Postone writes, 'The breadth and systematic nature of Marx's critical theory … can only be fully grasped through an analysis of its categories, understood as *determinations* of social being in capitalism.'[48] Form-determination *produces* rather than solely *controls* subjects, eliminating the possibility of deciding to remove oneself from its constitutive procedures.[49]

The production of subjectivity, however, is not universal or uniform. The form of the subject is differentially deployed and regulated, with some subject groups consigned to reproduction and survival and others to the constant threat of imminent death. Premesh Lalu has recently studied the contemporary development of political technologies designed precisely to differentially produce and control subjects. In *Undoing Apartheid*, Lalu situates the origin of the dominant neoliberal temporality of speculative capital in the South African apartheid, which functioned as a blueprint for experimenting with the temporal subsumption of subjects. South African authorities justified apartheid by claiming that it was a necessary tactic to avoid inevitable race war. By keeping whites and blacks apart, the collapse of the nation was averted through a suspension of an inevitable future. An imagined past of neatly divided races that pre-exists the global mixing of peoples was enacted as the permanent present.[50] Everyday life became a futureless invocation of an abyssal past, a repetition of an act that never took place, all in the service of denying a future that apartheid authorities claimed was inevitable. What Lalu calls 'petty

48 Postone 2003, p. 18.

49 The dynamic of production and control in relation to subjects is fully explored in Michel Foucault's *Discipline and Punish*. See: Foucault 1995, p. 11, p. 217.

50 Lalu 2022, p. 175.

apartheid' ensued: the present became a constant process of self-withdrawal and denial, a movement away from the terrifying slippage of today into the race riot of tomorrow.

The difficulty of maintaining this standardised temporality of permanent self-policing in the service of an ever-expanding now is that it is reliant on the denial of simultaneous and surviving temporalities, which emerge at moments of 'riotous assembly.'[51] For Lalu, a radical possibility resides in 'the way we apprehend the competing temporalities necessary for conceiving of revolution that defies apartheid's grand and petty designs.'[52] Within the anxious enforcement of a universal temporality of regulation and surveillance, other temporal modes survive, as Saidiya Hartman studies with intricate attention in *Wayward Lives, Beautiful Experiments*.[53] Every instance of survival is the exposure of another temporality of assembly, another way of being together against the grain of accumulation, privatisation, and petty apartheid.

To segregate lives into perceivably differential categories – the black and white parts of the city; productive, unproductive, nonproductive, and reproductive labour; 'Arab nationality' within Israeli citizenship – the temporality of value cannot be imposed in a truly universal form. The backwardness of racialised life,[54] assigning certain lives a temporal lag in apartheid South Africa, would be impossible if the capitalist present were fully universalised. Capital needs different temporalities – the backwardness of racialisation or the unproductive stasis of the feminised present – in order to maintain the illusion of a consistent present that is differentially afforded, assigned only to those subjects deemed potentially productive of value.[55] Capital cannot bear what it needs: the survival of differential pasts and fugitive temporalities, which maintain the social life of those removed from potential value-productivity.[56]

The slow, unproductive time of domestic labour would be indistinguishable from the fast-paced production of masculinised public labour if a subtly differentiated temporality were not suspended precisely at the border between these gendered forms of life. The very construction of a universal temporality

51 A version of this phrase is used throughout Hartman 2018. It originally derives from the 1771 Johnston Riot Act, which prohibits 'tumultuous and riotous assemblies.'
52 Lalu 2022, p. 179.
53 Hartman 2019.
54 Tadiar writes about this also in the Philippine context: Tadiar 2009, pp. 132–3.
55 While also focused on the visual arts, this is the central concern of Bradley 2023. See: p. 245.
56 Peter Osborne argues that this covering of different temporalities is a necessary ideological function of the modern notion of history that has held since the eighteenth century: Osborne 2022, p. 53.

of subject-production – both productive *of* subjects and operated *by* productive subjects – is reliant on the internal difference of suspended temporalities.

Lalu's project of undoing apartheid apprehends these suspended temporalities. When gathered as the unproductive temporality of lag, demanding a future released from the permanent fantasy of the present, a total catachresis destabilises the claims of authority. Its illusion of maintaining a pure past is upended, and a future opens in the excess of the totalising time of petty apartheid.

Marina Vishmidt finds similar unruly temporalities at work in art, exposing an exception to the regulated universality of production. Vishmidt seeks 'the *actualisation* of exceptionality', not as an abstract proposition but as the assembly of unexpected and uncountable parts.[57] Historically and structurally, the anomalies of social norms have been the 'free resources' of capital: 'women, the racialised and colonial subjects', as well as nature itself.[58] These resources are appropriable and expendable without remuneration because they actualise an exception within the framework of '(ac)countability':[59] they do not count, where not counting means both not mattering and being merely matter, merely nameless bodies reduced to a body count, shown in its most shocking form in the daily increasing number of lives lost to Israel's genocide of Palestinians in Gaza, lives that do not count as a function of their mere countability. The art practices that Vishmidt studies are the actualisation of a temporality that exceeds the form-determined present of value-production, exposing the primacy of insurgency in excess of individual being.

In their recent respective works, Lalu and Vishmidt seek to uncover these disjunctive temporalities of social survival in visual art. In *Poetics of Value*, I pursue the same fugitive temporalities in contemporary poetry. There is a particular antagonism that poetry presents to the temporal order of the present, which I attempt to bring out through close readings of four American poets: Alli Warren, Rob Halpern, Rowan Ricardo Phillips, and Fred Moten.

4 Poetic Temporalities

In the mid-2020s, we find ourselves in the twilight of American global dominance, at the sharp end of the ideological structures that uphold neoliberalism,

57 Vishmidt 2018b, p. 591.
58 Ibid., p. 592.
59 Vishmidt 2008, p. 26.

with a neotraditional far Right eradicating the brutal pillar of small-state privatisation that obtained since the 1980s, animating a further contortion of individuating and insular brutality.[60] Generalised political programmes are distrusted at every level, and despite the largest ever numbers of people gathering in protest, counterinsurgent authorities double down on ignoring and oppressing insurgency.[61] In this moment, the form of constitutive and immanent crisis that has long been the axis of the value-critical tradition *Wertkritik*'s radical refusal of capital is itself in crisis. Capital can no longer maintain the precarious border between function and crisis, and form itself collapses. Insofar as the potential valorisation of life is dependent on the possibility of sociality being marked as a form – a form that can be designated as potentially productive of and determinable by value[62] – the crisis of value is the crisis of crisis itself as a determining form. Crisis is in crisis.[63] Or rather, what is exposed is the fact that the crisis has always been the *continuation* of capital and its global project of violation and brutality; crisis is not a function of the *arrest* of the system, but its *survival*. The crisis of capital fails to maintain its own determining form, which also fails to maintain that which is form-determined by value, i.e., sociality as subjects.

In this crisis of form, Osborne finds a radical 'structure of temporal experience, … a new con-temporality, a bringing together or a disjunctive conjunction of socially different times'.[64] The temporal form of value's form-determination breaks open in the crisis of capital's continuous crisis, exposing other ways of being, which so far have largely been studied within the visual arts. Here, building on Judith Butler's concern with the duality of performativity, as both discursive violence and discursive resistance, each of which manifests in and mobilises the materiality of social life,[65] and Amy De'Ath's work on poetic rebuttals to the performativity of value,[66] I move away from the dominant focus on visuality and the visual spectacle of violence, and turn instead to the discursive exposure of fugitive temporalities. What I call the poetics of value is an attempt to antagonise the production of value and its determination of subjects, principally at the level of language and time, by way of the exposure of surviving modalities of insurgent sociality.

60 See: Rasmussen 2021; Butler 2024.
61 Bevins 2023.
62 Bradley 2023, p. 247.
63 Osborne 2022, p. 38.
64 Ibid., p. 117.
65 Butler gives many examples of this duality of performativity throughout their corpus. See: Butler 2021a, pp. 128–33; Butler 2004b, pp. 40–4. I discuss this further in chapter five.
66 See: De'Ath 2017; De'Ath 2023. I discuss this further in chapter two.

As Denise Ferreira da Silva writes in *Unpayable Debt*, 'explanations or justifications of police shootings of unarmed black persons' function at one level as spectacle, as the monstrously living continuity of enslavement, lynching, the Black Codes, and the Middle Passage.[67] At another level, this violence must be justified logically; something must translate the 'politically constituted ... colonial juridico-economic structure of slavery' into 'expressions of an organically determined moral deficit'.[68] A discursive practice translates the history of racialising enslavement into the immediate justification for the eradication of black lives by the police. This is the direct, murderously material violence of discursive justification, which I want to antagonise through politically radical poetry. How does this discursive practice of translation function? And how does it simultaneously expose an unwitting 'black residuum' of fugitive survival through the very fact that blackness itself – *black life* as opposed to *black lives* – is never killed?[69]

As José Felipe Alvergue writes, poetry is widely practiced in insurgent assemblies. By reading insurgent poetry, the poetics of insurgency itself is actualised. A certain way of communing and communicating with each other develops despite the spatial dispersal of fugitive lives.[70] What Alvergue calls 'lyric redress' is a formal disjunction that disturbs precisely the formality of address, held between expected modes of communication and the form of citizenship. In those instances where formal personhood is denied by way of and within the formal universality of citizenship (say, in the genocidal apartheid state of Israel or for black people in the US), lyric redress

> *of* the formal and informal institutions that manage sociality, and from the vantage of public expression, recognizes the impossibility in material redress through an expression of the impossibility for affiliation through existing memories of collective nationhood – those legitimated in the deliberative homogeneity of dominant theories of the social.[71]

The delegitimisation of the formality of personhood comes out of these lyrically redressive modes of communication. Following Alvergue, I pursue this

67 Silva 2022, p. 123.

68 Ibid., p. 124.

69 Bradley 2023, p. 240. See also Simone's focus on the unplanned practices of social survival that expose this fugitive excess, not through the production of art but by 'simply' living: Simone 2022.

70 Alvergue 2018.

71 Ibid., p. 222.

delegitimisation in poetry, recovering and actualising the antagonistic survival of sociality despite and in the excess of value.

My focus here is on the ways in which poetry exposes an antagonism in the calculation of value-productivity as the standardised and commodified temporality of abstract labour. By way of four contemporary poets, I seek a point of exposure for value-critical Marxisms and communist organising to the primacy of insurgency promoted in black studies.

5 The Coming Poets

The four poets I focus on synthesise my primary theoretical concerns. The first two – Alli Warren and Rob Halpern – are communists who explicitly build on earlier Marxist traditions in American poetry, foremost the Language poets and their commitment to poetry's political and material operation in the world. Developed in the United States since the late 1960s, the Language poets refuse the notion of the poet's autonomous production of meaning, instead folding the world and the poem together as a site of struggle, often by reproducing and reforming texts that already exist rather than writing poetry *about* an existent object. For them, the reader is the primary creator of meaning. Following the contemporaneous rise of postmodernism in critical theory, and against the 'narrowness and provincialism of mainstream literary norms', as they write in their 1988 manifesto 'Aesthetic Tendency and the Politics of Poetry', these poets 'challenged and exploded … the self as the central and final term of creative practice'.[72] This formal decentring of the self, placing readers and other objects in the world as the focus of poetry, has given rise to a whole genre of radical Left poetics.[73]

In contemporary poetry, though, a clear political distinction between the 'traditional' lyric self and its 'radical' refusal is more difficult than ever to maintain.[74] The use of a lyric 'I' is nowadays always critically built on the unstable ground set up by the Language poets, even for the most seemingly lyrical poets, among the foremost of whom, in the contemporary American canon, is Rowan Ricardo Phillips, whose poetry I study in chapter four.

Warren and Halpern directly respond to the developments of the Language poets over the last decades of the twentieth century. While they both use an 'I' that seems to quite coherently refer to the poets themselves, they follow

72 Silliman et al. 1988, pp. 262–3.
73 Rasula 2004; Spahr 2001. See also: Ashton 2005.
74 Houen 2014, p. 15.

the Language poets in building on the material formality of poetry, accessing their own subjectivity and subjection through the material history and struggles of the world. This practice contributes to a specifically communist poetics focused on the contemporary neoliberal production of subjectivity, which refuses both subject *and* object relations. In our data-driven contemporary, even the stability of *objects* cannot be assumed; the 'reader' may be a machine algorithmically calculating meaning, or a phone camera that mediates between a stanza, Instagram, and the infinite pursuit of subject-validation by way of views, followers, and likes.

In Warren's poetry, objects are terrifyingly autonomous, dominating the emotional life of each poetic scene, while in Halpern's poetry objects are indistinguishable from human subjects: soldiers in uniform, the weapons they carry, and the value that accumulates within them all excite a frenzied response in the confused and manic poetic speaker, who is no more a subject than the bloodthirsty erect penis he is guided by.

Both Warren and Halpern live in the San Francisco Bay Area, with its long history of radical poetry schools, which stages their poetry as a uniquely direct confrontation with the primary technology of subject-production today: Silicone Valley as the site of an unimaginably vast accumulation of privatised, profit-driven data. Warren and Halpern are on the frontline of what Yanis Varoufakis calls 'technofeudalism',[75] the brutally polarised infinite growth of profit (if not necessarily surplus-value) as life-time, set against a background of economic, climatic, and subjective collapse, poeticised in acute detail by these poets.

The latter two poets – Rowan Ricardo Phillips and Fred Moten – have been chosen for different reasons. Phillips, as I study in chapter four, is rare among his contemporaries in that he is an obsessively formalist poet. He almost never uses lineated prose, or free verse, and all his poems are profoundly informed by the history of poetry, with references and suggestive links filling every line. But he is also an explicitly political poet, often engaging with racist police violence and geopolitical events. This uniquely peculiar disjunction of form and content very clearly lays out my primary contention here: the *form* in and as which subjects are determined by value never fully subsumes the *content* of social life, which operates in excess of its own form.

While Phillips is a supremely *poetic* poet, whose poetry is a study of the possibility of poetry, Moten, whose poetry I study in chapter five, barely distinguishes between his very influential scholarly texts and his poetry. Moten writes

75 Varoufakis 2024.

as he speaks, whether that writing comes out as a philosophical monograph or a poem, with a profoundly theoretical idiolect and an endless allowance for digressions and subclauses. His poetry is written without any strict form. It is far more concerned with the social life that surrounds the page than the page itself. Since his first poetry collection, *Arkansas*, in 2000, he has been developing a striking mode of writing poetry as a social invitation, erasing the singularity of authorship and staging his poems through scenes in which friends and comrades emerge as the action. The coming together of an assembly is the event of the poem, to the extent that the poem itself is only formed of the gathering of the poem's own social life.

As the focus of the last of the four chapters that study contemporary poets in *Poetics of Value*, Moten gives me the opportunity to conduct a simultaneously poetic and theoretical refusal of the temporality of value, opening the present instead to a multiplicity of fugitive temporalities that survives antagonistically within and against the form-determination of subjectivity.

Over the coming chapters I move from Marxism to black studies, attempting ultimately to open a specific theoretical limitation of the former to the fugitive temporal imaginary of the latter. While certainly not wanting to dismiss other radical traditions that organise around the same temporality of primary insurgency, black studies seems to me to be the contemporary critical modality most concerned with (1) poetic expression as a performative disjunction in the norms of academic scholarship, and (2) the radical celebration of fugitive survival, seeking to 'renew our habits of assembly', rather than 'studying the failure' of assemblies, as Harney and Moten write, following Manolo Callahan.[76]

All the poets I focus on here work at universities, three as academics and one (Warren) in administration. For my purposes, this provides a far more direct opening between their poetry and contemporary scholarship in critical thinking. These poets are, to varying degrees, explicit about their reading and study practices and the ways their work is informed by theory, which allows me a smoother transition between the jargon-heavy esotericism of radical theory and poetry. Indeed, this smooth transition is not coincidental: these poets – especially Halpern and Moten – follow the general tendency of creative literature in developing their poetry *out of* theory. The critical literary theory that supposedly *responds to* creative writing is increasingly *generative of* its sociolect and critical apparatus.[77] For a project like this with a broad theoretical back-

76 Harney and Moten 2021, p. 30.

77 Andrews 2023. See also: McGurl 2011.

ground, which attempts to stage a disjunctive meeting of traditions, it is very helpful that the poets I study are already versed in these critical approaches and responding directly to them.

One of the principal questions that arises out of these concerns is: why American poetry? In her study of Philippine literature as an active reflection on and enactment of ongoing and possible insurgencies, Neferti X.M. Tadiar writes,

> literature is here not to be taken as a representation of the lived experiences of particular people. Works of postcolonial literature are rather to be viewed as experiments in broader social projects, indeed, in the very imagining of modern political communities.[78]

By focusing on poetry written in the United States, by American poets, I aim to access this imagining of modern political communities in the fading emblem of contemporary neoimperial, neoliberal, capitalist global power.[79]

6 The Coming Chapters

In *Poetics of Value*, I aim to posit the primacy of insurgency as a methodology for Marxism by taking fugitive, poetic routes into black studies and the Marxist tendency of 'value-form theory', which I prefer to place under the rubric of 'value-critical Marxisms', given the vast differences of these approaches, which are united only by their attentiveness to Marx's criticism of value. This practice is necessarily experimental, placing disjunctive discourses together. To set a firm grounding for the problems that arise out of value's general temporality of subject-production, I spend Part 1 – titled 'Subjects of Value' and formed of chapters one, two, and three – approaching matters of concern to contemporary Marxist discourse. Alongside my focus in chapters two and three on two contemporary poets – Alli Warren and Rob Halpern respectively – I complicate the temporality of value-critical Marxisms by setting up debates with other disciplines.

First, in chapter one, I provide an overview of value-critical Marxisms and the importance of these tendencies for understanding and antagonising the

78 Tadiar 2009, p. 6.

79 Given this focus on the US, I should add that this is a project very much conducted from the outside of its object of study: none of this book was written in the US, but rather by an English author living in Sweden.

contemporary development of capital. My contention with this critical mode is that, as it stands, it has no means of exposing its revolutionary project to the social life that survives in the excess of the capitalist present. The stakes of this limitation are brought out here by a comparative reading of black studies, with its dedication to the primacy of insurgency, and value-critical Marxisms, with their broad dedication to capital as a system that homogenises expended time, rendering subjects equal in the circulation of their commodified labour.

In chapter two, I focus on Marx's understanding of commodities as mystical and fetishised objects that carry the living labour of human bodies into exchange, and how Alli Warren's poetry stages a satire of this fetish-character. In Warren's poetry, the fetishised form of labour is presented in its most extreme performance. The poetic speaker is always alone in a vast and confounding world of animated commodities. This lonely confusion emphasises the monstrous character of value that speaks on behalf of its producers. Distorting this relation through a play on the history of commodities in American poetry, Warren opens the possibility of mystical belief in a social form that survives despite form-determination.

In chapter three, I explore the singular effect of living as capital personified. To closely investigate the perverse and paradoxical individuation of a standardised form – the subject – that serves the sole purpose of expanding value, I turn to psychoanalytic theory, which allows an especially dedicated focus on the personal and singular production of social violence. Here, I read Jacques Lacan's and Judith Butler's theories of the subject by way of two contemporary critical psychoanalytic theorists, Samo Tomšič and Lorenzo Chiesa, and the long debate on the inevitability of crisis in two German value-critical tendencies – *Neue Marx-Lektüre* and *Wertkritik* – in relation to the rise of a peculiar, acute anxiety in American culture.

In Rob Halpern's collection *Music for Porn*, the imperial military industrial complex of the USA's murderous economy is no mere political abstraction; it is expressed as the speaker himself, who is mourning his partner, a soldier in the US army. This loss is marked by the global movements of debt and military expansion to such an extent that the lonely, individuated speaker has no means of socially processing his trauma. Instead – as a synecdoche of America itself – he resorts to projective repression.

Published in 2012, Halpern's collection gives voice to the traumatised US subject, depleted by a decade of constant war, economic crisis, and the collapse of the material basis of the American ideological system. Halpern's poetry expresses the most brazen and brutal affects of a nation-state in its dying breaths, pushing out one final burst of spectacular violence before it succumbs to its defining wounds. I am interested in what Halpern exposes beneath the personal and subjective effect of these global movements in US economics and politics.

In Part 2 – titled 'Socialities of Value' and formed of chapters four, five, and six – I turn to the precise form of primary insurgency and the means by which undetermined social life survives as an antagonistic, fugitive temporality within the expansive present of capital. Where in Part 1 my concern is with the ways in which capital determines subjectivity, in Part 2 I turn to the fugitive social and artistic practices that survive despite this determination.

In chapter four, I am concerned with the form of value. Building on what I have outlined in previous chapters as value's suspension of time through the retroactive valorisation of labour, I argue here that the conceptual apparatus of this temporality arises from Kantian morality. For Kant, before any material experience of social life, each moral actor has access to the fundamental *a priori* coordinates of moral reason. Using his favourite example of friendship, Kant posits that one knows already what a friend *should be* before one ever makes a friend. However, I follow Christine Battersby and Adriana Cavarero in arguing that Kant's own life and archives present a very different portrait, one in which the material presence of *friends* always gives rise to the morality of *friendship*. I read this primacy of friends in relation to Rowan Ricardo Phillips's 2020 poetry collection *Living Weapon*, in which some strikingly anti-Kantian scenes are staged. The principal movement I trace is across two poems in the collection. In the first, '1776', Phillips's poetic speaker goes on a heroic, path-breaking flight to the top of the One World Trade Center Tower in New York City. This independent exploration is archetypally Kantian. In 'Golden Hour', however, the whole artifice of independence is removed, and the lonely speaker crashes into someone else who can also fly. The confused, ambivalent invitation that ensues exposes a constitutive social life that has been working beneath and before the sole flight of the speaker all along. I read this as the exposure of the materiality of *friends* before the ideal form of *friendship*.

In chapter five, I arrive at Moten's poetry and its insistence on the primacy of insurgency, which I stage in discussion with Judith Butler's complicated temporality of struggle, sociality, and power. Reading Moten and Butler with and against each other, I find a tripartite temporal schema in which these three historical forces confront, condition, and constitute one another. Placing these temporalities in the context of Althusserian interpellation and Gramscian hegemony, I propose a model of primary insurgency, located in Moten's poetry.

In chapter six, I turn away from close readings of poetry and take a broader view of black studies and Marxist philosophy. Having posited social life as a multiplicity of temporalities of survival in an undetermined, fugitive other – present beside the dispossessive temporality of value, in this chapter I ask what it is *in poetry* that exceeds its form of presence. I attempt to access this excess by way of two pages in Darell Wayne Fields' 2000 monograph *Architecture in Black*. On these pages, a peculiar artwork is displayed: two black boxes, titled 'Intentionally Left Black (by author)', parts I and II. Studying the *intentionality* of this *leaving*, the agency of this absence, I read this diptych as the insurgency of poetry that exceeds the symbolic format of poems on a page. Revealed in these two black boxes, satirically left untouched by the author's intentions in the most anti-Kantian way possible, is the fugitive excess of poetry, the para-symbolic social life of literature that reveals a scandalous survival within the form of poetry itself.

Poetics of Value ends with a short afterword, in which I briefly reflect on the insurgent political application of these poetic and fugitive temporalities of survival against the form-determination of value.

PART 1

Subjects of Value

Introduction to Part 1

The three chapters in this part of *Poetics of Value* begin by presenting my proposition for value-critical Marxisms: value is a mode that temporally homogenises the present as a form-determining process of abstraction, subsuming differential social lives in the determination of productive labour, which disallows the survival of coeval social temporalities. It is these social temporalities that I attempt to introduce as a disjunction in the temporality of value. I posit black studies as the critical mode dedicated to the social assemblies occasioned by fugitive temporalities, which survive within but are not fully subsumable into the dominant temporal mode of capital. This chapter opens the central theoretical challenge I aim to study and go some way towards satisfying in *Poetics of Value*. My aim is to expose value-critical Marxisms to the fugitive survival of social temporalities that black studies scholars locate and celebrate.

The following two chapters attempt to further explore the mechanisms of form-determination and subjection that define capitalism's temporally homogenising project. I do this by way of two contemporary poets who write in a very specific local context. Each is concerned with a particular kind of Bay Area communism. Alli Warren's poetry, the focus of chapter two, is a subtle and satirical movement inwards, an introspective pursuit of the emptiness of the capitalist subject.

What I find in Warren's comedic scenes is a peculiar ritual of belief in a formlessness that precedes subjectivity. Warren's poetry is situated in a world of monstrously animated commodities, so animated that the only living human body in the text is mostly mute. The form of subjectivity through which she accesses the world is an insufficient means of speaking; it cannot bring her to the material presence of social life. It stops, miserably, in the face of coagulated artefacts of labour. Pursuing some form of sociality to provide the basic mutual recognition of living beings, Warren is failed by the form of 'we'. There is no community she can operate into being by refusing the life of commodities.

The lonely character of Warren's poetry is mostly deprived of other humans. Instead, she is surrounded by animated commodities. All her love is reserved for objects, services, and commodified relations. By setting up this strange world of living things, Warren gives voice to commodities, who always seem to speak before the human subject of the poems. It is here that I find a link with black studies, which has long been concerned with the way commodities speak. While Marx famously asks what would happen *if commodities could speak*,[1]

1 Marx 1990, pp. 176–7.

this misses a crucial part of capitalism's history: enslavement is the commodification of people who continue to speak. Slaves are speaking commodities.[2] Warren gives life to a world in which speaking commodities are everywhere, and the social life of value exceeds the administrative rigmarole of human existence. Warren places the meaning of her poetry in its objects. In her often riotously funny poems, there is no material social life that precedes the commodifying abstraction of the present. There is, however, *belief*. Warren persists in poeticising belief in a form of meaning that exceeds the process of abstraction.

In this chapter, I trace this expansion of speaking commodities up to its limit point in belief: suddenly the determining abstraction of value disintegrates as Warren gives poetic dedication to belief in a social life that may not be real, may not be here, but is nonetheless possible; it survives somehow, in some hidden past or once-possible future.

In chapter three, I look further into the singular subjective effect of this expansive temporal abstraction on individual beings. Rob Halpern's poetry, like Warren's, is largely focused on a sole subject, alone in a world of war, violence, and commodification, but where Warren nonetheless invests in a formless belief that pursues a surviving social life in the excess of subsumption, Halpern poeticises the life of subsumption itself. Halpern's speaker is a depressed and destructive nihilist, unable to encounter any meaning in the perverse ubiquity of violence that surrounds and constitutes him. He is barred from grief and his only means of dealing with his unbearable pain is self-annihilation. In my reading, this lonely, aggressive subject is a synecdoche of America itself.

While the psychoanalytic theory I use to access the nihilistic core of this synecdochic subject may appear at first incompatible with the value-critical Marxisms that structure Part 1, I think it is useful to work fully into the contradictory form of the capitalist subject, in order then to move out of its boundaries in Part 2, where I will pursue alternatives to this prescriptive form in the survival of sociality, or what I am calling the primacy of insurgent sociality.

My general critical impulse in this project is to read disjunctive, even antagonistic, traditions together to bring out a social life that survives in the excess of form-determination. In chapter two, the disjunctive tradition placed in conversation with value-critical Marxisms is Marxist-feminism and the poetic tradition of mysticism. In chapter three, it is psychoanalytic theory, mostly focused on Judith Butler, Lorenzo Chiesa, and Jacques Lacan.

---

2 Moten 2003, p. 13, pp. 251–4.

CHAPTER 1

Critique of the Temporality of Value

1 The Operation of Form-Determination

In Marx's analysis, the form of labour that is productive of value is not the sensuous movement of each working body, but rather the standardised and generalised expression of people's activity. 'The total labour-power of society, which is manifested in the values of the world of commodities,' he writes at the beginning of *Capital*, Volume I, 'counts here as one homogeneous mass of human labour-power, although composed of innumerable individual units of labour-power.'[1] This labour-power is consumed by capitalists, who then exchange it as abstract labour, which produces surplus-value by adding the commodified form of partially-remunerated labour to exchanged commodities or services.

Beginning with the example of a coat, made of linen by tailors and weavers, Marx writes,

> the act of equating tailoring with weaving reduces the former in fact to what is really equal in the two kinds of labour, to the characteristic they have in common of being human labour. This is a roundabout way of saying that weaving too, in so far as it weaves value, has nothing to distinguish it from tailoring, and, consequently, is abstract human labour.[2]

As abstract labour, commodities and services are circulated without the differences of 'innumerable individual units of labour-power' that produced them. That is, their future in exchange obscures their past in production.

---

1 Marx 1990, p. 129. While it is outside the scope of this project to fully compare translations or discuss their respective merits, there are some very important differences in the latest translation of *Capital* into English by Reitter. This cited section is rendered as follows: 'All the labor-power represented in the values of the commodity world, the sum of a society's labor-power represented in them, counts for something here as one and the same human labor-power, even though labor-power belonging to innumerable individual people goes into it.' Marx 2024, p. 17. Rather than being a *unit* that composes commodities, labour-power here *belongs* to workers, presupposing a logic of possession that is incompatible with Marx's theorisation, in which workers are understood to be specifically deprived of the possibility of owning their labour-power (see: Marx 1990, p. 677). Fowkes' earlier translation (Marx 1990) is certainly closer to the original meaning in German, in which the final clause of the passage is: 'obgleich sie aus zahllosen individuellen Arbeitskräften besteht'.

2 Marx 1990, p. 142.

In the scene of production, the act of labouring is experienced as *concrete labour*, in which racialised, gendered, and variously determined groups are distinguished through the productivity of labour. As Beverley Best summarises, 'in capital, labour time, as such, can neither be gendered nor racialized, while labour time's bearers always are.'[3] Once these differentiated concrete labours are exchanged as 'congealed quantities of human labour,'[4] their difference appears to be eradicated: commodities function only as a relation to other commodities, through which abstract labour is represented.

A split occurs in the moment between production and exchange, and that split appears to have erased difference. For Iyko Day, this moment is precisely the brutality of this system: 'the principal violence of capitalism is in the way it abstracts (or renders homogeneous as commensurable units of labor) highly differentiated gendered and racialized labor *in order to create value*. It is therefore the law of value that obscures the racial and gendered character of labor power.'[5] Value obscures the difference required for its own production, while the cultural totality of capitalism that necessarily accompanies the expansion of value is dependent on the enforced continuation and entrenchment of this same difference.

Capitalism's profound investment in countless kinds of violence – racism of all kinds, including anti-black, anti-Indigenous, anti-Jewish,[6] and anti-Arab, misogyny and sexism, transmisogyny, homophobia, colonisation, imperialism, nationalism, ableism, and so on – is placed solely in the past, before the standardising moment of abstraction in which difference is obscured in order for commodities to relate solely to each other as abstract labour, represented by quantities of what Marx calls a congealed or gelatinous mass, but which I follow Seb Franklin in understanding as the *computation* of differential time.[7] Value works back from the scene of exchange onto the scene of production, *computing* that which is productive of itself as the standardised form of temporal accumulation, i.e. abstract labour. This is the process of form-determination: the form of concrete difference in the past is determined by the abstracted homogeneity of the future. Difference is retroactively determined according to its potential or impotential commodifiability as labour-power, which is used by capitalists to expand value.

3 Best 2023, p. 264.
4 Marx 1990, p. 141. In Reitter's translation: 'bare gelatinous blobs of human labor' (Marx 2024: 27).
5 Day 2016, p. 9. Original emphasis.
6 For the insufficiency of the term 'antisemitism' and an argument for the use of 'anti-Jewish racism' instead, see: Bakan and Abu-Laban 2024.
7 Franklin 2021, p. 7.

What I am foremost concerned with here is how the innumerable social differences at the site of production – understood as differential temporal modes of being – survive disjunctively in the present and future of exchange. That survival, as I will argue throughout *Poetics of Value*, is a living antagonism within and against the project of value.

Capital requires both *a single, abstract, and homogenised expenditure of time* for value-production to occur, and *differentials in productivity* for populations to be internally divided and individuals to be separated by mutual competition. Marx's focus when confronting this seemingly contradictory dual purpose of the mode of production is on capital's own dialectical history. In notebook VI of the *Grundrisse*, Marx notes that, by way of capital's historical dissolution of barriers to expansion in the form of 'compulsory guild membership, government regulation, internal tariffs and the like', the notion of capitalism as '*laissez faire*' competition gives rise to 'the even greater absurdity of regarding [capital] as the collision of unfettered individuals who are determined only by their own interests – as the mutual repulsion and attraction of free individuals, and hence as the absolute mode of existence of free individuality.'[8] What appears as the eradication of the barriers to the development of this free competition among the human actors of production, exchange, and consumption is in fact the eradication of the barriers to capital's own development.

> The historical side of the negation of the guild system etc. by capital through free competition signifies nothing more than that capital, having become sufficiently strong, by means of the mode of intercourse adequate to itself, tore down the historic barriers which hindered and blocked the movement adequate to it. But competition is very far from having only this historical significance, or merely being *this negative* force. *Free competition* is the relation of capital to itself as another capital, i.e. the real conduct of capital as capital.[9]

The people enlisted into this process of value-production are the carriers of the freedom of capital, and by this act of carrying capital they become determined by its requirements.

Placing this freedom of capital in a contemporary context, Marina Vishmidt gives the example of 'the debt burden and privatised social services which

8 Marx 1993, p. 649.
9 Ibid., p. 650. Original emphasis.

reduce the incentive for workplace militancy, while the dwindling of workplace militancy reinforces the truth of atomisation that supports the "human capital" version of human nature and its social implications.'[10] That is to say, each stage of the production of value negatively moves back against its grounding condition, which in its own turn moves against that which it grounds; capital eradicates its own barriers through the illusion that it is freeing its human bearers. As Marx continues, 'Free competition is the real development of capital.'[11]

The capitalist subject is free to carry the freedom of capital, free to move in accordance with the necessary movements of capital's freedom. The barriers pulled down by the development of capital are barriers *to capital*, and as such their absence allows for the freedom *of capital*. In 'the pure conditions of capital',[12] individual human freedom is produced as the erasure of the social difference of the past. Living labour is flattened out as dead labour through its computation as the mere commodified capacity to sell not what one *has* but what one *has been reduced to being*, i.e. labour-power. The production process eradicates all markers of singularity in this labour: it circulates only as standardised abstract labour, which does not belong to the bearers of the original living labour. It is separate from the sensuous singularity of their bodies, circulating instead as a possession of capitalists; this same claim on the possession of labour severs the connection between living, labouring bodies in the present and their group-determined difference in the past. In the constant present of the commodification of labour, there is neither a future nor a past for workers.

Workers in capitalism are suspended in an abyssal present without connection to either a future of value-expansion or a past of living difference. Individuals, then, are simultaneously produced and prohibited in capitalism, leaving them no means of subjective emancipation. As Vishmidt writes, 'the very notion of emancipation is "form-determined" by the circumstances from which the subject would emancipate itself.'[13] For emancipatory movement, we have to look elsewhere than the form of the subject.

In the future moment of exchange, the surplus-value produced through the consumption of productive labour is brought to fruition through its mediation by money, which then retroactively valorises the labour posited in produc-

10 Vishmidt 2018a, p. 45.
11 Marx 1993, p. 650.
12 Ibid.
13 Vishmidt 2018a, p. 46. On this 'form-determination' of subjectivity, see also: Marx 1993, pp. 676–7, p. 694; De'Ath 2017; Starosta 2016, cf. p. 191.

tion, rendering the commodities or services produced as value-bearing: the value of already-completed labour is valorised only once the product or service that bears exchange-value is exchanged.[14] That past labour is thereby differentiated according to its productivity, even though it is passed over into the future moment of exchange as a universalised form that does not distinguish between those who expend that labour: they are simultaneously expending *concrete labour* and *abstract labour*, the latter of which arrives from the later moment of value's realisation to determine the whole process. The subjectivity produced in this relation of labour, then, both *removes* individual distinctions between workers, separating them from each other and from their meaningful social groups, and *differentiates* people's working conditions dependent on their future determination by the extent of value's realisation in exchange.[15] The capitalist labour process generates at once homogenisation (as abstract labour) and differentiation (as differentially valorised life-forms).[16]

This differential valorisation of life-forms, which remains consigned to the past in capital's tripartite temporal schema (*differential past – commodifying present – abstract, homogenised future*), is persistently invested in the production of many forms of difference. As Iyko Day and Denise Ferreira da Silva, among many others, have shown, differential valorisation is the mechanism by which racialised difference among populations is systematically maintained.[17] It is also a gendering and sexuating procedure, as Alva Gotby, again among many others, has studied.[18] The productive sphere is reliant on the unproductive (unwaged) labour of the reproductive sphere, but also on a general ethics of care. The possibility of determining people and the infinite difference of their social lives as a homogeneous commodity is upheld by an implicit environment of care into which one is already given, and which constitutes each person.

This given environment is what Stefano Harney and Fred Moten call 'sharing,' which 'is not an interpersonal relationship. ... One doesn't share. One is shared.'[19] Sharing is not a choice or an active political decision; it is the

---

14 Marx 1991, p. 392. In the following chapter, 'Commercial Profit' (pp. 394–416), Marx goes on to show that these temporally divided processes are the source of profit for industrial and merchant capitalists respectively.

15 For perspectives on this particular temporal movement of value, see: Vroey 1981, p. 177; Kurz 2016, p. 72.

16 On the multiple forms of social violence that arise from this homogenisation, see: Endnotes 2010, pp. 20–51; Franklin 2021; Spivak 1988.

17 Day 2016; Silva 2022.

18 Gotby 2023.

19 Moten and Harney 2020a, minute 41.

structural requirement of survival for both the capitalist subject-form and that which exceeds its determination: the sociality ongoing despite capital's subsumptive reach. As Harney and Moten emphasise, we 'cannot be anything but already shared and already sharing.'[20]

In this sense, the subjectivising imperative of capital is forced to allow for the continuation of certain social practices of care, despite their removal from value-production. Capitalism is a system that is profoundly reliant on what it cannot bear. While it must allow other temporalities to persist in order for social difference to survive, capitalism nonetheless has systematic means of nullifying the political antagonism of these social temporalities of nonproductive difference. As Joshua Clover and Juliana Spahr write, for example, capital turns *differences* into *differentials* in order to separate populations according to potential productivity: 'Gender functions *for capital* not as difference but as differential, as a socially arbitrated and ideologically naturalized gap in wage levels (whether women are waged or not) across which surplus value flows.'[21] The form that difference assumes here is relatively arbitrary: in certain historical instances, sex and gender are the most efficient means of dividing populations according to the need or lack of the need to remunerate productive efforts, but there are other forms of difference that can achieve the same aim: differentials of race, nationality, status, caste, and so on can also be used. What matters is the systematic production of certain parts of populations, and certain global populations, as surplus and expendable.[22]

By maintaining these divisions of difference at the site of production despite the homogenised form of labour in exchange, capital ensures that individuals will operate through a primary claim to potential self-possession: people will understand themselves not as members of a society, but as the potential to competitively accumulate more commodified time than others. Behind, before, and beside this violent present, though, a past of difference – of different social temporalities – lives on; it survives in and between the form-determined claimants to labour-power. 'The hegemonic form of subjectivity in capitalism – possessive individualism – simultaneously disavows and depends on a feminised subjectivity of care,' as Gotby writes. 'A radical politics of emotional reproduction is one which seeks to undo these gendered forms of subjectivity.'[23]

20 Harney and Moten 2021, p. 122.
21 Clover and Spahr 2016, p. 299. Original emphasis.
22 See: Floyd 2016, pp. 79–80.
23 Gotby 2023, p. xix.

By way of poetry, this book accordingly attempts to undo capital's determination of subjectivity as the prohibition and disavowal of the practices of sharing that constitute sociality. Each of the poets I focus on evades the full determination of subjectivity by exposing the survival of sociality in the excess of individuation. The political ambivalence of this excess – which distinguishes it from the project of abolition, whose ambivalence arises after its enactment, in that, for example, the abolition of slavery in the US led to the Black Codes and the rise of the carceral state, entrenching the racialising violence of slavery – is that it could both be subsumed into the project of capital, adding to capital's tendency to adapt to resistance and refusal, and continue to survive without antagonism, simply exposing a methodology of social survival that contributes to the wellbeing of workers without disrupting the expansion of value.

In the following chapters I hope to politicise poetry's insurgency by focusing on the capacity of four contemporary poets to expose a sociality that is *necessarily* antagonistic as a function of its survival. First, however, I study the respective temporalities of black studies and value-critical Marxisms in order to locate the necessity, and the necessary antagonism, of the primacy of insurgency.

2 Marxian Primacies

The creation of a determined subjectivity amenable to the requirements of capitalism has never been inevitable or natural. Twentieth-century US industrialists – not least the behemoths Henry Ford and Frederick Taylor – were explicitly in pursuit of a reformed subjectivity that would allow workers to adapt to the regulated temporality of machinic production. As Matthew Huber writes, citing Taylor, 'the real challenge for scientific management was to produce "a complete change in the mental attitude of the working men." Thus adapting to the demands of mechanized production required not only new work methods but new subjectivities.'[24] The questions that remain open in Marxism are what *precedes* these new subjectivities, what forms of being are *appropriated into and as* the form-determined subject, and are these subjectivities *totalising* or do other ways of being persist beside them?

In the 1844 *Paris Manuscripts*, Marx seems to celebrate the existence of a prior and pure sociality that has been stolen by the regimented temporal order of capitalist production. Observing French socialist workers on their lunch break, he writes,

24 Huber 2013, p. 31, citing Taylor 1911, p. 140.

> Such things as smoking, drinking, eating, etc., are no longer means of contact or means that bring together. Company, association, and conversation, which again has society as its end, are enough for them; the brotherhood of man is no mere phrase with them, but a fact of life.[25]

The historical primacy of these social relations based on a fraternal ethics of sharing is further theorised by Marx and Engels in *The German Ideology*, written in 1846. There, they list four relations and their simultaneous production and satisfaction of the basic needs of life: (1) the production of the means to produce food, clothing, and housing; (2) the production of new needs for those means of production, i.e. maintenance and temporal and social organisation; (3) the bourgeois family, which ensures the production of subordinate workers; and (4) the process of turning this history into ahistorical nature and ideology, making it appear 'on the one hand as a natural, on the other as a social relation – social in the sense that it denotes the co-operation of several individuals, no matter under what conditions, in what manner and to what end.'[26]

In this brief history of capitalist development, the appearance of the nature of historically specific capitalist relations is produced by prior relations: people were already assembled at the site of social reproduction, which was subsequently produced as the grounding of the means of production. An original social impulse guides both the French socialist workers whose sociality is 'no mere phrase' but 'a fact of life' and the social units that develop the organised means of producing and satisfying needs. Their social gathering is historically primary; it is later appropriated by the means of production.

As Marx and Engels continue in *The German Ideology*, individual subjectivity emerges only *after* these relations that produce relations:

> Only now, after having considered four moments, four aspects of primary historical relations, do we find that man also possesses "consciousness". But even from the outset this is not "pure" consciousness. The "mind" is from the outset afflicted with the curse of being "burdened" with matter.[27]

In a footnote to this passage, Marx writes: 'Men have history because they must *produce* their life, and because they must produce it moreover in a *certain* way: this is determined by their physical organisation; their consciousness is

25 Marx 2007, p. 124.
26 Marx and Engels 2010, pp. 41–3.
27 Ibid., pp. 43–4.

determined in just the same way.'[28] The access that individuals have to their world is determined by the necessity of prior productive relations; the social gathering that results in social needs then produces the individual consciousness that organises the satisfaction of these needs in a specifically capitalist form.

In this historical staging, sociality is the *a priori* condition that is appropriated by capital. First, a certain siblinghood and practice of sharing presides, but that is taken by the division of time into units of commodified labour and its attendant production of possessive individual subjectivity. Sociality here resolutely precedes individuation, but individuation imposes a totalising production of history onto and *as* consciousness, producing subjects who see themselves as permanently and naturally individual, competitive, and guided by relations of possession.[29]

Later in the same manuscript, Marx and Engels ridicule Max Stirner's 'nonsense about born poets,' which presumes a poet '*remains* what he *is* from birth' unless unfavourable circumstances stop him from 'becom[ing] what *he could become*.'[30] They go on to argue that 'the development of an individual is determined by the development of all the others with whom he is directly or indirectly associated, and that the different generations of individuals entering into relation with one another are connected with one another.'[31] Yet what individuals were before their computation by value and continue to be despite and in excess of value is never clearly stated by Marx and Engels. After the 'indispensable communist revolution … individuals' consciousness of their mutual relations will, of course, … be completely changed,'[32] but whether that form of mutuality will be the survival of a previous form or the instantiation of a new form is difficult to know.

In the part of *Capital*, Volume I, on 'so-called original accumulation', Marx is resolutely dismissive of what could be read in his earlier works as a romanticisation of precapitalist communities. Satirically defining the brutalities of colonisation – the dedicated eradication of Indigenous people in the Americas, the appropriation of all Indian resources, the enslavement of Africans – as the 'idyllic proceedings … of original accumulation', Marx argues that this arch-capitalist movement uniquely involves the collaboration of multiple conflicting forces:

---

28 Ibid., p. 43. Original emphasis.

29 See: Iacomo 2020, p. 86 f.

30 Marx and Engels 2010, p. 423. Original emphasis.

31 Ibid., p. 438.

32 Ibid., p. 439.

> the combination embraces the colonies, the national debt, the modern tax system, and the system of protection. These methods depend in part on brute force, for instance the colonial system. But they all employ the power of the state, the concentrated and organized force of society, to hasten ... the process of transformation of the feudal mode of production into the capitalist mode.[33]

The emergence of a unity of means of production, peculiarly bound by mutual competition, requires the continuation of brutal violence. Here, Marx's criticism is at its most astute, highlighting the necessary aggression of capitalist production, since it is founded on a contradiction: capitalists must work with each other and the state to maintain the conditions of exploitation in which labour-power – embodied as workers – must return to work every day, while each capitalist wants to take as much as possible from all other capitalists, investing only in the individual fantasy of ultimate self-accumulation.

In *Capital*, Marx suggests that whatever existed before the capitalist individual is – at least from the historical vantage of capitalists – unknowable and lost in the brutal subsumptive force of capital. This is emphasised in the *Grundrisse*, where Marx argues that capital produces 'a stage of society in comparison to which all earlier ones appear as mere *local developments* of humanity and as *nature-idolatry*.'[34] The social life preceding capital *appears* to have been a pure form of community in which nature is lived with rather than used 'merely as a ruse so as to subjugate it under human needs'.[35] The only indication Marx gives of what this social life actually was, and how it survives, is given in the *Paris Manuscripts* as workers sharing food, drinks, and stories with each other, as Alfred Schmitt studies at length.[36]

Numerous Marxists – most explicitly, though not most successfully, Erich Fromm[37] – have attempted to adapt Marx's appeal to a seemingly prior sociality into a clear historical trajectory from a pure premodern community to the competitive capitalist individual. Marx, though, is never concerned with a simple and smooth movement of history, in which two undetermined elements are folded into mutual determination through the expanding logic of value's self-accumulation, but rather, as one of the original value-form theorists, Hans-Georg Backhaus, writes, on the 'perverted existence and independ-

---

33 Marx 1990, pp. 915–16. Translation modified.
34 Marx 1993, pp. 409–10.
35 Ibid., p. 410.
36 Schmidt 1983, p. 16 f.
37 Fromm 2001.

ent laws of motion' of 'the objective substance of economic matter'.[38] It is the life of objects assuming a perverse and monstrous form, and the infinite and unresolvable complexity of their dialectical emergence, that holds Marx's focus.

Marxist theory has long struggled to grasp this perverse life of objects and its resistance to any kind of clear historiography. Hegelian dialectics, as Theodor Adorno – whose later lectures gave rise to the tradition of value-critical Marxisms – frustratedly notes in *Negative Dialectics*, has done little to bring about the antagonism of history, instead 'rolling along, however often it may urge the contrary. If the thought really yielded to the object, if its attention were on the object, not on its category, the very objects would start talking under the lingering eye.'[39] An exposure is required at the level of thinking in order for objects to emerge as animated by a monstrous, hidden form of speech. The process of exposure, however, is anything but conceptual. The dialectical formation and determination of subjects and objects in history is not exhausted through the realisation of one in the other; it is the aimless and contradictory encounter of antagonisms, formed by 'a *play of* determination and *in* determination,' as Louis Althusser writes, where the point is the play itself, which is not solely *descriptive* or *prescriptive* but also *inscriptive*, in that it *inscribes* in history the viewpoint from which the tangled process can be observed.[40] Dialectics is observed dialectically.

Dialectics, for Adorno, is a negative process that reflects its own conditions of emergence, never separable as a critical method from the historical process it mutually creates and is created through.[41] The dialectical form observable in and as history necessarily mirrors the form through which it is observed: the dialectic of consciousness. The critical vantage of the present sees unity and clarity in the past that appears to have been broken by the disunity and chaos of the living present. 'No universal history leads from savagery to humanitarianism, but there is one leading from the slingshot to the megaton bomb,' as Adorno writes.[42] Nothing necessarily arises from the movement of history; no progress is inscribed in the passage of time, for Adorno. But the violence of the present is produced by the accumulation of the past. Dialectical history negatively accumulates possibilities and deploys them with increasing force in the present. Adorno here exposes dialectical history to its own negativity, but

38 Backhaus 2005, p. 15.
39 Adorno 2004, pp. 27–8.
40 Althusser 2020, p. 145. Original emphasis.
41 Adorno 2004, p. 141.
42 Ibid., p. 320.

his broad concern with the negative history leading from the slingshot to the megaton bomb misses the intricate social differentiation obscured by this historical process. In the world of the megaton bomb, slingshots persist, not as a primitive relic but as the disjunctive survival of other pasts and other forms of insurgency.[43]

Adorno's negative dialectics remain totalising, disallowing the survival of differential presents. What Adorno and Althusser do not allow is the simultaneous *differentiating* function of the dialectical determination of the value-form. Withholding fugitive pasts from operating in the present, the play of dialectics functions as an antagonism against antagonism, as the maintenance of dialectics itself against the continuity of slingshot insurgencies. But what happens to those pasts? What happens, as Sven Lütticken asks, when the *object* becomes an *obstacle*?[44]

Following recent scholarship in black studies, while reviving Marx's ambivalence regarding the possible survival or subsumption of communities as anticapitalist sociality, here I posit sociality as an irreducible modality that survives despite its form-determination by value and its computation as (im)potentially productive, while avoiding any presupposition of an *a priori* communal order from which individuals were brought by capital into agency and isolation. The irreducible sociality I posit here survives by way of fugitive temporalities beside the present of value-production, which I will attempt to show in the chapters to come.

First, in the next section of this chapter, I study contemporary value-critical Marxisms, revealing how they have moved away from Marx's own ambivalent theorisations of sociality and turned instead towards a totalising present of value-production that forecloses the living antagonism of other temporalities and socialities. Then, in the following section, I show how one Marxist tendency – *operaismo*, which has become 'autonomism' in the Anglophone tradition since the 1990s – argues for a very similar primacy of struggle. However, this autonomist primacy is held back by numerous limitations, which I discuss at length. I then present the multiple ways in which the black radical tradition can open anticapitalist thinking to the survival of fugitive temporalities without abandoning a Marxist dedication to the precise study of value.

43 This is the focus of Tomba's study, which pursues the survival and reactivation of other modes of organising against the dominant hegemony of private property: Tomba 2019, pp. 45–52.

44 Lütticken 2023, pp. 16–17.

3 The Primacy of Value

While very little else unites them, the Marxist tendencies concerned foremost with value and its criticism – which I call value-critical Marxisms – take a far more resolute approach to the temporality of sociality than Marx did. Building on Adorno's movement away from differential pasts that persist in the present, and abandoning Marx's ambivalence regarding the social grounding that not only gives rise to capital but continues within its processes of individuation and dispossession, value-critical Marxists all seem to agree on the totalising historical primacy of value. In these understandings, value arrives as a totalising force, eradicating the possibility of any sociality that historically precedes it. Sociality becomes fully determined by value, the former functioning solely in the latter's service.

The value-critical tradition of *Wertkritik* (value critique) is perhaps most explicit about this binary historicisation of the history of modes of production, in which the relations of other forms of gathering are erased by the arrival of the value-form. For them, given value's function as the abstraction of commodified time in the present, there is no continuity in capitalism between the past and the present. Capital is a totalising temporal rupture. Robert Kurz – still, despite his death in 2012, the principal theorist of this loose tradition that publishes the journal *Exit!* – writes that one of the defining features of contemporary capitalism is its 'inability to assemble armies of abstract labor,' removing any coherence in the association of class.[45] Workers are not united by a local context of value-production, but rather relate to a global imperative concerned only with value itself. This fetishistic fantasy is deprived of local coordinates, for Kurz, making all appearances of relativity ultimately 'subject to conditioning by social forms that imply relations of fetishism, power and force.'[46] These relations are imposed as universals in 'the commodity-producing system of Modernity', so the appearance of difference is itself ideological: 'alternatives remain to date unknown'; the fetishised form of dominated relations is constitutively undifferentiated.[47] Any class struggle becomes meaningless in this formulation since there is no social coherence between specifically determined groups. The local ties of class-determined cooperation are wholly withdrawn into a universal fetish and therefore can pose no threat to the value-determined future of abstract labour.

---

45 Kurz 2014a, p. 350.
46 Kurz 2016, p. 8.
47 Ibid.

In his critique of 'postmodernism' – in which, in a critical style typical of *Wertkritik*, he never explains what he means by the term nor cites any of its theorists – Kurz argues that any dedication to alternative temporalities and social formations that he sees as impossible 'fail[s] to develop any criterion for keeping apart the reference levels of relativity within human history as a history of "cultures" or social formations on the one hand, and determinateness or the absolute in a limited historical space of determinate formation that is itself relative, on the other.'[48] That is, in a world in which the fetish form of the universal is itself historically contingent and relative, any proposition for *other relative particulars* cannot account for the reason for the universal having become the universal, given that it is itself a universalised particular. Value is not born universal but *universalises* itself as the form-determining relation of productive time. Kurz argues that what he calls 'postmodernism' is unable to explain this difference in relativities, because if everything is a 'construct' then the '*substantiality* of the historical social formation remains unreflected and therefore also uncriticised.'[49] Although Kurz's text is marked by its own uncritical failure to specify what he is actually criticising, the point is nonetheless clear: focusing on the differential persistence and particularity of other modalities of being within the universal form of value leaves value's own necessary universality uncriticised; this is because, as Kurz writes, 'abstract labour ... comes first.'[50]

Given that all activist and organisational pursuits for class-based gains are limited to local contexts, with unions representing workers only in a particular industry and particular area, social movements are a mere distraction for *Wertkritik*. Instead, for Kurz, Marxism must concentrate on the form that creates and maintains this oppressive global structure, i.e. value, which *Wertkritik* is intent on abolishing: 'the head of real abstraction must be guillotined'.[51] While the project has no utopian dimension, instead seeing the present as a doomed totality of subsumption in the violence of abstract labour,[52] the abolition of value would give rise not to a Leninist proletarian party-dictatorship, but rather to a society in the absence of class. The crucial attribute of this society would be its freedom from the determining categories of the value-form, i.e. a society in which form-determined subjectivity no longer applies.[53]

---

48 Ibid., p. 10.
49 Ibid., p. 11.
50 Ibid., p. 83.
51 Ibid., p. 22.
52 Leslie 2014.
53 Kurz 2014a, p. 350.

The influential tradition of the *Neue Marx-Lektüre* (NML), with its anglophone variant that includes Christopher J. Arthur and Moishe Postone, is in agreement with *Wertkritik* on this movement away from the workerist concern with class struggle. NML seeks a return to an 'esoteric Marx' who understands capital as 'a form of impersonal domination,' as Amy De'Ath writes in her overview of these traditions.[54] This return is enacted by drawing on Alfred Sohn-Rethel's theory of 'real abstraction,'[55] which emphasises the physical and social force of value despite its immateriality. It is an abstraction with direct material consequences, operating through what Søren Mau, after Marx, calls mute compulsion.[56]

These value-theoretical traditions, as Samuel Chambers emphasises, following Ricardo Bellofiore and Tommaso Redolfi Riva, focus on the *form* of value and its reason for existing as the expression of labour, which undermines the need for a workerist struggle centred on the continuity of the class-form as it has been determined by the requirements of value-productivity.[57] Within the world determined by value, the working class is formed by the forced withdrawal of the capacity to make any claim on one's own labour, which becomes a commodity (labour-power) that must be sold to and consumed by a productive capitalist in order to be valorised; value requires as its mode of operation a living body through which its own productive exchange is facilitated. Class, then, is not an identity, as Nicholas Thoburn states, but rather the process of tearing apart the conditions of survival of a certain part of the population.[58] In the absence of that determining world, those bodies need no longer be determined by the form of class. For the workerist struggle, the revolutionary capacity of the proletariat is its labour, its activity as workers, which it seeks to actualise as an antagonism, while for value-critical Marxisms – especially *Wertkritik* – the revolutionary struggle is the abolition of value, which can only be undertaken at the global level of undifferentiated commodified time at which value operates, rendering meaningless the local concerns of unions, parties, and workerists.

In this value-critical understanding, the revolutionary abolition of value opens a currently unimaginable future, an opening in which current relations of production are functionally impossible since ownership and abstract labour no longer exist. *Wertkritik* attempts to move towards this future, despite not

54 De'Ath 2022, p. 230.
55 See: Sohn-Rethel 1978.
56 Mau 2023.
57 Chambers 2018, pp. 108–9.
58 Thoburn 2024.

knowing what will emerge in the absence of class, unlike the Marxist traditions that have, as Kurz writes, kept abolition in 'an incalculable future' that the present struggle cannot plan for.[59] For Kurz, these traditions – especially those that give primacy to class struggle, from Leninists and Trotskyists to autonomists, which Kurz summarises as 'labour movement Marxism'[60] – cannot counter capital's temporal logic, which impels workers towards the ever-increasing productivity of labour in order to maintain the constant present, to keep everything the same, while – in capital's third industrial revolution – systematically removing any meaningful relation between members of a class.[61] As Kurz's comrade in *Wertkritik* Norbert Trenkle writes, struggling *as* a class is hopeless, since it only affirms the form of labour produced by value. 'The future,' for Trenkle, 'belongs not to class struggle, but to an emancipatory struggle without classes.'[62]

For these value-critical theorists, the current communist struggle cannot hold onto the determining categories of the present, since those categories are precisely that which must be removed for the project of communism. For Trenkle and Kurz, traditions like black studies and feminism that focus specifically on a group-determined struggle – a struggle for black and feminised lives – amount to a fatal compromise with capital's own defining categories, since it is the historical requirements of value and its systematic exclusions that has determined those struggles as black and feminised. The limitations of this value-critical contention are made clear by Søren Mau's attempt to bring the project of value's abolition to a theory of difference.[63]

In his exposé of value's mute compulsion, Mau argues that the past is accumulated in capitalist subjects as '*transcendental debt*,' i.e. 'the continuing presence of the historical origins of capitalism; it is the existence of the past *in* the present.'[64] Through this accumulation of debt, the objective domination of subjects is instantiated para-subjectively: not *in* subjects but *as* the form subjectivity assumes.[65] So far, this disjunctive temporal continuity of the past in the present fits with the temporality of insurgency I am positing here. In the following chapter of *Mute Compulsion*, however, Mau applies this to the production of difference, which is when the 'past' that survives in the present is deprived of its crucial difference.

59 Kurz 1999, p. 97.
60 Kurz 2016, p. 10.
61 Kurz 1999, p. 111.
62 Trenkle 2014a, p. 221.
63 For a substantial critique of Mau's theory of difference, see: Fisher 2024.
64 Mau 2023, p. 135. Original emphasis.
65 See: Roberts 2017, p. 92.

Mau relies on a 'classical sex/gender distinction' to tentatively argue that while sexual difference is ahistorical,[66] gender does 'not *arise* from the logic of capital, even if [it is] in practice completely entangled with the latter.'[67] In his subsequent discussion of race, Mau copies the same logic: 'It is perfectly possible to hold that racism is a social phenomenon which does not *originate* in the capital form yet is conducive to and reproduced by the latter.'[68] What, then, is the actual *difference* of difference? Are race and sex/gender practically distinct in any way? And, most crucially, does their persistence *qua difference* in capitalism have any effect on the totalisation of capital? Do these modalities of being have any function other than providing a permanent ground for capital to homogenise in its commodification of time?

For Mau, the debt carried by subjects as their objective domination is itself undifferentiated. When he later argues that abstract labour does not homogenise proletarians, then, there is no way of understanding how capital determines and appropriates inter- and intra-social differences.[69] Workers are subjected in the past by a compulsion expressed as gender, race, and other differences, but Mau provides no means of differentiating those differences, resulting in a necessary homogenisation of difference and a dismissal of those contemporary discourses concerned precisely with difference. Moreover, the antagonism that this difference continues to stage against capital is neutralised; all generative power is given to capital: it is capital that fully decides the extent of difference allowed to survive within its temporally homogenising project.

For Mau, the past that continues in the present does not carry with it the difference that is nonetheless appropriated by capital from a previous and subsumed mode of production. The difference of the past is withdrawn into the present, but this past is determined only as debt, functioning as a method for disciplining those who diverge from potentially value-productive activities. While Mau's monograph is internal to value-critical Marxisms, and therefore cannot be faulted for its lack of concern with other disciplines, this refusal of the difference carried into the capitalist present from the past misses an opportunity to focus on a living antagonism in the present.

This is a problem common throughout contemporary Marxism, with influential theorists like David Harvey and Ellen Meiksins Wood understanding class exploitation as *constitutive* of capitalism, but race, gender, sex, and other

66 Mau 2023, p. 160.
67 Ibid., p. 162. Original emphasis.
68 Ibid., p. 167. Original emphasis.
69 Ibid., p. 172.

modes of oppression as *incidental* to capitalism.[70] As Ashley J. Bohrer writes, by arguing that class is *logically necessary* to capitalism, while race, gender, and sex are merely *historical coincidences* of capitalism, these theorists presume that logic and theory can be separated from history and materiality.[71] For Bohrer, though, there is no theoretical vantage from which to divide the historical practice of capitalism into necessary and contingent oppressions, since the logic of capital is infinitely intertwined in its historical practice. Moreover, '[t]here has never been a capitalist society that has not relied on gender, race, and sexuality as central structures of exploitation, dispossession, accumulation, and violence,' as Bohrer writes, so there is no historical evidence that shows capital in its ideal function *without* modes of oppression other than class.[72]

By understanding non-class modes of oppression as contingent, the complexity of capitalism's reliance on differential social life is undermined in favour of a paradigm that seems to pursue nothing but surplus-value: capital becomes a seamless process of homogenisation without internal antagonism from the persistence of difference. In this view, there is only one valid form of radical organisation, and it is the pursuit of the abolition of value. But why, then, do so many forms of supposedly non-capitalist oppression not only persist in capitalism but receive such extremely enthusiastic support from capitalist societies? Why do capitalist societies respond with such reactive violence to any assembly of nonproductive social groups, despite their lack of threat to blocking the expansion of value, from black people in the USA and queers in Russia to women in Iran and Palestinians in Gaza?[73] These social groups continue to exist in and with temporalities that are not wholly computed by potential value-production. Their living difference is the focus of an obsessive pursuit of erasure by the forces of capital. Both the survival of these temporalities and oppressive forces' adamant erasure of them exposes their crucial importance as living antagonisms in the project of value.

To find the persistence of these temporalities of difference, Massimiliano Tomba turns to Marx's readings of capital's temporal force in the *Grundrisse* and *Capital*. In Tomba's reading of Marx, capitalist history begins with a range of societies organised by different forms of violence (which he calls '*auctoritas*', in the Roman tradition) and 'cooperative bonds'.[74] In England, the history

70 Harvey 2015; Wood 1988.

71 Bohrer 2019, p. 188.

72 Ibid.

73 Bohrer provides many examples of such capitalist responses to oppression that have no grounding in the economic necessity of expanding value: Bohrer 2019, pp. 187–96.

74 Tomba 2013b, p. 405.

of which Marx studies closely in *Capital*, the dominant temporal order in the beginnings of capitalism was that of the church, which needed to be disbanded in order for 'the chronometric time of the market' to fully dominate.[75] In the sixteenth century, idleness was criminalised, vagabondage was severely punished, and labour was enforced as a moral and legal duty, all while the emergent global proletariat was divided into a disciplined market of living labour in which each body is a competitive capacity of potential production, placing each against and in competition with others. In this sense, for Tomba, slavery is not an anomaly consigned to 'the proto-history of capital', but a necessary threat that displays the most extreme form of temporal discipline – the total ownership of the person who expends labour-time, rather than the ownership of that expended labour-time – potentially available to all workers.[76]

In this narrative, noncapitalist societies are distinguished by their differential temporalities, with oppressive and cooperative relations maintaining separate temporal modes. The emergence of the capitalist state as the organiser of private accumulation is, for Tomba, necessarily the 'encounter and combination of different temporalities', which the state synchronises.[77] This temporal synchronisation is 'the constitutive element of capitalist modernity from its origins'; capitalism is the ongoing and constant violence of synchronising difference through 'a combination of different and relatively independent moments: violence of state, production of proletarians and formally free labour, colonisation, slavery, dissolution of ancient forms of *auctoritas*, enclosures, separation between producers and means of production, discipline of the wage-workers.'[78] Importantly, though, this synchronisation is never totalised. Capital uses, and even *produces*, differentials in productivity 'in order to set the price of migrant labour-power and to determine ethnical divisions of labours', as Tomba writes, but this incurs a necessary encounter with the resistance contained in the living and persistent difference to labour-power's standard form.[79]

While capitalism can often maintain modes of domination that are not strictly capitalist, these come accompanied by modes of cooperation that are resistant to specific forms of violence, leaving capitalism not only with other modes of domination but other modes of resistance also.[80] The temporalities that coexist with capital are not simply residues that passively continue

75 Ibid., p. 406.
76 Ibid.
77 Ibid., p. 405.
78 Ibid.
79 Ibid., 409.
80 Ibid., p. 408.

in the present, but living antagonisms against the possibility of homogenisation.[81] Value-critical Marxisms have so often missed out these other modes of resistance and survival in favour of a critical analysis of the other modes of domination and their gradual subsumption in the homogenising expansion of value. At rare moments, value-critical Marxists acknowledge the necessity of other temporalities and the temporal specificity of capital's totalisation. Kurz, for example, argues that '*the quality of time as such* differs historically and only becomes destructively "economised" in the modern sense in the functional space of capital,'[82] which understands the temporality of value as surrounded and punctured by difference. However, Kurz depoliticises the persistence of other temporalities by arguing that they remain as a mere residue without antagonism.[83] For him, the residue quietly awaits subsumption, rather than living as an active organising modality against the possibility of homogenised time.

For Tomba, to understand the complexity of the survival of difference within the fundamental synchronisation of capitalism, a historiography of original accumulation is needed. That is, we need to understand both the modalities by which capital imposes the normative temporal order of value-production homogeneously onto all forms of human life *and* how differential social temporalities – those of care, of cooperation, of resistance, of mutual aid, of sharing, of poetry – survive despite this homogenisation, asking how they enact a constant antagonism against their subsumption into homogeneity. This is what Tomba will go on to explore in his later monograph *Insurgent Universality*. Scholars in value-critical Marxisms, though, have resolutely ignored Tomba's appeal for a historiography of differential temporalities.

4 Cultural Presents

The general political demand of value-critical Marxisms is the abolition of value. This abolition, however, contains the same ambivalence that pervades other abolitionist demands: what comes after abolition? If racialised, gendered, sexed, and otherwise determined forms of social life are already computed as *impotentially* or *less potentially* productive of value than those determined by whiteness and cisheteromasculinity – that is, if the present and its homogenising temporality of commodified labour is split by differential temporalities that maintain racialised, gendered, and otherwise determined pasts – then the

81 Ibid., p. 410.
82 Kurz 2016, p. 47.
83 Ibid., p. 30.

future of value's expansion has already inscribed the past with its homogenising codes: the black past is already computed as the impotential production of value, since that past carries the accumulation of having been a commodity (enslavement) rather than having been the bearer of a commodity (proletarianisation) into the present, and the feminised past is already computed as the nonproductive labour of reproducing productive labour-power. These pasts will be brought into *any* future, whether it is dominated by the capitalist value-form or not.

The issue here with abolition is that the future contains within it already the differential determination of value, even in the absence of value, since it has determined the social relations through which abolition is enacted. Currently, value-critical Marxisms miss out the survival of differential temporalities and their political use as a disruption in the homogenisation of commodified time. A part of this absence in value-critical Marxisms arises from their general dismissal of any critical tradition that appears to interpret the determining force of value 'purely culturally', as the theorist of *Wertkritik* Roswitha Scholz writes.[84] For her, these traditions – feminism, queer theory, postcolonial theory, and black studies – are totally blind to the material content of capital's violence. She goes so far as to ridicule these traditions as only able to celebrate a softened form of their own exploitation.[85]

Scholz's critique of Judith Butler exemplifies the problem of this position. Scholz argues that contemporary capitalism requires dislodged, deterritorialised, undefinable subjects, detached from particular social groupings with their own determinations of meaning and limitations of practice. To deal with the current fall in the rate of profit and the simultaneous massive proliferation of material wealth, subjects are required to constantly shift their productive activities and circulate capital in innovative ways, including – or especially – when their activity is not directly remunerated with a wage. Scholz sees Butler's theory of gender performativity – which, like many Marxist criticisms of Butler, reads Butler solely as the author of *Gender Trouble* – as simply proposing the full subsumption of the gendered calculation of being into this adaptable and abstract obligation.[86] With their 'passion for the "middle position",' Butler is limited to offering ways in which determined subjects can reposition themselves within the framework of power's restrictions.[87]

---

84 Scholz 2014, p. 139.

85 Scholz, 2011b, pp. 201–2.

86 Scholz 2014, p. 135.

87 Scholz 2011a. Mau offers a similar dismissal of Butler (without any citation): Mau 2023, p. 159.

The fatal problem of this feminist model, for Scholz, is that it merely certifies all gender performances as part of the same oppressive structure that ordinarily regulates heteronormative binary gendering. 'Instead of critiquing both classically modern and the modified, flexible postmodern gendered imaginary,' Scholz writes, 'Butler ultimately merely affirms postmodern (gender) reality.'[88] By constructing nonnormative gendered ways of being as equally constitutive of the productive relations accessible within capitalism and its oppressive order, otherwise subversive socialities become legitimised as essentially productive of power's maintenance.

While eliding the crucial distinction between *performance* and *performativity* that constitutes the core of Butler's early project, resulting in a critique that has nothing to do with Butler's actual intentions,[89] the important point for my purposes here is that Scholz misses the simultaneous regulation of the social practice of freedom which accompanies the enforced ideology of individual freedom. While capital, indeed, promotes the bastion of individual liberty as the task of each entrepreneurial worker, who must distinguish themself by simultaneously producing and circulating value in numerous economic areas, this occurs in tandem with a more traditionally oppressive *restriction* on the practice of social freedom.[90] One is free to be whatever one is, as long as one remains untied to what one becomes. As Fanny Söderbäck emphasises, one can be nonbinary, trans, and/or queer as long as those are productive practices, as long as they operate through individuated entrepreneurial frameworks.[91] Being queer, however, is absolutely banned if what it provides is a nonproductive social life, i.e. a social life unmediated by the production of value. The need for this social life to be prohibited exposes the antagonism it presents to capitalist order.

What Butler sees (as I discuss in chapters three and five) and Scholz misses here is the subtlety of oppression, which is not limited to a single level of universalised productivity: the conditions of production are always differentially assigned. Missing out the differentiating function of the cultural and societal forces of capital that accompany its economic requirements – including, for example, the law, the media, logistics, and the regulation of urban space – leads

88 Scholz 2014, p. 135.

89 Valentina Moro and I discuss this in the introduction to Mason and Moro 2025.

90 This is a mistake most emphatically made by Slavoj Žižek throughout his corpus: he sees only the shift from forcible and explicit oppression to constitutive libidinal compulsion, without ever noticing that the previous form of direct force still survives but is directed against certain populations. The regular murder of black people in the US by police officers, for example, is obviously not a postmodern form of libidinal compulsion; it is the absolute necropolitical force of authority.

91 Söderbäck 2019, pp. 39–40.

to an obfuscation of the living antagonism of different social modalities within capitalism. Queerness is not only a productive possibility for neoliberal capital; it is also a multiplicity of nonproductive social modalities, which, by way of its indirect relation to production, presents an antagonism to the homogenisation of value's temporal order.

The issue with Scholz's criticism is that, while rejecting the capitalist computation of subjects according to the brutal prescriptions of gender, race, sexuality, and other relations of authority, she also refutes the social practices through which groups of determined subjects generate an internal meaning that exceeds the logics of power brutally assigned to them. Scholz's critique of Butler misses the *present* survival of certain social groups. It is this survival that is celebrated in black studies, as I discuss below. For those critical projects concerned centrally with the persistence of difference, like feminism, black studies, queer theory, etc., difference is studied both as part of a project of abolition – abolishing the structural and historical violences that compel and constitute these determining forms of difference – and an opportunity for a meaningful social life internal to those specifically determined groups.

In one of the original turns from the post-Frankfurt School German tradition of value-critical Marxism to an anglophone branch of the *Neue Marx-Lektüre*, Moishe Postone argues explicitly against a conception of value as the determining relation of 'a unitary whole' that disallows the internal production of antagonistic subjectivities. Those Marxist traditions that argue that 'the possibility of critical, oppositional, or revolutionary consciousness must be rooted ontologically or transcendentally – or, at the very least, in elements of social life that purportedly are noncapitalist' afford too much power to value, conceding the entirety of social production to its unitary system.[92] While he 'does not deny the existence or importance of residual, noncapitalist tendencies, which may introduce some heterogeneity into the dominant order and promote critical distance to it,' in *Time, Labor, and Social Domination*, Postone understands 'capitalism as a contradictory society [in order] to indicate that the possibilities for critical distance and heterogeneity are generated socially from within the framework of capitalism itself.'[93] As Marina Vishmidt and Zoe Sutherland emphasise, this is the Marxian critique of totality: 'As an ongoing process of the articulation of mediations, the Marxian critique understands the social totality not as an undifferentiated system, but as internally fractured and contradict-

92 Postone 2003, p. 38.
93 Ibid.

ory in determinate ways.'[94] There is, for Postone as much as for Vishmidt and Sutherland, no need then to look outside of value's own constitutive totality for differential antagonisms, since value's own apparently unitary whole is reliant on its containment of a difference that it can never fully subsume, homogenise, or compute.

Postone argues against a sole political focus on 'residual, noncapitalist tendencies', which he understands as historical antecedents. For him, any tradition concerned with 'noncapitalist tendencies' is rooted in an unpolitical residue, rather than a living antagonism. The numerous tendencies he summarises as 'traditional Marxism' had invested in historically anterior forms of subject-production and social life. This theory of anteriority, Postone argues – correctly and importantly, I think – concedes too much to capital in that this celebration of anterior sociality requires an understanding of capitalism as an uncontradictory historical totality. As Vishmidt and Sutherland point out above, though, this view misunderstands what Marx means by totality.

What I find in black studies, as I argue below, and in contemporary poetry, as I propose in the chapters to come, however, is not sociality as *solely historically antecedent to capital.* Instead, I insist that the residue of insurgent socialities persists *before*, *beside*, and *in the excess of* the present, which is not understandable on a strictly linear temporal model: *before*, in this understanding, means both *behind*, positioned sneakily in a way that anticipates its temporal subsumption into an apparent linear anteriority, and *in the face of*, in front and in refusal. The sociality I pursue here emerges *from and within* the conditions of capital – from its mutual production of the bourgeois individual and the cooperative social conditions of labour[95] – but not *as a function of* capital; it is not produced by capital, but neither does it clearly and smoothly precede capital and continue within its mode of production as an unchanged and unchangeable form.

At times, Marx gestures towards this before-and-beside temporality of social life, positing a gathering of shared desires for communal survival that arises in moments of insurgency – in the Paris Commune of 1871 or the barricades of 1848 – in which revolutionaries realise a sudden capacity for caring that exceeds both the productive cooperation of capitalist labour and the competitive antagonism of bourgeois individual relations. In these instances, which I explore in the afterword, the 'residual, noncapitalist tendencies' that introduce heterogeneity to capital, as Postone writes above, are not simple antecedents, but rather disruptive modalities of social gathering that cannot be positioned on

94 Vishmidt and Sutherland 2022, p. 68.

95 Postone is particularly attentive to this interplay throughout Postone 2003.

a linear temporal scale: they *are already*, but they *are not how they were*; they exist *in constitutive and disruptive relation* to capital, but are neither *formed by* nor *formative of* its totalising social order.

It is, for this reason, important to maintain a nondeterministic understanding of the primacy of insurgency as surviving, despite capital's always incomplete process of historical totalisation and homogenisation, in a temporality that is *before, beside*, and *in the excess of* the present.

The disruptive and contradictory grounding of differential temporalities celebrated in black studies, which I engage with in more detail below, is elided by Kurz, Trenkle, Mau, Scholz, and Postone, among other value-critical Marxists, who want to erupt out of capital without concern for the differential temporal accumulation stored in different subjects and social groups.[96]

In the next section, I analyse the Marxist traditions that have focused on what appears to be a very similar temporality to the primacy of insurgency that I centre this study around, while also bringing out some of the political problems with this temporality.

5 Antagonistic Primacies

One tradition in Marxism has, since the 1950s, rooted itself firmly in the primacy of struggle that I am proposing here: *operaismo*. Centred around the journal *Quarderni Rossi* (*Red Notebooks*), the *Sinistra operaista* (the workerist Left) was never a strictly coherent party. 'Despite its "-ism,"' as Gigi Roggero writes, 'operaismo always refused ideology and any loyalty to sacred scriptures.'[97] Operaismo was formed in response to new struggles between Italian workers in the 1950s and '60s, as workers from the South moved to the rapidly industrialising North, where the sudden scale of their arrival caused local workers to turn against them.[98] This tension turned into a possibility for the young, militant communists who became the *operaisti*, including Mario Tronti, Raniero Panzieri, Antonio Negri, and Romano Alquiati, all of whom began as organisers and later became theorists.

The most explicit formulation of a temporality of struggle among the *operaisti* is by Mario Tronti, whose great 'theoretical discovery', as Jason Read writes,

96 Among the theorists listed, Postone is the exception in that he recognises and names these differential temporalities, although he positions his project explicitly against these 'residuals'.

97 Roggero 2023, p. 1.

98 Checchi 2021, p. 99.

'was to invert the dominant interpretation of capitalism. Rather than analyse the structures and transformations of the capitalist mode of production, Tronti argued that it is necessary to examine the history and movement of the working class.'[99] This is not, however, a solely logical argument, but historical also: for Tronti, we have 'to start again from the beginning: and the beginning is the class struggle of the working class.'[100] It is not only that we have to *study* working class struggles first, but that those struggles *historically precede* their appropriation and division by capital.

The political demand of this historical primacy is, as Read writes, to be *disturbed* by the problem of capital; we live in a system that depends on the abstraction of labour, turning 'the antagonistic force of living labour' into 'abstract, unskilled, and interchangeable units'.[101] Our political stasis in these conditions comes from the assumption that our labour is reliant on its consumption by the capitalist mode of production: presuming the exploiting force to be primary, we give our living labour over as the generator of our own exploitation, permanently maintaining the systematic requirement of the process of abstraction. The *operaist* project affirms both that the cooperative impulse of living labour is resistance, and that resistance is primary, which, if accepted, does not only *disturb* us and our stable temporal assumptions, but exposes us (and our living labour) *as a disturbance.*

One consistent criticism of this position, as Marco Checchi explores, has been its lack of empirical, historical evidence. Although to some extent satisfied by others outside of *operaismo*, those in the tradition itself are yet to provide a historical treatise on the primacy of resistance.[102] For Checchi, however, as for Roggero, this is a strength of the movement, rather than a fault: the primacy of resistance is

> a concept that is never demonstrated as it is always busy in anticipating the future, in reading those tendencies within the present, in exploring the materiality of possibilities. This is the strength of the primacy of workers' struggle: an axiom, a method, a new mode of tracing conceptual trajectories.[103]

99 Read 2023, p. 220.
100 Tronti 1979.
101 Read 2023, p. 226, p. 221.
102 Checchi's own book is an attempt at this, though more through the history of philosophy than of social movements. Tomba 2019 and Chakrabarty 2000 are also important contributions to a history of social movements in which resistance is primary.
103 Checchi 2021, pp. 101–2. See also: Roggero 2023, p. 1.

Operaismo is theory-in-action, moving with the constant resistance of living labour as an antagonism to its abstraction: it is the *practice of philosophy*, as Negri proposes.[104]

With the publication of Michael Hardt and Antonio Negri's *Empire* in 2000, the *operaist* temporality entered global academic discourse. For these post-*operaisti* writing in English – also called autonomists, following the name of an Italian faction of the *operaisti* that split from the original formation in the 1970s – the class struggle precedes the exploitation of the proletariat by capital: 'The power of the proletariat imposes limits on capital and not only determines the crisis but also dictates the terms and nature of the transformation,' as Hardt and Negri write. '*The proletariat actually invents the social and productive forms that capital will be forced to adopt in the future.*'[105] The general principle followed here, directly indebted to Tronti, is: 'resistance is prior to power.'[106] This temporal assertion, however, is not intended to be *historical*. What Hardt and Negri pursue is not historical evidence of the primacy of resistance, but the political effect of taking this primacy as an axiom.[107] Citing Gilles Deleuze, they write, 'this axiom is that desire is active and power is reactive. Or rather, with respect to power, "*La résistence est première*". Resistance is temporally and ontologically prior to power.'[108] The methodological axiom of this primacy is not substantiated historically, which is, according to its proponents, precisely its radical invitation.

This optimistic insistence on the primary activity of resistance and the reactionary reactivity of power gained enormous influence in the academy. As Roggero writes, however, the radicality of this proposition was watered down by its popularity. In the 'liberal form of freedom' of universities, 'you can say whatever you want, as long as nothing you say affects the relationships of domination.'[109] The diffusion of the project's militancy happened by way of *Empire*'s broad acceptance, which took Hardt and Negri as posing a new *truth* for Marxism, a new discourse to be followed as a categorical praxis. But precisely the novelty of the *operaisti* was their dedication to the fact that the primacy of resistance refuses any stable truths or systematic forms of authority, even revolutionary forms. If resistance is primary, then nothing is stable and never should be. *Empire* was received as a primary authority, which completely undercut its

104 Negri 1999. See also: Read 2023, p. 219.
105 Hardt and Negri 2000, p. 268. Original emphasis. See also: Read 2003, p. 13.
106 Hardt and Negri 2017, p. 78.
107 Hardt and Negri 2002, p. 13. In Checchi 2021, p. 101.
108 Hardt and Negri 2002, p. 4.
109 Roggero 2023, p. 3.

insistence on the primacy of resistance. Roggero—somewhat unfairly in my view—blames the authors themselves for the depleting effect of the popularity of their work.

Of greater concern for my intentions here is Hardt and Negri's separation of the production of subjectivity from the mode of production. 'After a new theory of value,' they write in *Empire*, 'a new theory of subjectivity must be formulated that operates primarily through knowledge, communication, and language.'[110] Here, the production of value is not understood as *already* the production of subjectivity, insofar as value is the relation that determines the form of productive labour embodied in and as workers; its determining function is the abstraction of labour, which is to say the computation of all human activity as potentially (or impotentially) productive of value. This is Hardt and Negri's clearest divergence from Marx's labour theory of value.

Rejecting the German tendency that understands value as the determining relation of the form of subjectivity, which occurs through the abstraction and generalisation of labour-power as abstract labour, they turn instead to the Italian tradition – followed still by Hardt, alongside Franco 'Bifo' Berardi and Maurizio Lazzarato[111] – that posits value as an adaptable method, as a central rubric of capitalism that can assume many forms, including cultural production and ideology as well as the extraction and abstraction of labour. 'The various institutions of modern society should be viewed as an archipelago of factories of subjectivity,' as they write; this archipelago, however, is not bound by value as its cohering force, but rather by an amorphous power.[112]

The institutions that fabricate subjectivity, for Hardt and Negri, are not necessarily capitalist; their primary function is not necessarily the production of profit. This disconnects the crucial insights of value-critical Marxisms, which link the production of (specifically capitalist) subjectivity and value. Instead, in their desperate attempt to *respond* to proletarian subjectivities that exceed subsumption, these archipelagos of factories of subjectivity turn workers towards 'immaterial labor',[113] relinquishing the strict economic mode of value and diffusing it into 'cultural phenomena'.[114] Thus diffused, for Hardt and Negri, all activity becomes productive of unspecific 'values', which forces labour into a 'tendency to become increasingly immaterial.'[115]

110 Hardt and Negri 2000, p. 29.
111 Berardi 2012; Lazzarato 2014.
112 Hardt and Negri 2000, p. 196.
113 Ibid., p. 269.
114 Ibid., p. 275.
115 Ibid., pp. 28–9.

The problem with this view is that value is and has always been immaterial; it is a relation, not an object. It nonetheless functions only through material effects; it determines labour as productive of itself, whether that labour is intellectual, speculative, or industrial. As Moishe Postone writes, taking a very sharp turn away from autonomism and what he calls 'traditional Marxism', 'Marx's theory provides the basis for a critique of the form of production and the form of wealth (that is, value) that characterize capitalism, rather than simply calling into question their private appropriation.'[116] This centring of the *form* of production emphasises the 'abstract form of domination' through which value functions as a determinant of class and labour, which results in the political impossibility of *using* labour as an antagonism *against* capital, since labour itself is historically specific to capitalism and required for the expansion of its form of production: 'the working class is *integral to* capitalism rather than the embodiment of its negation,' as Postone argues.[117]

Hardt and Negri's account of the diffusion of value into numerous institutions and immaterial forms of labour has numerous obfuscating effects on anticapitalist criticism. Firstly, it misses the specific means by which value determines subjectivity as the general project of capital, displacing the fundamental insight of Marx's economic criticism. Autonomism thus fails to situate the violation of social life in the specific historical conditions of capitalism, thus obscuring the historical specificity of labour as a uniquely capitalist form. The material socialities that exceed value's determination of labour and persist within capitalism precisely as difference then become intangible and indefinite, since they cannot be separated from the strictly commodified temporality of capital and its subjective form.

Hardt and Negri's political project is to withdraw the 'immanent antagonism' of labour before it is commodified as labour-power, operating the cooperative conditions of the scene of production as a refusal of the diffusion of labour into immateriality.[118] For Tronti and the autonomists who follow him, it is the conditions of capitalist labour that provide the collective cooperation from which a revolutionary working-class vanguard is realisable. In this understanding, the primacy of struggle is still reliant on capitalist labour for its cooperative assembly. That is, the antagonism of this primary resistance does not *exceed* the form in which capital determines the individual lives of sociality and the social lives of individuals. They remain consigned to capital's determination

116 Postone 2003, p. 17.

117 Ibid. Original emphasis.

118 Checchi 2021, p. 103.

of their assembly. As Tronti writes, 'the working class should materially discover itself to be a part of capital if it wants to then counterpose the whole of capital to itself. It must recognise itself as a *particular element* of capital if it wants to present itself as its *general* antagonist.'[119]In this model, the form-determination of workers' subjectivity by the process of producing value is reproduced and maintained. Workers do not access an excess that is undetermined by value, or communally erase the marks of determination by refusing the form of subjectivity; rather, they antagonistically operate the subjective form of collective labour-power that has been determined by the specific requirements of the expansion of value, which are historically unique to capitalism. The mode of production that constitutes capitalism, then, is required for the general antagonism of workers to be used antagonistically: anticapitalism necessarily follows capitalism. Not only does this afford primacy, after all, to capital (if not to *power* understood as a general, ahistorical force), it also requires revolutionary actors to have already become uniformly capitalist. The time of insurgents' lives must be determined already as potentially value-productive, which ignores the many populations systematically excluded from this potential abstraction.

In autonomist understandings of the primacy of resistance, it is not possible to practice *differential primacies*, i.e., to actualise the obscured social lives of those groups who have specifically been denied the format of homogenised labour-power. They foreclose the possibility of a specifically *black primacy* that precedes and exceeds whiteness, *queer primacy* that precedes and exceeds cisheteronormativity, or *Palestinian primacy* that precedes and exceeds genocidal Zionism, for example. For them, instead, *living labour* is primary, which does not account for all those forms of social life that have been specifically denied the form of potential productivity, including feminised, colonised, and enslaved populations.

6 Moten's General Antagonism

As I discussed in the introduction, the temporal and historical primacy of difference *qua* insurgency is the focus of Fred Moten's work, often in collaboration with Stefano Harney. While his proposition for a 'general antagonism' includes the logical primacy of the *operaisti*, Moten is adamant that the primacy of insurgency is historical.[120] As he writes in the first sentence of his first mono-

119 Tronti 2019, p. 31. Original emphasis.
120 Harney and Moten 2013, pp. 100–59.

graph, 'The history of blackness is testament to the fact that objects can and do resist.'[121] Africans were turned into objects through enslavement, but those objected people never stopped resisting: they escaped, they jumped overboard, they formed fugitive communities, and they continuously rose up against their enslavers to insurgently refuse their status as objects, turning *objectification* into *objection*. Moten's political and theoretical task, as he writes in the footnote to the sentence above, is to expose the transgressive performances and performativity of blackness:

> Blackness, in all of its constructed imposition, can tend and has tended toward the experimental achievement and tradition of an advanced, transgressive publicity. Blackness is, therefore, a special site and resources for a task of articulation where immanence is structured by an irreducibly improvisatory exteriority that can occasion something very much like sadness and something very much like devilish enjoyment. To record this improvisational immanence – where untraceable, anoriginal rootedness and unenclosed, disclosing outness converge, where that convergence is articulation by and through an infinitesimal and unbridgeable break – is a daunting task.[122]

The condition of violation that marks black lives today is both maintained and disrupted by the history of blackness, in that the persistent project of racist violation was constantly exceeded by the 'irreducibly improvisatory exteriority' that marks black social life. Blackness is sustained in the excess of its violation through the material, public performances of black sociality, which range from – as I cited from Harney and Moten at the beginning of the introduction – barbeques to music.[123]

As the above passage clearly shows, though, Moten's style often does more to obscure this historical primacy than to expose it. While maintaining an insistence on the historical primacy of resistance to oppression throughout his corpus, as I explore in chapter five, this is often conveyed through poetic statements that come across more as scripture than scholarly arguments. In *All Incomplete*, for example, Harney and Moten argue:

> Prior resistance to individuation is both the primary mode of our perversion as well as the structure and activity of persistence that is most

121 Moten 2003, p. 1.
122 Moten 2003, p. 255n1; see also, p. 258.
123 Harney and Moten 2021, p. 121.

> essentially productive of value. In this regard, perversion is total education's primary object and justification insofar as all our efforts at social reproduction must be deemed wrong, insufficient, and weak.[124]

At first, here, social life is revealed to be rooted in *prior resistance*, which comes before *individuation*. There is already a historical argument at work here, even if not clearly outlined through historical analysis. This social life is *perverse* in that it is not reducible to the normative form of individuality. This perversion both allows for the survival of sociality as prior resistance *and* feeds capital with its endless energy: it is the activity of social assembly that impels people to constantly gather in productive ways, which can be appropriated for value-production. Through this process, the repressive regime of 'total education' (taken from Foucault[125]) appears to be the generative power, producing perversion in order to control it. However, perversion is in fact the *justification for* total education insofar as the latter is reliant on the prior excess of the former: perverse sociality always exceeds the format of aggregated individuals.

I focus on this passage to highlight the poetic attention that is required to withdraw a specific historical analysis and political programme from Moten's thinking. Moten has to be read, to some extent, as a poet even in his critical scholarly texts; to access the excess he is constantly celebrating, a certain speculative investment in the excess of the words themselves has to be practiced. This is what makes him crucial to a poetic study of value. However, this obscurity is not limited to style; it is also a feature of his historical and critical frameworks, which has caused abundant criticism.

Two of the most familiar, and superficial, criticisms of Moten concern his life and the experience of reading his work. The former concern emphasises the immediate disjunction of a widely renowned senior professor, awarded Guggenheim and McArthur fellowships and employed at the most prestigious universities in the US, who nonetheless operates under the image of an 'anti-scholar', an 'insider-outsider', who attacks the bourgeois and white supremacist structure of the institution from within.[126] The second, and connected, familiar response to Moten's writing is its impenetrable difficulty. With his frequent use of unexplained neologisms, digressions upon digressions without a summar-

124 Ibid., pp. 63–4.
125 Ibid., pp. 61–2.
126 This criticism, however, turns very quickly into a simplistic and reactionary call for a mythical return to the simple purity of the universally accessible Good and True. For an archetype of this reductionism, see: Keegan 2022.

ised central point, and poetic mode of criticism, his writing requires a reading practice more akin to faith than criticism.[127]

While Moten, unlike Judith Butler, has never written a defence of his difficult style,[128] listening to interviews with him shows that this is not a style limited to his academic texts; he speaks in the same way. Moreover, he does not come from a bourgeois academic class, where the structural maintenance of privilege and exclusion of others is entrenched by jargon; rather, he is a poet who works as a professor and writes in a complex and poetic way because he is a poet writing about complex problems.

Moten is, of course, an academic, and works at a university; he also provides multiple important ways, both practical and theoretical, of criticising and refusing the structures he works inside. As he and Harney contend in response to claims of the hypocrisy of working at institutions they are against, *quitting* the Dodge automobile assembly factories in Detroit was never a demand of General Baker and all the workers in the wildcat strikes he organised in the 1960s. Necessarily, they were both the *workers* and the *antagonists* of the automobile industry in Michigan.[129] While Harney and Moten are professors at universities, not workers at a car factory, their refusal of the institution is nonetheless bound up with their work at those institutions. Either way, I am far more concerned with the political implications of Moten's theoretical project than these dismissals of his difficulty (and the same goes for Butler[130]).

The more substantial criticism of his writing centres on its tenuous link to political practice. George Shulman studies Harney and Moten's reading of the Black Panthers in their first book, *The Undercommons*, in which they argue that the revolutionary group was revolutionary because it had *no politics*; it was not a group gathered under the name of shared interests, but was rather a social assembly that emerged precisely as the continued practices of their specific and local sociality. 'The Panthers theorized revolution without politics,' as Harney and Moten write, 'which is to say revolution with neither a subject nor a principle of decision. Against the law because they were generating law, they practiced an ongoing planning'.[131] Their practice was the survival of black sociality rather than the representation of united subjects under a set of common interests.

---

127 Dues 2024.

128 Butler 1999.

129 Harney and Moten 2020a.

130 Moro and I have written about this in our introduction to Mason and Moro 2025.

131 Harney and Moten 2013, p. 18.

Shulman questions this withdrawal of politics: 'By shifting the revolutionary from politics to sociality, by depicting Panthers engaged only in planning as social reproduction but not in politics, their agonistic refusal to be governed appears only *against* "politics," not *as* a politics or a tension within politics.'[132] Harney and Moten's political withdrawal creates a binary in which everything that engages with politics is complicit in the bourgeois, white supremacist form of the subject and its discourse of mutual interests, while anything that exceeds politics is deemed truly revolutionary.

The challenge of this antipolitics may depend on the meaning of excess, to the extent that Moten seems to uncritically celebrate *any* excess to the normatively political. As Shulman notes, Moten's absolute idealisation of the *ante*-political excess of politics lacks a historical materialist grounding in that those historical and contemporary cases of political refusal – Shulman lists 'Native tribes, maroons, or Zapatista activists' – ultimately have to return to a certain conception of grouped interests based on political subjectivity.[133] They have to realise themselves at some point as a coherent subject-group in order to protect themselves from internal divisions. However excessive to normative politics the group may be, it becomes split by 'inequalities of class, gender, or homophobia', and then it needs an appeal to a coherent political interest that supersedes these divisions.[134]

Kevin Ochieng Okoth's criticism similarly encounters in Moten a possible absence of political application, which Okoth finds by equating Afropessimism with Moten's 'black optimism'. Afropessimism is one of the two main traditions in contemporary black studies – which is also called the black radical tradition – alongside black optimism, although Moten no longer uses this term. Most importantly for my purposes here, while Afropessimists are certainly anti-capitalist, they explicitly refuse political action. They argue that black life is already lived as death, already closed to the possibility of Being insofar as Being is the ontology of whiteness.[135] While Moten's 'black optimism' might seem directly opposed to Afropessimism, Okoth argues that ultimately Moten's celebration of life, and his emphasis on the survival of black sociality despite the insistent enforcement of its death in white ontology, is nothing but a slight variation in terminology: Afropessimists say 'death' and Moten says 'life', but ultimately, for 'both Afro-pessimists and Black Optimists, the afterlife of slavery

132 Shulman 2020, pp. 288–9.
133 Ibid., p. 291.
134 Ibid.
135 See: Hart 2018.

is characterised by the social death of the Black/Slave'.[136] This social death situates all political activity in a prior negative ontology from which blackness can never emerge; blackness is not, in Okoth's reading of both black radical traditions, a social grouping organised around common interests, and therefore cannot be elicited into revolutionary abolitionist projects.

While Okoth quotes Moten as noting 'the slightest most immeasurable reversal of emphasis' that separates his project from Afropessimism,[137] the former's inattention to the significance of this reversal makes his criticism miss the entire point of black optimism. This reversal is made clear by Harney in an interview:

> There's so much misunderstanding, especially in Afropessimism, about Indigenous sovereignty. ... That comes from putting things backwards: imagining sovereignty precedes the rebellion. And ... that's just not correct. Historically, ... the experience of Indigenous struggles is that one can find a ... fugitive home [in a] land that's not sovereign.[138]

In this historical understanding, the Indigenous use of land as a social and fugitive home precedes its forced accumulation into the sovereign privacy of capital and settler colonial claims. While Indigenous land is then subsumed into the form of property, the 'fugitive home' nonetheless survives. It lives on in a fugitive temporality, within and against the subsumptive present.

As one of Afropessimist's primary theorists, Frank B. Wilderson III – whom Moten calls 'the last great theorist of the subject'[139] – writes, Afropessimism understands Black people as the 'baseline other' of white Humanity.[140] The world of Humans, for Wilderson, is constructed on the scene of the slave plantation, where (white) Humans are embodied subjects and (black) Slaves are the negative non-identity of Being, produced and maintained by whiteness. As Wilderson writes, 'the Slave wakes up in the morning wondering, What will these Humans do to my flesh? A hydraulics of anxiety that is very different than exploitation and alienation.'[141] The operation of the world, for Wilderson, is mechanical and automatic: racism does not arise from the bad intentions

---

136 Okoth 2020, no page numbers.
137 Ibid.
138 Moten and Harney 2020b, minutes 31–3.
139 Moten and Harney 2020a, minute 24–5.
140 Wilderson 2020, p. 164. For this discussion of Wilderson's texts, I follow his style of capitalisation.
141 Ibid., p. 303.

of misguided people, but is the structural groundwork of the possibility of Humanity *qua* whiteness, which forms the central axis of Being and its impulse to consume and destroy its negative impossibility, i.e. blackness.

In this sense, the nonbeing of blackness exceeds working-class exploitation, Indigenous dispossession, or misogynist patriarchy. 'Slaves *themselves* are consumed, not their labor power. Slaves are implements, not workers,' Wilderson writes.[142] This total negativity is structurally necessary to the world-making project of whiteness, for Wilderson, which opens a multiform impossibility that constitutes the adamant pessimism of his project. All pursuits of redemption, in any form, including critical theory and revolutionary struggle, must ultimately realise themselves in the form of the World, which is a constitutive part of whiteness, making any movement an affirmation of the nothingness of the Slave. There is no possibility of promoting or even experiencing the 'fugitive home' in which Harney grounds the primacy of insurgency. 'Afropessimism,' for Wilderson, 'is a looter's creed: critique without redemption.'[143]

Black optimism contests the looter's creed by arguing that we do not loot in response to our property being taken, nor are we formed by the imposition of possession or its absence; rather, social life is already riotous, already looting before there is anything to loot.[144] The subsequent question is: what to do with the loot? Black optimism is not far from a looter's creed, in its celebration of the radical excess of black sociality that disrupts the oppressive order of every racialising institution in its project of the general antagonism, but its next step is to share the loot. The looter exceeds the logic of property, taking and sharing instead of appropriating and accumulating. Their possession of property is public and shared, not private and expansive. 'Homelessness is the condition in which you *share* your house,' as Moten says. 'Literally, it's the condition in which you *give your house away*, constantly, as a practice of hospitality.'[145]

This is 'the slightest most immeasurable reversal of emphasis' that Okoth uses to homogenise the projects of Afropessimism and black optimism, but the difference is vast: for Moten and Harney, sociality is the prior condition of life, the survival of which is constitutively insurgent; social life is the constant insurgent practice of sharing. This sharing precedes its appropriation into the logics of private property, and remains despite appropriation: people continue to be socially constituted by the fundamental generative principle of sharing and being shared. Carried into the world of private property and racialising

142 Ibid., p. 304. Original emphasis.
143 Ibid., p. 174.
144 Shulman 2020, p. 284.
145 Moten and Harney 2020b, minutes 13–14.

violence, this sociality of sharing persists as an internal insurgency, disrupting the possibility of the full totalisation of private property. For Wilderson, meanwhile, the process of appropriation produces a necessary nothingness that is constitutively dependent on the productive project of whiteness and its regime of private property. For Afropessimists, there is nothing to go back to, and no surviving remnant in the present, while for black optimists, the fugitive survival of insurgent sociality in the present is the revolutionary project always on the brink of actualisation.

Afropessimism's temporality of struggle is peculiarly aligned with that of value-critical Marxisms, with each positing power as the prior totality, which produces subjects in their differential social forms. Both autonomist (post-)Marxists and black optimists stage instead a reversed temporality in which social life is primary and constitutively insurgent, while power is a reaction to that primary insurgency.

From the perspective of a critical methodology, then, I see the most generative tension as that between autonomism and Afropessimism on the one hand, and value-critical Marxisms and black optimism on the other. Given, though, what I have argued above are my disagreements with autonomism, and my dedication to value-criticism as the primary critical modality for understanding the complex operation of the production and form-determination of subjectivity, I find the latter tension to be the most generative for radical theory and communist praxis.

The crucial point of Moten's and Harney's project in black optimism is that blackness is prior to the racialising ontology of capital, not produced by – or in a dialectical totality with – Being *qua* whiteness. 'As opposed to seeing blackness as an ontological status that is introduced or even produced by anti-blackness,' as King-Ho Leung writes, 'Moten argues that "blackness is ontologically prior to the logistic and regulative power that is supposed to have brought it into existence".'[146] That is, ontology *qua* whiteness is *in relation to* blackness *qua* nothingness. Nothingness here is absolute; it is the prior and persistent condition of being, from which Being seeks to extract an ontological project of white supremacy and racialising order. But, as Leung argues, the 'distinction between "relative" and "absolute" nothingness is what fundamentally distinguishes [Moten's] paraontology from Afro-pessimism.'[147]

This paraontology is the philosophical aspect of Moten's work that separates it from the equivalent temporality of insurgency in autonomism. Moten's

---

146 Leung 2023, p. 47. Citing Moten 2013.

147 Leung 2023, p. 50.

is not a political argument; it does not, as Tronti's originary formulation of the primacy of resistance in *operaismo* does, attempt to assemble the working class of a particular industry, but rather to assert the *anti-* and *ante-*political affirmation of blackness as the absolute nothingness on which the modern metaphysics of whiteness relies. This is a philosophical argument that asserts paraontology as the antagonistic excess of ontology; it posits the absolute and prior nothingness of blackness as preceding and exceeding Being.

This argument, despite the political force with which Moten conveys it in interviews, has no immediate political grounding, while the equivalent autonomist temporality *only* has a political grounding: the latter is a claim drawn from the struggles of industrial workers insofar as their struggle is understood to precede capital and force its totality of authorities into a constant reaction and defence. Moten's claim, as Shulman writes, is instead the operation of a fugitive imaginary as constitutive of social life in the excess of its form-determination, formed of 'depictions of impasse as nominations that could be otherwise; as organizing fictions whose world-building effects we must trace and assess; as speech-acts we can take up, revise, or refuse.'[148] This is at once a *poetics* and a *praxis* that reconstitutes the ontological grounding of Being, undermining its absoluteness by drawing out the paraontological primacy of blackness as the negative absolute.[149]

Moten's philosophical argument for paraontology is in need of a political grounding. While *Poetics of Value* is not precisely that political grounding, it is an attempt to find and expose literary and social openings into that political grounding, which I then hope to more fully actualise in subsequent projects. The criticisms of Moten's obscurity or insistence on a historical grounding that he never explicitly provides often result in a dismissal of Moten's work and of black studies generally as an important tradition in radical theory and philosophy.[150] My intention here is to bring out Moten's theory of primary insurgency by situating its historical claims in contemporary poetry, in order to provide not exactly a precise historical grounding – which others have done and are doing[151] – but an access point to that insurgency in the literary practices of our contemporary.

---

148 Shulman 2020, p. 273.

149 Proctor argues for the necessity of this kind of specifically imaginative, speculative and creative theorising in black studies, which she finds in the works of Moten and Saidiya Hartman: Proctor 2018.

150 C. Warren 2017, p. 220. See also: Leung 2023, p. 46.

151 I outlined many of the theorists doing so in the introduction. Notable are the works of Neferti X.M. Tadiar, Saidiya V. Hartman, Massimiliano Tomba, R.A. Judy, and Denise Ferreira da Silva.

Despite the criticisms of his work, then, I find Moten's poetic dedication to a prior sociality, in its constitutive insurgency, not only stylistically useful for a poetics of value but crucial in framing the uncapturability of this excessive sociality. I am not claiming that a simple undetermined remnant of social life remains operative in the present without determination by the requirements of value-production, and without affecting production. Instead, I am arguing that the form-determination of subjectivity by value in capitalism is *reliant* on a constitutive excess that survives as insurgency, which is *exposed* – however mutely or minutely – through certain forms of discursive and social gathering. The crucial aspects of this primary insurgency are that it *precedes and exceeds* capital, capital *needs* it, and it can be *actualised* as an antagonism against capital. The way I read the four poets in the chapters to come is as discursive and material openings to a perverse social life, whose perversion – as Harney and Moten write above – is the modality of both its violation and its survival despite violation.

Moten's poetics of primary insurgency brings out the emotional and social complexity of the 'irreducibly improvisatory exteriority that can occasion something very much like sadness and something very much like devilish enjoyment'.[152] What this emotional intensity makes possible is not just a critique of value by means of poetry, but a *poetics of criticising value* that turns the activity of criticising into social insurgency itself. This is what I find so necessary about Moten's project, despite its limitations, which range from its unstable historical grounding to the possible synonymy of his vast idiosyncratic idiolect, in which *fugitivity, insurgency, sociality, anaoriginality, incompleteness, insistent previousness, the general antagonism, black optimism, blur, irreducible improvisation, friendship*, etc., may all just be ways of saying the same thing. That thing, I nonetheless maintain, is worth saying.

My proposition for an opening of value criticism to the fugitive social temporalities of black studies arises foremost from engagements with Fred Moten's work, to which I turn in Part 2 of *Poetics of Value*, especially chapters five and six. However, this temporal poetics is not exclusive to Moten. Fugitivity and insurgent survival are studied throughout the black radical tradition. In the final section of this chapter, I study some of the other ways these temporalities are theorised. I focus on the ways in which contemporary scholarship in black studies locates the survival of antagonistic socialities that persist within the present, not as the simple continuity of a pure and prior past, but as the disjunctive survival of those forms of life whose survival is specifically prohibited by capital.

152 Moten 2003, p. 255n1.

7 The Routes and Roots of Survival

In *Ordinary Notes*, literary theorist and black studies scholar Christina Sharpe posits the accumulated brutality of the past as the living marker of survival: in a world in which the 'crime is being Black and surviving,' it is an extraordinary, 'strange miracle' to witness generalised '[r]efusals of brutality.'[153] This practice of refusal is the basis of Sharpe's temporal wish: 'I want acts and accounts of care as shared and distributed risk, as mass refusals of the unbearable life, as total rejections of the dead future.'[154] The temporality of Sharpe's demand here is striking: the death of the future has already determined the very possibility of speaking, of criticising the conditions of futurity.

As a graduate student, Sharpe developed a compulsive gesture, which she was unaware of at the time. As she spoke, her fingers would rise up to her neck and stretch around it: the gesture 'was, for all intents and purposes, self-strangulation.'[155] The possibility of speech was already determined and prohibited by a vast accumulation of forced silence, of innumerable scenes of strangulation. Regardless of the lived conditions of the present – being a graduate student in the time of the story, or a renowned critical theorist, writer, and professor in the time of its narration – the strangulation of speech persists as the determination of feminisation and racialisation, eradicating the possibility of *any* future absent of strangulation without first contending with the living continuity of the past in the present. 'I was strangling words before they even left me throat. Speech and speechlessness; each one has a cost.'[156]

The future is not the site of a possible opening for Sharpe; it is already determined as the wounded wake of this brutality. Instead, it is the multiple meanings of the 'burning past', as Frantz Fanon poeticises,[157] that holds the general antagonism of this refusal. The strangling hand has been trained to encircle its own throat, but it can be trained on other throats, and into other shapes, instead.

Media theorist and black studies scholar Rizvana Bradley calls this twisted temporality 'the black residuum', which names a condition of irreparable opacity: this 'opacity is constitutively bound to the abyssal, which dispossesses any teleologies of repair,' but also contains a uniquely persistent antagonism, in

153 Sharpe 2023, p. 332, p. 350.
154 Ibid., p. 333.
155 Ibid., p. 277.
156 Ibid.
157 Fanon 1967, p. 4.

that the racialising regime of modernity 'needs opacity but can neither abide its irreducibility nor eradicate the traces of its exorbitance.'[158] The irreparable and irreducible life-form of opacity – i.e. blackness – functions through a certain 'antesight'[159] that allows for a peculiarly disjunctive position in modernity: while 'value, as such, and its derivative, capital,' as Beverley Best writes, is 'a system of social averages of social productivity objectified as production costs',[160] blackness survives as both a crucial condition for the emergence of value and a residuum that 'constitutes a dehiscence within every moment of valuation'.[161] Survival here is meant in the etymological sense of living *on top of*, *in the excess* and *over*: *sur-vivre*. Blackness lives in excess of its production as the condition for value to emerge.

The extreme brutality of the refusal of black time, black history, or blackness *qua* a certain erased time and history, was so totalising in the Middle Passage and its living wake today that the possibility of the survival of blackness was both *erased* and *opened into a fugitive excess*. For Sharpe and Bradley, being black in capitalist modernity is both always impossible and always fugitive, always foreclosed and always exposing a wholly different possibility of being: 'each primal scene constitutes that which cannot be further reduced without a *remainder*,' as Bradley writes.[162]

In the world-making and world-ending scene of subjugation of the Middle Passage and its attendant slave plantations, an excess is simultaneously *exposed* and *produced*; it neither simply *was* and lives on, nor *was not* and had to be made from scratch. Instead, as Bradley describes the black residuum, 'this exorbitant materiality can be continuously concealed, disavowed, and displaced. But because this materiality is vestibular to the very metaphysics which interdicts it, it can never be completely eliminated.'[163] What Bradley calls the anteaesthetics of the black residuum, as the specific condition of blackness in capitalist modernity, and what I am calling the primacy of insurgent sociality, as the general condition of all social life in capitalist modernity, cannot be borne by that which requires it and that which it antagonises by surviving.

Here, survival and antagonism function as mutually constitutive and intertwined forces. The survival of difference is an antagonism because the expans-

158 Bradley 2023, p. 245.
159 Ibid.
160 Best 2023, p. 260.
161 Bradley 2023, p. 247.
162 Ibid., p. 240. This 'remainder', as I discuss in the afterword, is explored at length in Tadiar 2022.
163 Ibid.

ive, homogenising movement of value is reliant on the incorporation of differential temporalities, but that incorporation is reliant on the survival of those temporalities. This is the general antagonism always borne within the dead future that Sharpe reads as the archetypal temporal imposition on black lives: despite the historical totalisation of antiblackness, blackness persists as a general refusal of the brutality that both produces and erases blackness. This refusal is the grounding condition of what constitutes black being in the present.

Iyko Day proposes a similar reading of Indigenous relations, which neither precede nor follow the colonial conquest of and claim on land, but rather survive as an antagonism within that conquest. Understanding Indigenous relations to space as a queer wasteland, Day writes that 'racialized sacrifice zones are necessary for capitalist social reproduction in reaction to Indigenous modes of relation.'[164] Within these conditions – in which, crucially, capital *reacts* to Indigenous survival, rather than vice versa – the wasteland itself operates 'as a non-chrononormative carceral space insofar as it suspends the progressive temporality of use and improvement central to reactionary settler-legal conceptions of land as property and resource.'[165] The survival of Indigenous socialities actively suspends the possibility of colonial-capitalist claims on the land as a productive possession.

This disruptive temporality of survival, for Day, Bradley, and Sharpe, can be actualised as a political break in the expansive homogeneity of capitalist time. As Day writes, 'the wasteland offers a productive reminder of the degenerative, unwanted, erased past, which is always potentially leveraged as a future site of expropriation and "improvement."'[166] That erased past and its attendant socialities persist, presenting the constant threat of incompletion to the capitalist requirement of temporal homogenisation. The project gathered under the name of this disruptive remainder 'is not a search for a way out, or even forward,' as literary theorist and black studies scholar R.A. Judy writes, 'rather, it is an effort to keep on flying.'[167]

This is the core of the *optimism* of black optimism, in that the unintended accompaniment to racist erasure is the exposure of racialised socialities that survive in fugitive temporalities, in a separate (dis)order of temporal relations, which has been given many names in black studies: black gathering,[168] black

164 Day 2022, p. 51.
165 Ibid., pp. 51–2.
166 Ibid., p. 52.
167 Judy 2020, p. 21.
168 Cervenak 2021.

speculative life,[169] stolen life,[170] and, in Judy's phrasing, the thinking in disorder of nonontological life, i.e., *poiēsis in black*.[171]

In *Poetics of Value*, following the arguments of the black studies scholars I have engaged with here, I understand the fugitive social temporalities that survive as impotentially or differentially valorisable lifetimes as constitutively insurgent, presenting a necessary antagonism to the full realisation of value's temporal homogenisation. The fundamental commodification of time that occurs between the difference of production and the standardisation of exchange is antagonised by the survival of irreducible social difference. I call these surviving temporalities the primary insurgency of sociality.

The aim of *Poetics of Value* is to propose the primacy of insurgency as a Marxist methodology, breaking open the limiting temporal imaginary of value-critical Marxisms, which have turned away from Marx's ambivalence concerning the persistence of differential social temporalities. To open value-critical Marxisms to the fugitive temporalities of the black radical tradition, I turn to poetry. In the work of the poets to come, I find modes of social time that survive in the excess of individuation, which are exposed through the catachresis and play of poetry. I call this the poetics of value.

169 Brown 2021.
170 Moten 2018a.
171 Judy 2020.

CHAPTER 2

Alli Warren and the Production of Subjectivity

1 Value's Poetry

While Alli Warren – a Californian poet who has been publishing consistently since the early 2010s – reveals very little biographical information in her poetry or elsewhere, her politics is clear: she is the author of adamantly communist poetry. Her texts are always balancing the quotidian experience of capitalist urban life and the mystical fetish-form that undergirds and determines every appearance. The scenes she constructs are of purchase, exchange, and exploitation, studded with stunning ruptures into liberatory demands:

> Who can live, who gets to eat
> what's a sidewalk, what's a street
> Let's loot the establishments
> I mean feed each other[1]

The difficulty with this communist poetry is in understanding exactly where the merging point between text and world occurs. At which point, and in what way, does Warren's poetry take on the form of revolutionary (anti-)politics? How does her poetry materially contribute to the struggle against capital?

I approach this connecting point between text and world through the German philosophical term *Darstellung*, which is staged in opposition to *Vorstellung*. Both are roughly translated into English as *representation*, but in very different ways. In *Vorstellung* – composed of the parts *vor*, which is the prefix *pre*, and *Stellung*, meaning *position* – what is represented is separate from the representation: a material distinction between original and copy is maintained. A representation is a separate object, removed from the mutual determination of what is represented. In *Darstellung* – with its prefix, *dar*, meaning *there* or *towards* – what is represented is present in the representation itself, with and within the form that representation takes, establishing a determining relation between observation and depiction, of being-present and re-presenting.

These terms are derived from Kantian aesthetics. The representation of judgement – which, as David Lloyd writes, 'governs or regulates this trans-

1 A. Warren 2017, p. 40.

ition from material particularity to formal universality'[2] – is *Vorstellung*. As George Hartley writes, this form of representation 'operates according to the inside/outside opposition of empiricism – a position operating in a space distinct from that which is re-presented there by its proxy.'[3] *Vorstellung* is the genus under which intuitions, concepts, and ideas are categorised for Kant.[4] The problem with these objective forms is that they do not correlate to the sensible subjectivity of perception. The alternative form – which is precisely presentation through the senses – is *Darstellung*, in which there is no hypostasis: what is represented is there, within the thing itself, given over as its own presentation.

In Warren's poetry, *Darstellung* is enacted by the text's representation of the forced absence of social life: the text *contains* the absence of sociality that it *represents*; it is itself the unfolding drama it poeticises. The struggle against determination by value is present in Warren's poetry as a rumination on the absence of social life; sociality is brought into the text through the affective elaboration on its enforced removal. Through the *Darstellung* of the capitalist subject, Warren's poetry places itself in the material social relations of the struggle.

By tracing the loss of sociality in Warren's poetry as *Darstellung*, the questions I ask in this chapter are: How does value produce and determine the form of subjectivity? How does social life survive despite this determination? And, what is the place of contemporary poetry in this surviving social life?

First, before getting to Warren's poetry, I work through current scholarship at the intersection of Marxist economics and literary theory. What I am trying to do with poetry in this book is slightly different to the Marxist studies of poetry I discuss below, in that I posit no formal equivalence between value and poetry. Instead, I read Warren's poetry as a moment of social exposure: her poetry does not *represent* value or its relations at all, whether in the form of a lyric 'I' or its refusal in a collective 'we'. Instead, Warren performs her poetry as the forced removal of sociality, presenting the actual process of capital and its original accumulation in her poetry. By giving catachrestic voice to certain social relations that nonetheless persist within the world of value, she unearths other social temporalities. Her poetry, in this sense, is the *Darstellung* of fugitive temporalities, with no need to formulate literary representations of what value is *like*, as in the metaphoric mode that many recent Marxist literary theorists have studied.

---

2 Lloyd 2019, p. 29.
3 Hartley 2003, p. 94.
4 Kant 1998, A320/B377.

Then, turning to Warren's poetry, I note its similarity to Marx's elaborations on fetishism and alienation. Warren gives life to the monstrously animated commodities that Marx also obsesses over. I then place Warren's poetry in its local context, showing its relation to the mystical writings of the San Francisco Renaissance. My aim here is to bring out the ways in which Warren's poetry elicits a form of belief in social life despite the monstrous melancholy of living among animated accumulations of exploited time.

2 Determining Forms

In his reading of Frank O'Hara, Joshua Clover writes that the only way to understand the structural logic of a poem in capitalism is by coordinating the 'global marketplace ... via the poem's syntactic and semantic activities,'[5] constructing a materialist understanding of poetics by comparing the self-presentation of language and value. The poem is itself meaningful in circulation, as is value, in Clover's *Neue Marx-Lektüre*-inspired reading, in which value is understood as fundamentally produced in exchange rather than in the commodified relations of production.[6] This is, he writes, 'why poetry takes on increasing significance alongside the increasing drive toward global abstraction and complexity, toward increasingly absent determinations.'[7] Poetry, for Clover, assumes increasing importance in financial capitalism because it is the abstraction of language, and, relatedly, finance is the abstraction of capital.

The introduction of poetics to the study of this increasing capitalist abstraction is based on two premises: (1) that poetry is the abstraction of the direct representation of meaning; and (2) that capital is increasingly abstract, that its neoliberal shift from industry to finance is a shift to greater abstraction. Can either of these claims be justified, though? And, if they cannot, then why exactly is poetry an important grounding in the critique of capitalism?

For Clover, the poem carries in itself the ideological structure of capitalism as the seeming continuity of global space. 'This is the world of *and*: the coordination of metropole and its invisible colonies'; the poem (specifically 'The Day Lady Died' by Frank O'Hara,[8] but in general too) refers to this world by performing the constitution of the subject through commodification, the scene

5 Clover 2010, p. 338.
6 Kurz 2016, pp. 70–83.
7 Clover 2010, p. 339.
8 O'Hara 2014, p. 21.

of buying things, of being bought, of constituting a self through engagements with the various appearances of value.[9] 'But,' Clover continues, 'the poem does not exactly describe that world. It gives account of the form of consciousness that world demands.'[10] The poem constructs its meaning in relation to the ideological meaning of capitalism through the reenactment of the conditions of consciousness it demands; to exist in capitalism – to become the Beings of Exchange, as Christopher Arthur writes[11] – one must attain, and constitute oneself within, the singular impulse to expansion: *like value, one must expand.* One must improve oneself constantly as the perfection of the being-in-circulation, as the representative of abstract labour, which occurs through narrative as much as exchange. 'Narrative requires motion and change,' as Clover writes in another essay, 'not simple replenishment; motion and change are exactly what constitute the general formula [MCM'].'[12]

In Clover's understanding of a 'renewed Marxist poetics,' poetry and value could simply continue as they do.[13] The increasing abstraction of finance capital – or what Moishe Postone calls 'a new, increasingly abstract form of social domination'[14] – matches the abstraction of language as poetry, for Clover, but poetry does not work back onto finance capital as an antagonism against its abstraction.[15] Value and poetry *reflect* each other, but do not *antagonise* each other, leaving poetry with no means of refusing the appropriation of its speculative form by value.

A more fundamental problem with Clover's reading is its presumption of the structural synonymy of poems and value as increasing abstractions. As Leigh Claire La Berge writes, the fundamental process of value-production, its commodification of time and its expansive increase, remains the same throughout capitalism, from hand-operated cotton factories to adaptive AI that accumulates data.[16] While there is no *historical* increase in abstraction, as La Berge emphasises and Elena Louisa Lange has also recently argued, there are nonetheless levels of abstraction within the expressions of value.[17] So, while abstraction does not *increase*, certain technological developments – which

9 Clover 2010, p. 342.
10 Ibid., p. 342.
11 Arthur 2001, p. 34.
12 Clover 2011, p. 36.
13 Clover himself recognises this, to an extent. See: Clover 2011, p. 38.
14 Postone 2003, p. 3.
15 Peculiarly, though, Clover elsewhere argues precisely against this way of reading poetry in relation to value: Nealon and Clover 2023, pp. 212–13.
16 La Berge 2022, p. 89.
17 Lange 2021, p. 14f.

are necessary for the maintenance of value's status quo – remove some of the necessity of muscular energies in the production of value. Fundamentally, there is not a historical increase in the abstraction of value; it is, rather, the production of abstraction *per se*.

If the relation of a poem to value is not, then, one of mimesis through a mutual historical increase in abstraction, what does this relation emerge from? In *Forms of a World*, Walt Hunter argues that the importance of poetry to understanding capitalism is in its especially *material* contribution to the production of value.[18] For Hunter, poems are the limit of speech, the logical point at which the communicative function of language is given over to an excess of signification. In poetry, language does not function to communicate, but rather to create itself as poetry, which makes reading poetry the act of witnessing the scene of production, rather than consuming a poetic product: in reading a poem, one is witnessing the self-construction of poetry. It is a form of language that always maintains an awareness of its own conditions of production, since it directly *communicates* nothing, remaining within its own production rather than giving itself over to an addressee. Poetry's interlocutor, for Hunter, is the production of poetry *qua* poetry.

Poetry etymologically is, of course, creation, a creation that renders its creator non-existent – as John Keats famously says, and Giorgio Agamben follows – because the poem is always before the poet, and the desubjectified poet is always ashamed of this paradoxical act of creating and eradicating themself.[19] This shame, Agamben writes, is grounded in the subject 'bearing witness to its own disorder.'[20] However, the poem survives the moment in which the poet witnesses their own eradication: the poem endures as a witness. For Agamben, this is its most remarkable feature: 'the poetic word is the one that is always situated in the position of a remnant and that can, therefore, bear witness. Poets – witnesses – found language as what remains, as what actually survives the possibility, or impossibility, of speaking.'[21] Poets are the peculiar producers who produce no product, but instead must bear witness to the self-production of meaning as poetry.

While investing in a notion of changing value that is incompatible with Marx's labour theory of value, for Hunter it is this loss of oneself in the moment of creation that allows poets to write critiques of those same conditions.

18 Hunter 2019, p. 214 of Apple Books edition. This is in sharp distinction to Berardi, whose point is that a *symbolic* synonymy presides over this relation: Berardi 2012.
19 Agamben 1999, pp. 112–13.
20 Ibid., p. 106.
21 Ibid., p. 161.

> Soldered to the mutations of a global capitalist system, the lyric does not withdraw from the traces of consumer goods that threaten it, as Adorno would write. It is the continually reasserted voice of that which has been made into a commodity and traded.[22]

That is, the poet has also been commodified: there is no escape from that subsumption. But the confrontation of the poet with the impossibility of speaking – and the particular impossibility of subjectivity in capitalism, as I discuss below – opens a complicated scene of witnessing in which readers adopt the shame of the desubjectified poet, leaving them in the scene of desubjectification while remaining bound to the social relations between consumers (readers) and commodities (poems): the relation is a remnant of the eradication of the productive subject.

It is important to note that this does not mean that poets are performing productive labour while writing poems, i.e., they are not subsumed into the wage-relation. Most poets are not paid by a capitalist to write poetry as a commodity, so their labour is not commodified as labour-power and their means of production are not owned by the consumer of that commodity. Their work is in fact 'useful labour' in that it is not directly mediated by the expansion of value and is not consumed as a commodity by a capitalist.[23] This is not in itself exceptional. All work in which labour-power is not sold as a commodity to a capitalist is not productive labour, but the social relations of those involved are nonetheless determined by the process of capital. Artistic labour is particularly complicated, as Marx discusses with a specific focus on poetry,[24] especially given the post-Kantian aesthetic tradition which understands artistic subjectivity as that of the 'non-worker': to be an artist is to be exempt from labour, turning the artist, by definition, into the one who does not work.[25]

Jasper Bernes approaches the politics of poetry from a position between Clover's mimetic abstraction and Hunter's materialist productive lyric. For Bernes, 'O'Hara takes the vast, impersonal world of 1950s Manhattan and makes it familiar, provides an intimate and therefore less threatening view of it,' which, he posits, is similar to the contemporary role of service workers, who play the part of mediating the violence of social relations through distraction and dis-

---

22 Hunter 2019, pp. 148–9.

23 For a general description of forms of labour in relation to the arts, see: Beech 2019. For Marx's distinctions of labour, see: Marx 1990, pp. 126–9. See also: Bottomore 2001, p. 1.

24 Marx 1990, p. 1044.

25 See: Woodmansee 1994.

tance.[26] 'Such workers are instructed to act "like a friend," to make the store or restaurant seem "like home," to compensate for otherwise disorienting social processes.'[27] Commodities are reliant for their circulation on the affective performance of their sellers, while the world described by poems is reliant on its potential poeticisation. For Bernes, the world is a vast store of possible poetic antagonisms, of potential symbolic links, which poetry can either actualise as a radical project, as I will argue Alli Warren does, or water down and turn familiar, as O'Hara does in Bernes' reading. The class struggle as history in Bernes' work is also the poetry struggle as society.

In a society in which 'O'Hara's charisma is the charisma of the salesperson,'[28] the literal exploitation of workers in the service industry is made possible by its subsumption into the non-commodified work of poetry. O'Hara had a job that was not writing poetry, at the Museum of Modern Art in New York, and his poetry only becomes a commodity when it is sold by a publishing company. The labour of everyone in involved, except the poet, is commodified as exploited labour-power: the bookmakers, the printers, the editors, the distributors, the bookshop sales staff. This situation is not the case for O'Hara, but his desubjectified placement of that remnant of the 'poetic word', as Agamben writes above, into the social discourse as a commodity removes the 'charisma of the salesperson' from its strict subsumption in value-production. Through the 'useful [i.e., indirectly market mediated] labour'[29] of writing poetry, O'Hara releases a relation into a totality of commodities, letting it linger there as the remnant of the impossibility of speaking productively; everyone speaks of sales, speaking for the ultimate sale, but the poem cannot be sold because it contains the remnant of something unspeakable. While this gives political agency to the *poem*, it further entrenches the exploitation of everyone involved in its circulation, turning the poetic world of their social relations outside of exploitative labour into more opportunities for exploitation and productive expansion.

For Bernes, there is an important dialectical determination between poetry and the society in which it circulates. There is never a neutral point of access to art, for Bernes; artists, with or without their knowledge, are employed in rendering the antisocial relations of capitalism into a consumable social product through the circulation of their works. When poems bring the public semiotics of advertising into the quiet space of reading poetry,[30] the affective distinc-

26 Bernes 2017, p. 25.
27 Ibid.
28 Ibid.
29 Endnotes 2013.
30 I am referring here to Kevin Quashie's multiform meaning of quiet: Quashie 2012.

tion between work life and home life is eradicated.[31] This method of poetry criticism finds any apparent homology between world and text as a dialectic in Fredric Jameson's sense of encountering endless and unresolvable incommensurables.[32] 'Art does not simply reproduce what it finds in the world but reconstitutes and reconstellates it to form models of prospective futures,' as Bernes writes.[33] These futures, moreover, determine the reach and meaning of poetry's past, as well as the conditions of the world grounded and opened in poetry.

3 The Real Abstraction That You Are

Amy De'Ath's reading of Alli Warren's poetry begins with value itself, understanding 'real abstractions as both the source and the consequence of a process in which the organization of capitalist society is *form-determined* by value,'[34] following the Marxian method in which, as Beverley Best writes, the form 'is inscribed in the object of analysis.'[35] Understanding value as form-determining, and capital as the subject of this determination, De'Ath reads Warren's poem 'Acting Out' as 'enter[ing] the space of mediation itself,' by which the poem 'is confined to its own humanist temporality and mediated experience,' but can nonetheless attempt – even if impossibly because of the form-determined subjectivity of the poet herself, and the poem's speaker – to describe this determination by organising the poem's scene as the interaction of objects independent of the speaker's consciousness.[36]

In the opening poem of Warren's 2013 collection *Here Come the Warm Jets*, 'Acting Out', the speaker herself is posited as an external object, using the second-person pronoun to situate herself in the scene.[37] This 'you,' for De'Ath, is 'an isolable particular' who has the function of forming incommensurability

31 Bernes 2017, p. 27.
32 Jameson 2009.
33 Bernes 2017, p. 33.
34 De'Ath 2017, p. 2. Original emphasis.
35 Best 2010, p. 61.
36 De'Ath 2017, p. 44.
37 Warren 2013, pp. 1–3. Note here that, while Bernes describes John Ashbery's familiar use of 'you' as the formation of 'a polyphony of writer and reader' that opens a 'cascade of characters and subjects,' Warren's use of 'you' is a *concentration* of singular being into the most universally knowable subject: *the other*, who is – in a society of necessary social relations through exchange – far better known to the subject than the subject themself (Bernes 2017, p. 73).

between the world as form and its perception through form-determination.[38] The subject does not enter a world given by the poem; instead, the world and the subject are constantly arriving at a disjunction between speaking and knowing, so much so that this attempt at *Darstellung* – at placing the presence of the thing itself in the scene – comes out as *Vorstellung*, as an absent meditation on what cannot emerge. The poem begins,

> You begin from economic fact
>
> You enter in overalls, a tart talisman
> distinguished by what you do and how you go about doing it
>
> You are a perceptible, finite and particular
> part of the scaffolding
>
> Your personal qualities should ideally be completely irrelevant
> chains of forgetting[39]

In these double-spaced lines, the split between subject and world – this syntactic awkwardness, as De'Ath calls it[40] – is for De'Ath operated through grammatical unease, with the middle of the noun phrase 'particular part' cut in half by a line break, displaced into the 'deliberately tack-on phrasal finish' of the following line.[41] The subject – who here enters *after* the economy, which is the poem-world's genesis – is already ridiculed by being positioned in this world, which is evidently made for labour and not for people.

This closely held relation between ridiculing humour and deadpan Marxism is a very recognisable feature of Warren's poetry, which, as De'Ath emphasises, scatters suggestions of subjective undoing throughout the poem. There is no eureka effect, no sudden awakening; the constant impossibility of the subject is, instead, gradually exposed by the list of aphorisms that never gets anywhere.

The peculiarly non-present subject of 'Acting Out' – who can never quite be spoken into being, like Agamben's poet or Kant's *Vorstellung* – is disturbed in the line 'You are a perceptible ... part of the scaffolding.' The subject is presented, in one sense, as *merely* perceptible, rather than real and existing in the world, creating an uneasy synonymy of essence and appearance. This is pushed

38 De'Ath 2017, p. 217.
39 Warren 2013, p. 1.
40 De'Ath 2017, p. 217.
41 Ibid.

further by the proximity of 'a' and 'perceptible' and the comma following them, which stops the reading movement: *a perceptible* becomes *a-perceptible*, i.e. not perceptible.[42] Instead of specific moments in the emergence of the subject into the economy-as-world, then, these 'chains of forgetting' that constitute 'personal qualities' are subsumed into a necessary social process, and a social process that eradicates the individual being of the subject, forcing subjectivity to appear less as perception of self and world and more, in De'Ath's words, as 'the movement of capital constantly renewing itself.'[43]

This poem may appear thematically similar to O'Hara's *Lunch Poems*. Warren also scribbles brief notes while working another job,[44] and the speaker of her poetry also joyously lists surrounding commodities, forming meaning in the world through the remnants of material production. The crucial difference though – which De'Ath brings out in her reading of Warren, beyond Clover's reading of O'Hara – is that Warren emphasises the defamiliarising force of individuation and its occlusion of autonomous subjectivity in the form-determination of value. Where O'Hara hopes to make the world of self-commodification more familiar through its poeticisation, Warren disorders the register of commodification by isolating it, removing its illusory social life, and highlighting the perverse antisociality of capitalism's social mode.

4 The Capitalist Abolition of Subjectivity

Despite her resolutely non-confessional poetry, what Warren does reveal is her dedication to California, especially San Francisco. Throughout her collections, the specific surroundings of the Bay Area are poeticised through the poetic speaker's acute relation to commodities. There are very few other human agents in Warren's poetry, unlike the sprawling social networks of the Beat poets and the New York School, which she explicitly draws from. Instead, the speaker is alone in a world of universalised objects, rendered reproducible and non-specific as animated commodities, but strangely in the very local context of the Bay Area. The objects are non-specific, but their setting is familiar and personal.

The isolation of the speaker distances the material conditions of politics and production from the text itself. Warren's lines are not – despite their semantic and formal appearance at times – presented as a manifesto. They are sites of

42 Ibid.

43 Ibid., p. 218.

44 Dodson 2020.

reflection, holding the constitutive semiosis of social relations without taking any material part in their formation. As Warren writes of reading generally, it 'is a way of looking in in order to look back out with altered vision.'[45] The social life of the text is formed as a recalculation of the reader's knowledge of the world, rather than as a stage in a simple telos that works inexorably towards the revolutionary synthesis. Poetry, Warren continues, 'is a technology of memory[,] building up community memory, humming these fight songs.'[46] It is a memory, though, of a possible future arising from abolished pasts rather than a memory of mute and closed conditions. In Warren's poetry, memory is in the process of being made, a memory that is deeply informed by the material life of capital and workers, and of literary history, as much as it diverges from any strict notion of continuation.

At one level, the dialectical reversals in Warren's poetry are performed through the constant cession of personal narrative for political statement. In 'Water and Power', an eight-page poem in her 2020 collection *Little Hill*, the condition for the personal is, firstly, the refusal of labour:

> Eating a freshly fried egg at 10am is one of the ways I
> indicate to myself I am experiencing a day without
> compelled paid labor[47]

This long line is an expulsion of the breathless imperative to produce, staged as the breathless imperative to produce poetry. An act is established as the refusal to act: she cooks breakfast in order not to work. Already the paradox of refusal is staged in the first line, concentrating the withdrawal from exploitation into an individual scene with the poet alone at breakfast. This is not organised strike action, but the personal impossibility of continuing to work.

What follows this opening is a gradual rise through scales, from the micro of one person's late morning meal to the macro of global conditions. The poem begins with a personal reflection on the semiotics of breakfast as a refusal of labour, then moves to the surrounding situation of the city, then further expands the frame to include commonplace platitudes, the macro scale of the symbolic order, then again further into broad definitions of society. But then, suddenly, it reverts to the analytic grounding of a social abstraction as a generalised material movement:

---

45 Warren 2020b.
46 Ibid.
47 Warren 2020a, p. 69.

> I've called in sick and it's warm, the sky's blue
>
> People say the light is different in California but I've been here all my life
>
> People say you can measure the size of raindrops by examining the colors in a rainbow but I've never tried
>
> I carry my symptoms to the pole past the metropole, waist deep in marsh muck
>
> The bell rings as the waters rise over the base, which is what generates the winds, with the flows and with the floods
>
> The population is assembled and made to produce a surplus[48]

On one level, the importance of this poem – like many of Warren's poems – as a rumination on the possibility of abolishing value is in the ways it erodes the lacuna between the theory and practice of communism, explicitly celebrating the practical refusal of exploitation. On a more fundamental level, it is the structure of this poem that makes it crucial to an understanding of the poetic rebuttal to capitalism's determining genres. To access the antagonism of that structure, though, it will help first to understand the structure of Marx's critique of political economy.

In *Capital*, Volume 1, Marx does not focus on the commodity because it is the *a priori* beginning of capital's expansion, but because it is the simplest expression of capital's duality of value. A commodity is purchased for its use-value, i.e. because it is useful to the buyer, but it is only exchanged because the seller calculates it as an exchange-value, which expresses the commodity's capacity to become a different use-value for different purchasers without any material change. Focusing on the commodity as the simplest expression of the logics of capital, the commodity reveals itself to have a universal expression as its immanent being.

Dialectically, this focus allows Marx to find within the commodity the duplicity of its appearance. What seems like the materiality of each commodity is in

48 Ibid.

fact its duality 'as an object ... possessing both use-value and exchange-value,' which itself opens the realisation that 'labour, too, has a dual character: in so far as it finds its expression in value, it no longer possesses the same characteristics as when it was the creator of use-values.'[49] Accordingly, 'heterogeneous forms of useful labour' are necessary for the production of commodities with a dual expression of use and exchange, meaning that the 'division of labour is a necessary condition for commodity production.' This brings us back to the isolated material conditions from which value assumes its appearance in commodities: 'Only the products of mutually independent acts of labour, performed in isolation, can confront each other as commodities.'[50]

These are the isolated conditions of specifically capitalist labour. In these conditions, the use-value of labour is also variable, and one worker can determine to a large extent the particular conditions of their own work. As the bearer of the commodity necessary for the production of value (labour-power), workers can sell their labour to another capitalist for a higher price, or, possibly, decide to work fewer hours in return for reduced living conditions, or choose the reverse and exchange more time for more wages (at the expense of other workers, as Marx notes[51]). However, what cannot be decided by the worker is the social determination of their individual conditions. This is the crucial moment of the form-determination of subjectivity in capitalist social relations, a moment which constitutes the violence of capital as the generalised abstraction of the individual conditions of labour.[52]

Capital's own dialectical structure is not simply a mimetic performance of the capitalist mode, but a necessary exposure of the hidden folds of its processes of subsumption and determination. The labour contract is revealed, as Magnus Granberg writes, as 'a strange legal suspension of legality through a formally voluntary surrender of subjectivity.'[53] As Gayatri Chakravorty Spivak says, moreover, it is precisely this subsumption of subjectivity *as* abstract labour that constitutes the historical grounding of capital's ontology. As capitalism historically develops fully, the coercion of workers is no longer necessary. Instead, what unfolds is 'the *historical* possibility of the definitive predication of the subject as labor-power. Indeed, it is possible to suggest that this "freeing" of labor-power may be a description of the social possibility of this predication.'[54]

49 Marx 1990, pp. 131–2.
50 Ibid., p. 132.
51 Ibid., pp. 781–802.
52 See: Starosta 2016, p. 134.
53 Granberg 2022, p. 290.
54 Spivak 1985, p. 79. Original emphasis.

The subject, as an economic actor in capitalism, is the force contracted to eradicate the possibility of individual subjectivity, grounding the social possibility of one's own determining impossibility in the conditions of labour, which is to say in the conditions of the universal abstraction of the material conditions of value-production. The subject in capital is the form-determined computation of value's potential valorisation. In this bind, the revolutionary subjectivity required for a radical break from the ontology of capital seems lost, fully subsumed in a process developed to eradicate its emergence.

Granberg above writes that subjectivity undergoes a 'formally voluntary surrender' to the labour contract. Stopping at the first level of the dialectics of subsumption, this analysis would assume that subjectivity precedes its subsumption in the operation of value-production; that there is a form of subjectivity independent of and prior to the conditions of capitalist production. What comes out in pursuing Marx's dialectical method in *Capital* beyond the analytic stage and into the synthetic stage is that the unity of the social labour of production, and its necessarily social form as abstracted from the particular conditions of the isolated labourer, occurs only after the moment of exchange: the abstraction of labour into a universal form is retroactively imposed from the future of exchange. This is the determinate, objective character of value, which expresses itself in capital as the social subject of the form of production in which labour (and the labourer's consciousness) has been commodified.[55] Capital is the (anti-)social life of capitalism, a process that removes the subjectivity of workers. As Guido Starosta writes,

> This is because, in reality, the whole of Chapter 1 [of *Capital*] (and, actually, the whole of *Capital*) has as its object the alienated consciousness of the commodity producer. However, the text starts out not with the alienated consciousness in and for itself, but with its most general *objectified* form of existence, namely, the commodity.[56]

Consciousness in capitalism is posited by capital as the illusory agency of the individual subject of capital after having been alienated through the commodification of labour-power; the capitalist subject is the loss of subjectivity.

Warren's speaker is acutely tangled in this illusory promise of capitalist subjectivity. For her, real subsumption has no history, since it is itself the abolition of any history independent of subsumption. The capitalist determination of

55 Starosta 2016, p. 140.
56 Ibid., p. 142. Original emphasis.

subjectivity is not a historical process, but rather the production of history. The subjective is the historical, and the historical is the subjective, leaving those forms of life that do not fit the format of the subject without history.

Lindon Barrett's anti-Marxist critique of value helpfully shows the historical mechanisms of this eradication of histories. For Barrett, value operates through a tripartite historical movement. There occurs first *value as force*, through which value is historically imposed as the determining relation of productive labour, then *value as form*, which regulates its appearances and distributes its differentially computed violences, then finally *value as denial*, through which value covers its tracks by retroactively subsuming its subjectivity as that of the economic agent.[57] It *produces* its own history as the retroactive designation of the subject as the agent of value, but this agency is imposed from the future circulation of value as abstract labour. It is the commodified, universal form of abstract labour that retroactively determines the history of living labour.

All the forms of life specifically excluded from the retroactive validation of value-production, however, are removed to the periphery of this violent but life-sustaining subsumption: those deemed subjects in and of history are forced to survive through exploitation. There is, though, a vast 'remaindered' population displaced from history, as Neferti X.M. Tadiar studies.[58] Those remaindered socialities are neither eradicated nor fully subsumed. They persist in the nonontological space that exceeds commodified subjectivity. That remainder – unlike in Clover's reading of O'Hara[59] – has no will or active agency. In Warren's poetry, it is precisely this poetic excess that is described not as *another kind* of subject, but rather as the form of life that lives as the absence of subjectivity, as the excess of subjection.

For Marx, individual subjectivity in capitalism is an illusory tangle of misinterpreted time, in which the individual sees themself as the creator of a natural process of valorisation, computed already in the ascription of value's differential coordinates (race, class, gender, etc.), which covers and refuses recognition of the actual process: the individual is the result of the fundamentally *social* operations of labour and exchange.[60] It is only, then, by the subject's belief in a subjectivity antecedent to exchange that the subject of capital engages in the

57 Barrett 1999, pp. 28–9.

58 Tadiar 2022.

59 Clover 2010, p. 335.

60 Marx writes, 'In the developed system of exchange … the ties of personal dependence, of distinction, of education, etc. are in fact exploded, ripped up …; and individuals *seem* independent (this is an independence which is at bottom merely an illusion, and it is more correctly called indifference).' Marx 1993, p. 163.

determining function of the value-form. The subject is required to believe in the possibility of their independence in order for their consciousness to be created by the suspended promise of value. The *ex post facto* subject of the value-form is not a subject at all in this regard, but rather the mystical and yet material groundwork of value's social force.

5 The Particulars of Water and Power

To return with this impossible subjectivity to Warren, the final line of the opening page of 'Water and Power' ('The population is assembled and made to produce a / surplus') posits the constitution of 'the population' as a singular entity *ex post facto*. Once people have been assembled as producers of value, the possibility of differential self-determination is removed, and a social abstraction formally subsumes these people as the population under the imperative to reproduce their own conditions of subjectivity: 'made to produce a surplus.' This brings the dialectic back to the material isolation of the first line ('Eating a freshly fried egg at 10am …'), in which the speaker withdraws from the imperative to production. However, without the possibility of redetermining herself as another kind of subject, undetermined by the valorisation of her labour-power, it takes only one sentence for her grasp of the world without work to be subsumed back into the general condition of the city ('the sky's blue'), leaving her repeating generalised and anonymous sayings ('People say the light is different') without recourse to the isolation which was itself the foundation of her subsumption, in that it was only by isolating the worker's conditions as 'mutually independent acts of labor' that the singularity of the worker could lose any trace of self-determination as subject.

Having established this complex formation of subjectivity in the first page, the rest of the poem examines the materiality of the subject form-determined by value. In the mostly disconnected, aphoristic lines, frequent references are made – as the title suggests – to water and power:

> They pump groundwater from boreholes
> …
> Every day I am covered in water twice and also uncovered twice
> …
> I throw my belongings out to sea and this brings me great prestige
> …
> The land is scrubbed and repurposed
> They build prisons on fallow fields because there had been drought

Because there had been drought fires rush across the land
To fight fires they use the labor of the people they imprison in cages
My brother says if people in cages accept pennies to fight
fires that's their choice, I ask my mom how he got this
way
My mom gave birth to me, child number three, when she
was 34, the age I am now, childless
What is the water doing before the ducks disturb it?[61]

In these lines, other people are present, but – aside from the speaker's brother and mother, which I discuss below – not as distinguishable individuals. They are only abstracted and universalised forms of action.

The anonymous 'they' are destroying the world through a planned imbalance of water and fire. Water is removed from the land, and the catastrophe of that removal justifies further catastrophe through planting fallow fields, which requires conditions of forced labour. The earth and the anonymised, general productivity of people are together constituting the eradication of their own conditions. No one decides; no one feels or experiences these movements as anything but the abstract concentration of what they do without knowing it.

With a clear semantic separation of lines, formally following the division of labour rather than aesthetic or poetic choices in line lengths, in the section beginning 'The land is scrubbed' the world that precedes labour is the destruction of the world itself. Everything is destroyed for the production of capital to emerge, which is the (always ongoing) stage of original accumulation setting the (always adapting) ground for real subsumption.[62] What follows, as 'prisons', is the subsumption of the labourers themselves into the desolation of the land. People and their world – the world and its people – are now imprisoned in production.

While this narrative sequence describes a general history of oppression and power in capitalism, Warren is also immediately referring to the increasing intensity of wildfires in California, which are often fought by teams of incarcerated people, who are led by professional firefighters and paid less than $5 per day.[63]

Directly following these political lines, the personal jarringly emerges. While Warren's theorisation earlier in the poem of her relationship with a cat is a

61 Warren 2020a, pp. 70–1.
62 For more on 'primary', 'primitive', or 'original' accumulation, see: Beech 2020, pp. 11–12; Roberts 2017, p. 193 f.
63 See: Uenema 2022.

familiar trait of her uniquely romantic-communist sentimentalism, the description of her family is a very rare moment of autobiography in her poetry. However, unlike the Language poets, who fold the world into poetry as data, disturbing the distinction between quotidian and poetic language, Warren's use of real conversations emerges *out of* the material conditions *in the poem*. The incarcerated labourers – building their own prisons on the earth that was drained specifically to become uninhabitable to them – set up the conditions for Warren to speak to her family. The conversation begins as a reference to the prisoners. Here, the production of the social is an attendant form of the conditions of capitalist labour. Warren's family is made through its reflection on exploitation; they come into being by positioning themselves in relation to the erasure of productive land and its replacement by exploited subjects.

The material dialectic that pushes contradictory incommensurables against each other is realised across social scales, from the large-scale prison industrial complex and the small-scale exploitation of its every prisoner, to the large-scale debates on the ethics of prisons and prison labour and the small-scale family dispute between siblings and their mother. Out of the particular and personal, the social is found again.

This complexity of political critique and intimate reflection runs throughout Warren's poetry, but here it is displayed on just one page, dialectically countering the scales of global and personal contradiction in pursuit of material and social change.

6 Let We Be Moral

'Water and Power' makes the reproduction of subjectivity as a relation between labourers and/as commodities apparent, placing the process of commodity fetishism and the social determination of value in front of the subjects of capital, but this is insufficient in itself to expose a way of being without subjectivity, or a subjectless sociality. At the end of the poem, though, a political proposition emerges. The final lines reveal the thirst that emerges from the drought conditions described in the poem, constructed from a moral imperative that cannot quite find its grounding.

> Let the fleece of our fleets be fruitful, let we be warm of
> thought
>
> Let the paper money men and goldbugs find their necks
> mud-raked

I want this like I want a long weekend, a kiss in a dark
bar, a slug's trace across some lichen

There's lots of little birdies hopping around in the grass,
the rich are running for their lives

They say it's an immaterial, promissory, and imaginary
feeling, although not unreal[64]

The language of morality here is confusing, with 'let we be warm' conforming to a general ethics of generosity but by misnaming the subject, using the subject rather than object pronoun. This semantic catachresis disorders the expected clarity of morality, which at one level reveals the complexity of the task of abolishing value, but also presents the duplicity of the subject itself. In the more formally correct command 'let us,' the active subject is in fact the object of an other's subjectivity; there is a power beseeched to *let us* act, which Warren's command eradicates, positing *us* – or better, 'we' – as the active agents of this ethics of generosity and warmth.

This catachrestic subject, rendered subjective against its presupposed objectivity, assumes the form of Marx's animated commodities, specifically his legendary example of the table, which, upon

> emerg[ing] as a commodity, ... changes into a sensuous extrasensory thing. It not only stands with its feet on the ground, but, in relation to all other commodities, it stands on its head, and evolves out of its wooden brain grotesque ideas, far more wonderful than if it were to begin dancing of its own free will.[65]

Beverley Best emphasises that Marx's use of catachresis here is not simply a literary flair, but rather 'expresses a particular historical, material, and social situation more generally.'[66] Catachresis gives rise to an awareness of the arbitrariness of forms, which grounds social positions as questionable rather than natural. As Warren returns through her own family to the exploitation of incar-

64 Warren 2020a, p. 76.

65 Marx 1990, pp. 163–4. In Fowkes' translation, the first sentence of this citation is rendered as 'a thing that transcends sensuousness.' As Michael Heinrich notes, this translation is incorrect. Marx's original describes the commodity as a 'sinnlich übersinnliches Ding.' In this citation I have replaced Fowkes' translation with Heinrich's. Heinrich 2004, p. 72.

66 Best 2010, p. 81.

cerated labourers, Marx presents the table as a grotesque distortion once it exists as a commodity among commodities. 'Something monstrous lurks in the most innocent of catachreses,' as Paul de Man writes; 'the word can be said to produce of and by itself the entity it signifies, [one that] has no equivalence in nature. When one speaks of the legs of the table or the face of the mountain ... one begins to perceive a world of potential ghosts and monsters.'[67] What Warren is searching for is a ground from which to move against the ghosts and monsters who constitute the Marxian world of commodities.

As Starosta posits against the grain of most Marxist theorists, 'Marx is not searching for a common property in commodities. Rather, he is searching for (i.e. not yet unfolding) the specific determination defining the potentiality of the commodity as a historical form of social wealth.'[68] Marx does not represent the dual appearance of the commodity through a *Vorstellung* that pursues the commodity's duality. Instead, he examines the commodity – which itself presents its duality when questioned dialectically, represented in the text through *Darstellung* – with the object of critique apparent and present in the critique itself, as its own form of representation.

Warren is similarly moving out of the form-determining prescription of subjectivity by a catachrestic poeticisation of the incommensurable social relations that might be 'immaterial' but are nonetheless 'not unreal.' Her poetry is positioned within the incommensurability of speaking of subjectivity through subjectivity, of formulating a poetics of subjectless sociality from the inside of form-determination but the outside of capitalist labour. Her poetry, like Marx's criticism, is itself a stage of incommensurability in the dialectics of subjectivity.

The uniqueness of Warren's criticism of the conditions that produce subjectivity is that she is not interested in a new form of subjectivity, but rather in what precedes and survives despite subjectivity. Is there a formless life, a generative sociality, that has been hidden by the historical force of subjectivity? Warren's poetry is the mystical pursuit of ghosts and spectres that live on despite the totalising moment of historical formation. As she writes, crucially proposing the incommensurability of her own poetics of value:

> Despite the blood red talk
> I am not a nihilist
> I believe despite myself[69]

67 Cited in Best 2010, p. 81. Best's ellipses.
68 Starosta 2016, p. 129.
69 Warren 2020a, p. 97.

7 The Structure of Belief

In Warren's poetry, a world is staged in which social relations are not social in the sense of creating meaningful bonds between human beings, but in the sense that people are abstracted into a universalised market that determines relations as the possibility of exchange. In that world, fetishised objects assume subjecthood in the operation of capital, an assumption that constitutes their monstrous character. This fetishised relation is not directly imposed, as Sandro Mezzadra points out, by a capitalist who owns the means of production and purchases workers' labour-power, but is rather formed by a collective will that produces the conditions in which workers' subsumption is necessary. This will is abstract and alien to everyone, but is nonetheless a real abstraction with material force, which appears throughout Marx's critique of political economy as the thread that forms the necessity of subjectivity-production in capitalism.[70]

Many political poets produce critiques of capitalism through poetry, and a part of Warren's poetry is firmly within the contemporary Marxist-feminist poetic tradition, building on the Language poets and their refusal of 'the self as the central and final term of creative practice,' as they write in their 1988 manifesto.[71] At other moments, however, her poetry strikingly portrays the experience of joy in relation to commodities. There is a social relation between objects of capital that is real, that is enjoyable, while also necessarily alienated, fetishised, and exploited. This ambivalence is what makes her poetry so romantic and humorous as well as critical.

For Marx, the conditions for the revolution are always borne within the capitalist form of relation itself. As he writes in *Capital*,

> As the number of co-operating workers increases, so too does their resistance to the domination of capital, and, necessarily, the pressure put on by capital to overcome this resistance. The control exercised by the capitalist is not only a special function arising from the nature of the social labour process, and peculiar to that process, but it is at the same time a function of the exploitation of a social labour process, and is consequently conditioned by the unavoidable antagonism between the exploiter and the raw material of his exploitation.[72]

70 Mezzadra 2018, p. 96.
71 Silliman et al. 1988, p. 262.
72 Marx 1990, p. 449.

By entering the necessary fetishisation and alienation of the wage relation, workers become the raw material of value-production. However, that relation is formed of a network of wider social relations, which abstracts the particular working conditions of each worker into their universal form, i.e. abstract labour. It is at this level that the antagonism between the relation of capitalist to worker and of labour-power to value-production is established. The input that requires a worker's individual subjectivity in having chosen to work and in having the ability to work is antagonised by the output that requires the worker's life to be computed as labour-power, i.e. as a commodity which is fetishised, reflecting 'the social characteristics of [workers'] own labour as objective characteristics of the products of labour themselves, as the socio-natural properties of those things.'[73] The 'social animal'[74] that is the human, in the ongoing moment of determination in the subjectivity of value-production, is turned into raw material for the reproduction not of people but of the purpose of this process: surplus-value.

Marx is always turning back from the commodity – with which he famously begins his study – to workers and their lives. Even his chapter on machinery and large-scale industry is ultimately concerned with the way in which machines shorten the working day – meaning less pay for workers – and increase the production of surplus-value, extending the reach of exploitation.[75] Warren's poetry, as I discussed above, is removed from a direct relation to value-production, since her poetry itself – as a book – only becomes a commodity when it is sold by a publisher, not when it is being written or read. Its antagonism in the production of value, then, cannot assume the same approach as Marx's criticism. Instead, Warren focuses on the personal relation between consumer and commodity, which is to say between alienated subject as potential labour-power-bearer and fetishised subject of capital as value-bearer.

The way Warren achieves these strange critical ruminations is through a focus on the mystical and the occult. The final poem of *Here Come the Warm Jets* is the eight-page, single-spaced 'Personal Poem', which removes from O'Hara's famous 'Personal Poem' any reference to the 'I' except in quotation marks, instead directing its often absurdist aphorisms at a nonspecific 'you'.

Warren's poem is not directly drawing on O'Hara's, but rather seems to take from it an initial sentiment, a flare for wandering and adamantly quotidian poetry with a focus on social relations. This direct but unspecified reference is a common feature of Warren's work, especially notable in this collection, named

73 Ibid., pp. 164–5.
74 Ibid., p. 444.
75 Ibid., p. 492.

after Brian Eno's 1973 album *Here Come the Warm Jets*, despite making no reference to it.[76] In its style of flaneur ethics, Warren's 'Personal Poem' seems more intertextually influenced by O'Hara's 'Personism: A Manifesto', in which O'Hara assumes the ironic savant's voice, wise but dismissive and unstable.

This intertextual link through O'Hara and Eno already forms a system of belief that invests deeply in the structure of tradition. Warren's dedication to the past fills the lines of 'Personal Poem', which implores its addressee to 'Be kind towards the paintings of the past,' to 'Keep in touch with your friends,' and to 'Call your mother on Good Friday.'[77] The dedication to tradition is mixed into a belief system in which dedication itself is the imperative. The typically comedic, powerful, and confusing sequence of lines leading up to the grand claim 'Astrology is real' presents all of this in its broad narrative reach:

> Remember the debt you're living off remember being exchanged
> for a few donkeys remember how bricks get made
> Treat the detritus around you as a talisman the permeable wreck
> don't claim to know what modernity is
> If your date uses the word "dialectics" don't get up and walk out but
> remember this moment it's important
> At the height of your priestly powers
> don't drink beer
> Astrology is real[78]

The imperative to remember is the semantic structure holding the rest of the dispersed narrative moments together, an imperative to remember not only *being* here but *having arrived* here. The most shocking proposition of this poem as historiography is its absence of any material antecedence to subsumption: a violent rupture enacts this moment in which the subject is 'being exchanged' as an ontic condition, but nothing precedes that moment. That subsumption is history itself. There is no suggestion of a way of being before 'being exchanged'; it is always happening because it is the condition of being a subject who remembers.

The way to think otherwise, without totalising the determination of subjectivity, is found in the material 'detritus' of the world, which functions as

76 In personal correspondence, Warren told me that she took its name simply because she likes the album.

77 Warren 2013, p. 92, p. 97.

78 Ibid., p. 95.

a 'talisman'. The world of objects is alive and informs the subject of its presence in the totalising present, to such an extent that 'modernity' cannot be known, instead appearing as permanent. This is the world of Marx's table with a 'wooden brain' and 'grotesque ideas'.

Indeed, like Warren, Marx is obsessed with the mystical horror of the commodity and value, describing them throughout his corpus as blood-sucking vampires in various guises. At its core, as Mark Neocleous writes, the literary gore in Marx's writings is 'nothing less than the horror of a property-owning class that appears to be vampire-like in its desire and ability to suck the life out of the working class.'[79] Marx emphasises this point by beginning with the observation that capital is not 'a value-producing entity in its own right;' it is rather 'nothing but accumulated labor,' which opens the distinction between 'accumulated labor' and 'labor *pe se*,' or 'living labor.'[80] It is the agency of this living form that animates the operation of capital.

> In capitalist production, then, "living labour appears merely as a means to realize objectified, dead labour, to penetrate it with an animating soul while losing its own soul to it." The appropriation by the capitalist of the worker's productive powers is a means by which "living labour makes instrument and material in the production process into the body of its soul and thereby resurrects them from the dead."[81]

The capitalist devours the life of the worker, expanding the capitalist form of life through the literal accumulation of time in the exploiting body against the exploited body.[82] The capitalist can enjoy this accumulated time through what Tadiar calls the regeneration of consumption, filling oneself and one's surroundings with the extended time of the commodity form, such as by having access to far quicker means of transport or to expensive health and relaxation treatments.[83] The other option for the capitalist is to resist these luxuries, in which case capital regenerates itself through investment in other forms of living labour. Capital, as Neocleous writes, 'becomes a phantasmal body, a monster which stalks abroad while its master sleeps, consuming the pleasures the master foregoes.'[84]

---

79 Neocleous 2003, p. 668.
80 Ibid., p. 680.
81 Ibid., citing Marx 1993, p. 461, p. 364.
82 See: Marx 1990, p. 667: 'In capitalist society, free time is produced for one class by the conversion of the whole lifetime of the masses into labour-time.'
83 Tadiar 2012, p. 784.
84 Neocleous 2003, p. 683.

Both the capitalist and capital operate as vampires, bringing to life the dead labour of accumulation. 'Because capital is dead labor,' Neocleous continues, 'the desire to live one's life through commodities is the desire to live one's life through the dead.'[85] It is the fetish that brings the dead to life. Commodities seem to be animated by a power inherent in themselves, arising out of the interactions of objects, while what is in fact taking place is a relation between people; what animates the commodities is the human labour-time valorised in them by the social relation of exchange.[86]

8 Life before Life

In Amy De'Ath's critique of Warren's poem 'Acting Out', the 'you' who 'begin[s] from economic fact' is simultaneously specific and universal: both a singular, labouring body, and an abstract representation of a form. The form, as De'Ath notices, is feminised labour, which has traditionally been unremunerated and domestic. The determination here is crucial, in that the expression of this 'economic fact' as both labour and as feminised pushes the gendered domestic form beyond the strict division of public/masculine and domestic/feminine. As De'Ath writes, 'the greatest job growth [since the 1990s] has taken place through the conversion of domestic tasks into paid work'.[87] As urban property is increasingly used as a commodity for the tourism market, cleaning becomes subsumed in the wage-relation and domestic feminised time – previously the unremunerated time of the mother/wife figure – is commodified as labour-power, distinguishing it significantly from a previous form of private cleaning as a use-value.

In this contemporary marketisation of labour, a glitch occurs. Certain kinds of domestic work were defined as 'feminised' because of their indirect relation to the market and the lack of freedom to choose other kinds of work. As that relation becomes direct through subsumption in the wage relation, the meaning of feminisation in capitalism shifts, losing its specificity. Moreover, through feminist struggle and the changing needs of capital, the feminised workforce becomes 'freer' to choose its form of labour. And yet the people performing this labour remain feminised, resulting in the same computation in the patriarchal coordinates of the misogynist economy.[88]

85 Ibid.

86 McNeil 2021, p. 44.

87 De'Ath 2017, p. 79. See also Bernes 2017, pp. 120–48, for how these same poetic passages can be insufficiently studied in the *a priori* assumption of the category 'woman'.

88 See: Endnotes 2013.

In 'Acting Out', domestic feminised labour is performed as poetry. The 'you' who begins from economic fact is now acted out as a poem, even 'accused of being a lyric poet'.[89] The assignation of feminisation to domestic labour does not occur through a simple narrative telos: one does not *begin* as a feminised subject who then undertakes reproductive domestic tasks, a process which then feminises that labour, until one's property itself – house, children, commodities – 'becomes an extension of you / set apart from all the world'.[90] Instead, as the traditional sexed distinctions of labour fade, at least in certain cultural contexts, the feminisation of certain workers seeps into the masculinised performance of public, productive labour.

Feminised labourers, in Warren's poetry, are not relieved of the determination of sex and gender at the moment of entering value-productive work; rather, they carry a disjunctive, catachrestic domesticity into the workplace. The traditionally feminised role of social reproduction is literally forced into the world of production in 'Acting Out', resulting not in the harmonious equality of sexes, but in the collapse of a seemingly natural sexed order:

> You mutually dissolve and engender your love
>   thus your mass
> You are the ceaseless excess of little green things[91]

Both worlds – the productive masculinised future of expanded production and the reproductive feminised past of preparation and survival – are undone in this meeting of temporalities, a literal destruction of physical form. However, something persists; 'the ceaseless excess' carries through in green things (dollar bills? nature? envy?) of which no description is offered.

In a very material sense, Warren disrupts the normative function of the liberal economy of labour by exposing the 'ceaseless excess' that survives in the performance of value-production, where a mutual dissolution is punctured by the survival of engendered love: reproductivity is carried through as a catachrestic practice in the masculinised productive economy.[92]

This disruption, though, is not only material. In addition to the collapse of sexed labour roles occasioned by the commodification of domestic spaces

89 Warren 2013, p. 2.
90 Ibid.
91 Ibid., p. 3.
92 Rebecca Carson calls this the 'immanent externality' of social reproduction, in that it functions as a necessary and internal part of the mode of production, but is nonetheless outside of it and never fully determined by the requirements of production: Carson 2023.

and the expansion of waged labour, especially into the industry of care work, a profound system of belief undergirds the violence of the misogynist economy Warren depicts. De'Ath reads the second line of the poem – 'You enter in overalls, a tart talisman',[93] which opens into the simultaneous conditions of labour and mysticism – as the 'sarcastic imitation of the individualism of the contemporary neoliberal subject.' The following line – 'You are a perceptible, finite and particular / part of the scaffolding' – adds the 'deliberately tack-on phrasal finish' to mimic the illusory antecedence of the individual, whom bourgeois capitalist ontology assumes as preceding the social.[94] Here, 'the scaffolding' as the social structure 'feels unnaturally clunky,' thrown onto an already-formed totality, i.e., the individual, represented in the first line of the couplet.

The genesis of the individual is not separable from the fetishisation of the individual as an inherently meaningful and self-constituting actor in the production of value. The poem's intentionally tedious taxonomy – listing the factors that create 'you' – constantly reenforces this genesis through the production of one's own value alongside an external value, circulated globally.

> You are the relations of exchange by way of this accumulation
>   audible in the following way
> Your property is an extension of you
>   set apart from all the world[95]

'Your property' is not only 'an extension of you' but also *precedes you* in this formulation of capitalist ontology; you are already what property you own, and that is all you are, defined only by this extension of yourself. It is precisely this antecedence of the property-relation – in which property *appears* to precede people's social relations, an appearance that arises out of the totalising form of subjectivity, which abolishes people's awareness of their way of being before and in excess of that subjectivity – that fetishises workers' labour, alienating it from themselves since their labour-power is presented as a commodity to be exchanged with capitalists.

What arises from this fetishism in Warren's work is not refusal or immediate strike action, nor is it simply playful engagement. In O'Hara's similarly wandering poems that encounter dead labour in commodities, the poetic subject is joyously celebrating these monstrous life-forms, exchanging them with friends.

---

93 Warren 2013, p. 1.
94 De'Ath 2017, p. 217.
95 Warren 2013, p. 2.

In Warren's poetry, no other people are apparent. This is a world almost exclusively formed of lifeless commodities that seem to be animated by their mystical value. This loneliness in the commodity-world is what De'Ath calls Warren's 'poker-faced sarcasm,'[96] but the emotional turmoil of existing in this fetishised world is beyond satire.

The life of exchange is presented in the monstrous form of a living commodity who cannot quite become a human subject, and yet restricts the human subject's subjectivity through this totalising world of fetishised commodity-forms. This theme emerges throughout the collection in humorous and critical lines, but what should not be missed is the tragedy of each satirical scene, a tragedy that profoundly invests in the sociality of belief.

Where for Marx it is the cooperation that exploitative capitalist labour requires, and its eradication of intra-proletarian difference, that provides the condition for a unified revolutionary vanguard, for Warren social life is grounded in belief. What brings people together is the loss of having been together. In mourning the social life prohibited by subjectivity, social lives are staged as the possibility of belief in accessing again that foreclosed 'ceaseless excess' that survives subsumption. This is the kernel of Warren's poetics of grief, opening her lonely poetic subjects to belief in the possibility of grieving what they have always been unable to be.

This dedication to belief is performed spectacularly in 'A Few Facts about the Thorax', a poem that incessantly abolishes its own attempts at becoming both criticism and romance. In the first line, Marxist criticism is erased for a drier mathematical scheme: 'Oh come, it's all over the faces of the ~~wage earners~~ figures.'[97] What could be criticism folds itself into a computed form without sociality. Simple numerical order takes the place of workers and their collective conditions. Later, this is concentrated into an impulse for gathering and its rejection by dispersal: 'We must sit around in sun and make sure ~~love~~ we does not escape.'[98] The first impulse here is to protect the feeling of the 'we', but the form of the poem – the structuring form of society as much as of the text in this *Darstellung* of capitalist subjectivity – removes this possibility, instead producing 'we' as a singular abstract entity external to the conditions of the subject speaking: *we* must not escape, where 'we' is an abstract referent rather than a collective subject pronoun.

In the final lines of the poem, the sociality of desire has fully split and all that is left is the rudimentary mathematics of sex, presented in Warren's famil-

96 De'Ath 2017, p. 221.
97 Warren 2013, p. 14.
98 Ibid.

iar style of deadpan grotesque humour, but with a strong mark of sadness as the potential for a meaningful relation to an absent other has been ripped apart by the short narrative of the poem:

> Oh come, won't you forgive me?
>
> One must never go to the country
>
> If you are in the country then I cannot lick your asshole
> And everything that is throbbing and heaving and sopping
> Will not throb and heave and sop[99]

At the beginning of the poem, the speaker longs for something other, a human form of relation beyond computation. This relation, though, can only be expressed in pornographic imagery – 'Oh come, it's all over the faces ...' – turning desire into work, subsuming sex into the value-productive industry of porn.

The loss of this possibility of any meaningful, unmediated relation with others is poeticised most clearly in the 'Astrology is real' sequence in the collection's long finale, 'Personal Poem', in which the mutual constitution of alienated subject and fetishised object is at play. Throughout the poem, the impossibility of presenting oneself is formulated. When a date uses the word 'dialectics', 'you' should not leave, but 'remember this moment it's important.'[100] There is a practice of belief that precedes the performance of subjectivity; before the human being emerges as a subject, an investment in belief has already constructed a different kind of being, a subjectivity subsumed within the practice of self-presentation.

The same logic appears at the beginning of the poem as 'Open your mouth and say what you think you might mean,'[101] in which the speaker's own subjectivity is a mysterious future that is yet to condition the acting subject who opens her mouth. The logic appears again later: 'When your niece pulls candles and bunnies from wall sockets / believe her she's a living relic,'[102] in which a mythical temporal twist places the existence of a niece in the long temporality of social relations preceding the world of commodities constructed in the poem, in an antecedent time that crucially has no form. The child is a relic, given form as a family member through belief. It is the social structure of belief

99 Ibid., p. 15.
100 Ibid., p. 95.
101 Ibid., p. 91.
102 Ibid., pp. 94–5.

that precedes and exceeds the subjective forms of family members in the normative reproductive temporality of capitalist modernity.

9 San Francisco Renaissance

This mystical system of belief and its erasure of the standard temporality of capital through poetic *Darstellung* shows Warren's poetry as an intensely local praxis. Beneath the abolitionist communism of her poetry's more theoretical moments, and beyond the homogenised world of exploitative commodity-production that it portrays, there is a specifically Californian literary history implicit in all these lines, especially referencing the San Francisco Renaissance.

The literary historiography of the San Francisco Renaissance has, ironically, become submerged in myth from the beginnings of its narrative reconstruction. A poetry reading at the Six Gallery in October 1955 is recounted as the mythical genesis of a whole Bay Area subsection of the Beat movement, not least by Jack Kerouac in *The Dharma Bums*.[103] The *Princeton Encyclopedia of Poetry and Poetics* mythologises the loose movement connecting Bay Area poets in the decade following the Six Gallery reading as simple creators of myths. Mythologically, these poets are mythologists.[104]

It is this mythological genesis that Robert Duncan, in 1982, saw as the remarkable feature of California as a poetic setting: its history of alternative religions and cults.[105] This appears in Duncan's essays as doubt in the implicit individuality of the self, where the fact of writing arises as the questioning of the writer: 'I am but a part of the whole of what I am, and wherever I seek to understand I fail what I know.'[106] The 'I' who knows is given through a mystical genesis that the 'I' who seeks to understand cannot grasp, which reappears in Warren as the detritus that acts as a talisman and the imperative to not make any claims on modernity.[107] It is the ruptures in the world, its broken subjects, who hold the experience of something else, despite the detritus and its false knowledge leading elsewhere.

Duncan's Californian belief systems are universal in a peculiarly Bay Area way. His fellow San Franciscan mystic poet Jack Spicer makes the magic of poetry even more explicit. Spicer invested in poets as 'singers' and 'entertain-

103 Davidson 1989, p. 3.
104 Ibid., p. 5.
105 Ibid., p. 11.
106 Duncan 1982, n.p.
107 Warren 2013, p. 95.

ers,' not as romantic turreted bards eliciting the eternal reflections of readers.[108] Poetry, for Spicer, is supposed to be accessible and useful, an embodied and social movement as alive as music. Most importantly, though, poetry is grounded in a mystical external force. Spicer rejected the 'big lie of the personal,' instead presenting the poet as simply a means of transmission.[109]

Placing even greater emphasis on the refusal of an agentive 'I', giving the agency of meaning-making instead to readers and language itself,[110] the Language poets emerged in the late 1960s and early 1970s from the conditions created by the San Francisco Renaissance. This turn to readers' autonomy was intended as an explicitly political project in the service of abolishing the bourgeois individual self.[111]

The self-stated 'inevitabl[e] ... social and political ['as well as aesthetic'] activity' of Language poetry comes out of 'the (various) measuring and questioning and composition of our references.'[112] Meaning is constructed through a network of discussions, developing poetry as a social practice. The Language poets' famous dictum of giving poetic agency to the reader is not so much a direct transfer between two stable subject-positions (the Poet to the Reader), but rather a process of turning poets into readers of other poets, to the point that the person writing a poem is foremost a collaborator in the social meaning of other poets' works. Poetry becomes a practice of belief in other poets and in poetry; it is a system of faith around which poets materially gather. The space of poetry brings poets together because the meaning of each poet can only be created in and as this gathering.

Building on the San Francisco Renaissance and the Language poets, Warren dodges direct reference to the personal in her poems, instead formulating a mystical investment in belief as the structure giving meaning to poetry, as a strange *Darstellung* of the commodity form's fetishism and alienation. However, if she simply posited a determinate revolutionary subjectivity as the escape route from the form of subjectivity and its *Darstellung* in her poetry, then the logics of capital would be reproduced, carried through to the poetry as a new but still productive mechanism for computing subjectivity.

Instead, Warren follows Marx – in Moishe Postone's reading – in positing 'the relation of individual and society in capitalism [as] not, as has been commonly

108 Davidson 1989, p. 6.

109 Gizzi and Killian, 2008, p. xiii. For more on the ambivalent politics of the San Francisco Renaissance, see: Harris 2009; Hickman 2015, pp. 9–11.

110 Spahr 2001, p. 6, pp. 12–14.

111 Hejinian 2000, p. 171.

112 Bernstein and Andrews 1984, p. x.

assumed, limited to a critique of the isolated and fragmented bourgeois individual'; criticism cannot simply 'positively evaluate the collectivity, in which all persons are parts, as the standpoint from which to criticize the atomized individual' because 'both the bourgeois individual and society as an abstract whole confronting the individuals were constituted as capitalism superseded earlier forms of social life.'[113] To push the dialectics of subjectivity beyond the simple celebration of 'we' over 'I', Warren complicates the subsumption of collective capitalist conditions, finding a sociality in the excess of subjectivity's form-determination: she does not look for 'we' before 'I', but for a social mode that persists despite the dominance of the bourgeois individual and the abstract whole of society.

Warren believes despite herself; she is not a nihilist.[114] In her belief, the fact of believing itself becomes the mystical animation of knowledge. Something monstrous arises in the knowledge of one's subjectivity, and that monstrosity is a belief in the possibility of a different way of being, of social life that exceeds the illusory *I* and *we* of capitalist ontology. Her critique of the mystical is itself her mystical praxis, which again binds her closely to her local literary history. But mostly, for my purposes in this chapter, what this critical poetics allows is the opening of sociality in the excess of the foreclosure of both the individual and collective renditions of subjectivity in the value-form.

Fredric Jameson attends to the problem of a singular subjectivity growing out of communist theory by regarding subject-relations as 'responses to situations' in which one person is capable of constantly adapting to the requirements of each social form.[115] Determination is then in social flux, bound to the necessity of each changing relation, which opens the subjective form of 'self-knowledge' to others, revealing knowledge to have always been the process of knowing the other: 'what has been called self-knowledge is not really a knowledge of the self, but rather a consciousness of its situations,' Jameson writes, 'a way of gaining and keeping awareness of precisely that multiplicity of situations in which the self finds and invents itself.'[116] The self is constituted as knowledge of its surroundings, its world of relations. This is exactly the formation of social life in the poetry of Duncan and Spicer, where 'the poem enacts in its own realm forces (whether psychological or physiological) that structure the natural world.'[117]

113 Postone 2003, p. 32.
114 Warren 2020a, p. 97.
115 Jameson 2009, p. 282.
116 Ibid.
117 Davidson 1989, p. 20.

The revolutionary movement in Warren's *Darstellung* is in bringing the process of subjectivation in front of its subjects, rather than where it usually happens, so famously 'behind the backs of the producers.'[118] While through this act, as Starosta writes, 'we do not *cease* to be determined as [the] personifications [of the value-form] and become able to affirm an abstractly free self-determining action,' a break in the norms of subject-production nonetheless becomes available to us: 'through the critical investigation of the value form we affirm our freedom because we come *consciously to cognise* our own determination as alienated social subjects.'[119] To present the conditions of subjectivity's subsumption in value-production through poetry as *Darstellung* is to see the manifold movements of sociality arise out of and away from the site of subsumption, to witness the survival of social being beyond the strictures of value's form-determining computation of subjectivity.

In Warren's poetry, sociality in the excess of subjection is not revealed through metaphor or poetic analogy. Her poetry, instead, enacts a belief in the constitutive sociality that exceeds both the determined forms of the 'I' and the 'we'; she actualises a general antagonism of excessive sociality that disrupts the productive form of alienated subjectivity.

10 The Emotive Poetics of Sociality

There is a subtle emotional arch within Warren's belief system. Something despairing haunts her poetry. Even her celebration of beauty – 'the joy of a child with a chocolate mouth / & the sun setting / & the sun setting'[120] – is held in loss, as if this were the final moment of wonder, before which everything collapses. Within the aphorisms of 'Personal Poem', the formal structure of this emotive complexity is revealed: 'Translate your sadness to anger then be done with it / everyone knows you're no good at staying mad.'[121] The sequence leading up to 'Astrology is real' represents this aphorism: it is the discursive practice of translating sadness into anger, the unbearable excess of which is then released. That is, the 'Astrology is real' sequence is the *Darstellung* of the later 'Translate your sadness' imperative.

This movement within the poem itself presents Warren's poetry as a praxis of study. Between the poet and the reader, before the subsumption of this book as

118 Marx 1990, p. 135.
119 Starosta 2016, p. 191, citing Iñigo Carrera 2007, p. 204. Original emphasis.
120 Warren 2013, pp. 96–7.
121 Ibid., p. 97.

a commodity and after its inevitable failure to enact the (anti-)political revolution it ruminates on, study is built as a stage in a revolution, which is yet to arrive but is always ongoing in a suspended temporality, ongoing but currently out of reach in the optics of subjectivity.

Warren is deeply serious about the meaning of belief, even if the referent of that belief is not specific: 'Celebrate the birthdays of your friends and the holy days even / if you're not a believer learn the tales eat the eggs.'[122] The fact of being present for the sociality of belief is important, regardless of the specific practice or object of belief. The excessive social world has chosen to believe, and it has led to this, which is why it is important. This does not mean that the past is simply accepted – revolutionary dedication is also maintained throughout the poem: 'Be kind we must overthrow the government'[123] – but that it is not rejected or forgotten. Fundamentally at work in Warren's poetry is the *Darstellung* of a poetic sociality opened discursively by belief. Warren's discursive sociality is a practice that materially withdraws social lives from the constitutive fetishes of alienated individuality and society.

This poetic counteraction to the formal subsumption of sociality in the computed subjectivity of capital is what I see as the importance of Warren's poetry. In this commodity, a subtle monster speaks, with a magical belief in a simultaneous contemporary that exceeds the temporality of capital's real abstractions. There is social life in the excess of subsumption, and a spectre within the semantics of exchange is revealing a little opening towards it. What is most important to emphasise is that this monstrously animated form, this mystical thing, is not metaphorical and cannot be described by any of the usual devices of literary studies: it is not a reference to or representation of labour and capital, nor does it symbolise or hypostatise or intertextually designate the truth of capitalist social relations. Warren's poetry is the *Darstellung* of the material dialectics through which revolutionary sociality emerges, working against the computation of social relations form-determined by value. Those relations are re-presented through their presence in the work, as opposed to the distanced metaphoric method of *Vorstellung*.

Alli Warren's *Darstellung* is achieved through a local praxis of poetics that refuses to stop its critical dialectics at the liberal celebration of the *we*, a collectivity so easily subsumed into the subjectivating process of value-production. The *we* is not an escape from the *I*, but the mere political aggreg-

---

122 Ibid., p. 96.

123 Ibid.

ate of many *Is*. In her hilarious, subtle, and profound poetic project, Warren is dedicated to a social mode that undergirds the fetishes of this commodified world.

The question remains, in the excess of *we* and *I*, of how subjectivity is experienced in and by its form-determined actors, and which social and poetic mechanisms are at hand for disbanding this oppressive form. These are the pursuits of the following chapter, in which I read Rob Halpern's poetry, studied through Judith Butler's and Jacques Lacan's psychoanalytic texts. By doing so, I hope to expose and criticise the constitutive fantasies that create the experience of being a form-determined subject.

In this chapter, I have attempted to uncover the persistence of a social life that lives in a temporality before and beside the present. Warren exposes this temporality through a practice of belief, which – by way of the method of *Darstellung* – allows her to situate repressed feminised, familial, and social temporalities within the commodified and fetishised relations of the present. Warren breaks open the alienation of the subject by exposing it to the social temporalities that form all the hidden connections upholding the possibility of social life.

In chapter three, I turn to the internal experience of alienated subjectivity, attempting to understand the network of fantasies and traumas that force us to remain within this computed, alienated form of subjectivity. Then, in Part 2 of *Poetics of Value*, I leave the fetishised forms that value imposes and look instead for the sociality that survives in its excess, reading Rowan Ricardo Phillips and Fred Moten as poetic means of accessing the 'ceaseless excess' that Warren has presented in this chapter as constitutively present but violently erased through commodification.

CHAPTER 3

Rob Halpern and the Crisis of America

1 Before the Pain

Rob Halpern's poetry is concerned foremost with the embodied experience of value, the experience of living as an animated site of accumulation. Throughout his collections, the formation of bodies is intimately bound up with the capitalist contradiction of individual feelings: one's body is obsessively individuated, prohibited from any meaningful social life in the absence of competitive accumulation, and yet the sentient experience of one's own body is always mediated by an external, regulatory relation: value. The antisocial force of capitalism is imposed by its dominant social relation. In Halpern's 2012 collection *Music for Porn*, this contradiction is displayed in its most obscenely spectacularised expression: the soldier's body as a militarised apparatus of prohibited and prohibitive feelings.

As a site of sentient prohibition, the soldier's body is the most concise representation of the contradictions of US culture, bringing together the economic and personal scales of this historically unique form of aggressive, anxious subjectivity. At the national level, as I explore at length below, there has been a significant rise in the ratio of unproductive compared to productive labour in the US economy. While most of this shift in the twentieth century was down to the rise in circulation labour, such as accounting, banking, and insurance, which redistributes existing surplus-value, in the twenty-first century a large part of this shift to unproductive labour is caused by the rise of care work. At the same time, however, the United States has been overcome by a crisis of care, which makes it both increasingly necessary and increasingly impossible to provide and receive the basic care required for survival.[1]

In this chapter, I explore the limits of contemporary American subjectivity by reading Halpern's *Music for Porn* and its spectacular fetishisation of the sexualised soldier's body in relation to its immediate historical context: the post-9/11.

Slavoj Žižek compares the months following the 9/11 attacks to 'those brief moments after we have been deeply cut, before the full extent of the pain strikes us. We do not yet know how the events will be symbolized, what their sym-

1 Fraser 2021.

bolic efficiency will be, what acts they will be evoked to justify.'[2] Suspended in the silence of pain but without recourse to any causal reasoning or social cure, unable yet to ask why or find meaning in the experience of a pain 'we' suffer, the modality of accusation is assumed.

In the days immediately following the 9/11 attacks, the New York Stock Exchange closed for four days, the rule of economic order put on hold. Endless discussions of Islam and its supposed inherent terrorist fundamentalism ensued, alongside defences of the global supremacy of capitalist democracy. The project of 'Infinite Justice' was begun, revealing the unconscious fantasies of America: 'it is easy to account for the fact that poor people around the world dream about becoming Americans[, but] what do the well-to-do Americans, immobilized in their well-being, dream about? About a global catastrophe that would shatter their lives,' Žižek writes.[3]

When the material armoury of the world's militarised chaos finally reached the United States in the ultimate spectacle of attack on 9/11, the narcissism of US subjectivity was revealed in a drive far more fundamental than the simple self-justifying fantasy of catastrophe. This fundamental drive is opened in psychoanalysis, which, as Samo Tomšič writes, 'debunks the modern myth of the narcissistic ego as the primary unit preceding socioeconomic relations as the indivisible social atom.'[4] There is no subject before the generative fantasies that animate collective subjectivity. Instead, Tomšič understands Freud as positing that 'there is no purely psychological, individual or thoroughly private resistance. Psychological resistance stands in direct continuity with the resistance of structures sustaining the social mode of production.'[5] The neoliberal social mode of production,[6] based on the speculative infinity of money and the permanent war economy,[7] is constituted by a libidinal force. Its guiding desire is to recuperate the heroic dominance the United States enjoyed from the late nineteenth century until recently,[8] an abyssal desire directly generative of the subjectivity that operates within the twinned projects of nationalist ideology and surplus-value.

---

2 Žižek 2012, pp. 55–6.

3 Ibid., p. 20.

4 Tomšič 2021, p. 108.

5 Ibid., p. 110.

6 I follow Keeanga-Yamahtta Taylor's definition here: 'above all, neoliberalism is a political, social, and economic rejection of the social welfare state and the social contract more generally. It is a strategic effort aimed at restoring the profitability of business and capital by undermining the social obstacles that had destabilized its primacy.' Taylor 2019, p. 232.

7 See: Kurz 2014b.

8 Arrighi 2010, pp. 336–70.

The subjects who perform this anxious Americanness not only carry but give life to the productive libido of the American economy. As Tomšič goes on in his reading of Freud, 'Who enjoys? Freud's answer is that there is direct continuity between the subject's enjoyment and enjoyment of the system. Or better, what enjoys in and through the subject is the system itself.'[9] This is exemplified in the domestic military fetish of the United States. The permanent war economy is the guide of essential quotidian conduct not only while at war in Afghanistan, but – especially – in civilian life.

War is increasingly conducted through drones from far away, every target calculated by distant satellites, but the expression of the joy of war is found in the system's animation of its subjects. Every American subject – in very different ways, of course, and with varying degrees of success – is a performance of the militarised ideology of Infinite Justice that proceeds as the ongoing reaction to the spectre of terrorism; these are the constitutive conditions of American subjectivity. The pain of America's Žižekian cut is yet to arrive, but the symbolic efficacy of blood is fully in swing.

This confusing and aggressive 'self-love' produces a peculiar temporality of subjection, as Tomšič writes. What he calls the primacy of narcissism 'may appear primary but is in fact a reaction formation, whose primacy is retroactively constituted, a form of resistance to the ontological lack and structural instability inscribed into the organism.'[10] Once the fantasy of the USA's vulnerability is made possible in reality, it must be repressed and aggressively dismissed. In the world that follows 9/11, American subjectivity is asserted as the material affirmation of the USA's financial reign as capitalism's arbiter. The way of being that is *American* is the anxious drive that conceals the vulnerability of *America*. To be American is to dismiss the impossibility of America as a coherent signifying system.

After 9/11, as Žižek writes, what collapsed was the unquestionable presupposition of America's world-ordering innocence, its *a priori* right to invade, manipulate, and depose any expression of power, anywhere in the world, according to American ideology. The big Other of America – its 'subject-supposed-to-believe' – disintegrated and finally it had to give explicit voice to its ideological exertion.[11] That very stance of anxious aggression – the sudden slip into the void of presupposed assurance, with every act a defensive reaction that attempts to destroy a phantasmatic opponent, which Israel has also

9 Tomšič 2021, p. 87.
10 Ibid., p. 114.
11 Žižek 2012, p. 60.

acutely fallen into since October 2023 – has left the USA since then on defensive ground, desperate to assert its synonymy with the universal telos of capitalist democracy.

In the scene of being wounded, in opening to one's wounding, as the wounded subject and the subject who wounds, one is confronted with a foundational vulnerability. It is, as Judith Butler writes, in the moment of injury that one is directed towards a possible ethics of the other, in which one grounds oneself in the obscure social causes of this pain, a network of traumatic feelings that finds one's stability in a general social condition: the condition of having been wounded. The wounding that inaugurates 'the fundamental sociality of embodied life' is staged in loss, and even 'if I do not already know what it is *in* another person that I have lost, it may be that this sphere of dispossession is precisely the one that exposes my unknowingness, the unconscious imprint of my primary sociality.'[12]

Grief forms an important agonism in the USA's archetypal refusal of its constitutive pain because, by grieving, one accepts that one is vulnerable to being changed. Ceremonies of mourning are social rituals in which subjects offer their illusions of homeostasis over to one another, relinquishing the claim to being self-made and self-sustaining. 'Perhaps mourning has to do with agreeing to undergo a transformation,' as Butler continues, 'the full result of which one cannot know in advance.'[13] Mourning is the practice that breaks the ideal subject's presupposition of foresight, of being able to conquer the future through projective plans. In grief, the expansive temporality of subjectivity recedes, leaving only the social vulnerability of an indescribable loss.

It is of course for this reason that the post-9/11 US production of subjectivity is so intent on foreclosing the recognition of pain, a foreclosure that forces what Sara Ahmed calls 'the promise of happiness' on individuated subjects,[14] prohibiting the bad feeling of grief: one must only see the bright and positive feelings of the seeable future, marking the time to come as fully accumulable value, barring grief precisely as the complexity of social life. America is the name for the infinite expansion of the gap between *being* wounded and *feeling* wounded, between the violence and the pain. The body's social precarity materialises the possibility of an ethics formed in the sharing of this general pain.

The body, however, does not only open in its vulnerability. Butler understands survival as dependent on 'a social network of hands,'[15] helping hands

12 Butler 2020, p. 28. Original emphasis.
13 Ibid., p. 21.
14 Ahmed 2010.
15 Butler 2016, p. 14.

that support and carry, but hands that also offend, also wound, also abuse. The vulnerable body, as Marina Vishmidt notes in her critique of the body in Butler's corpus, marks a paradoxical and antagonistic limit, simultaneously separating and binding resistance to being touched and the need for social touch.[16] As Maya Rivera writes, the necessity of interhuman contact also demarcates the body as the site of contact's erasure, as the limit of one's capacity to be touched, to be reached by the Other.[17]

Engaging with current debates in value-critical Marxisms, in this chapter I explore the economics of the USA's contemporary militarised ideology, which I stage as a debate between 'primary narcissism' and 'primary sociality'. Halpern's poetry opens acutely into this complexity, maintaining a focus on what Silvia Federici notes is absent throughout Marx's works: the generative desire of capitalist subjects.[18] Why do we keep reproducing these unbearable conditions? What impels the continuation of this militarised drive to surplus? These are the deeply personal questions Halpern responds to in his military poetry of desire.

Like Alli Warren, Halpern is a San Franciscan poet who writes very consciously in the tradition of his local area. Where Warren is concerned with the everyday life of domestic American commodities, though, Halpern's focus is largely on the international exertion of the USA as a cultural and aesthetic commodity itself, represented by the US military's imperial interventions as global police. This poetic concern with international military politics and the endless scandal of American capitalist aggression gives Halpern's poetry a brutal mood, a feeling of nihilist oppression, where Warren's poetry is more occupied with the quotidian futility of the USA's obsessive commodity culture.

In *Music for Porn*, the speaker's lover – a soldier in the US army – has died, and the speaker's reaction is sexual and military aggression, in which the urge to fuck, to kill, and to accumulate are indistinguishable. At the same time, the speaker is Halpern, an academic, a Marxist theorist, who is aware of his subsumption in the abstract deployment of the militarised economy, anxiously covering the need to globally circulate value, and of his fundamental determination by value at the level of subjectivity.

At turns shocking, revealing, disgusting, and beautiful, Halpern's poetry nestles into the heart of value's world-constituting operation. The principal

---

16 Vishmidt 2020.

17 Rivera 2015, pp. 5–7.

18 Federici 2021, pp. 80–1. In his early writings, though, Marx is somewhat dedicated to a potential passionate subject of communism, even from within his humanism. See: Marx 1992b, pp. 355–6.

experience of being that arises from these reflections – the defining coordinate of the American subject's placement in the world – is shame. The profoundly ashamed, militarised subject responds to this unbearable experience with murderous aggression, which opens the intriguing possibility of a psychoanalytic reading of the subject-determining force of the value-form. That psychoanalytic understanding of the aesthetics and ethics of the USA's contemporary military economy is the focus of this chapter, pivoting on Halpern's poetry and essays.

2 In the Face of Failure

The feeling that spreads throughout the painful, oppressive prose of Rob Halpern's *Music for Porn* is a peculiar shame without cause, an expansive experience that does not require the ashamed subject necessarily to have transcended any social prohibition. The shame of being comes before any shameful act. By existing in this body, holding oneself up in the chorus of unending confusions, one is already given away to the solitude of shame.

> Upon being hailed, I'm completed by the sudden awareness of my own hideous shape, all feeling dead at the base of my balls. But behind the veneer of these earnest comments lies my excrement and cum, gross product, this residue of debt, cruddy yield thru which we seek transit, a justice in excess of any legible demand. Whereupon I awake with visions of the prison house, abattoirs positioned along peripheral fades, exquisite creatures of social waste, and all the things I'll never see that make me what I am.[19]

But what gives rise to the conditions of this feeling? What terror underpins these foundations of the anxious, impossible subject?

The speaking subject is only a 'residue of debt,' the result of the accumulation and empty promise of value-accumulation. He has proceeded from a productive economy, productive both of value and of himself. And through that production, his own capacity to reproduce has been curtailed: his balls are dead and his own hideous form emerges from the scene of hailing. However, something lies before this, something hidden in the folds of ideology: 'behind the veneer' is his own waste, the waste of his reproduction, which codes this

19 Halpern 2012, p. 8.

residue as male. This man, awash in scenes of violence, of abattoirs and prisons, is formed in the gendering ceremonies of militarised shame.

In *Totem and Taboo*, Sigmund Freud poses sacrifice as a suspended promise held before every emergent male subject as potential patricide.[20] In Jacques Lacan's reading of this scene, shame is the feeling that gives meaning to the event.[21] It does not matter whether the murder takes place; the possibility of murdering one's father is the instantiation of a shame that pervades the subject *qua* subject. Placed already in shame as the condition of being an adult who has emerged from a primary caregiving scene, the subject is founded in an identification with what it must eradicate. To enter adulthood, mired in its perennial fantasies of independence, those who make the child must be killed.

This is 'the pacifying function of the ego ideal, the connexion between its libidinal normativity and a cultural normativity bound up from the dawn of history with the *imago* of the father,'[22] whose pacifying function occurs through the feeling of shame that exceeds the totemic murder, leaving an 'Oedipal identification ... by which the subject transcends the aggressivity that is constitutive of the primary subjective individuation.'[23] Becoming *one* requires an identification with an Other who is and is not wholly separable, an identification by which the seemingly primary given features of the subject are also determined, as Lacan writes of gender/sex: 'the statement, "I'm a man", ... can mean no more than, "I'm like he whom I recognize to be a man, and so recognize myself as being such." In the last resort, these various formulas are to be understood only in reference to the truth of "I is an other".'[24]

The intergenerational identification of the gender of the son with the gender of the father, and the father with the grandfather, and so on, goes, for Lacan, all the way back to 'the dawn of history,' a point at which the father, in 'the mythical circularity' of this complex, is only a mythological event meaningful precisely by his absence.[25] He has already been killed, and every son is already constituted in a perennial guilt coded as man. Men, however, continue to pursue the repeated scene of this fantasy as the primary guide of their enjoyment, their objectless *jouissance*. The only enjoyment possible is this aimless attainment of an erasure that has always-already happened: the apparent independence of these gendered actors – Father and Son, man-maker and man-made – arises

20 Freud 1978. See: Chapter IV, 'The Infantile Recurrence of Totemism'.
21 Lacan 2001, pp. 9–32.
22 Ibid., p. 25. Original emphasis.
23 Ibid.
24 Ibid., pp. 25–6.
25 Ibid., pp. 25.

as a function of their mutual destruction. As Tomšič writes, the political and the private are here intimately merged, with no way of being separated.[26] The social is productive of the subject, and the subject is erased as a subject through exposure to the social.

This is what Tomšič means, in his reading of Freud, by the *enjoyment of the system*. One's apparent enjoyment is not a subjective release into the world, but rather an anxious merging of the subject's determined social roles and the fantasy of independence that produces a desiring subject: 'social links are internal and external to the subject, [so] enjoyment cannot but take place inside and outside the subject's mental apparatus.'[27] This externality of desire produces and maintains the unbearable anxiety of desiring. Every act of desire is the confirmation of the subject's instability, in that it confirms the ingestion and subsumption of external norms. As Žižek writes, this Lacanian *jouissance* is 'the abyss of traumatic/excessive enjoyment which threatens to swallow us up, and towards which the subject desperately endeavours to maintain a proper distance.'[28] The subject wants to be distanced from this terrifying external imposition but has no means of operating other than through this ambivalent desire.

For Lacan, then – whom Tomšič, Žižek, and Lorenzo Chiesa (on whom more below) closely follow – both the subject and the other are 'no more than mirages' constituted by a desire that exceeds them both.[29] By speaking, the subject pursues the recognition of the other.[30] When unencumbered by projective aggressive fantasies, this is the possible ethics of desire. To arrive at that point, though, the subject needs to stop imagining themself as a stable site of projection into the world, a projection inevitably productive of shame and aggression, and instead see that 'there is no speaker, no subject of communication preceding and underlying the relations that constitute discursive reality,' as Tomšič writes. 'There is, however, a subject that is produced out of joint as soon as a body begins to work, think and speak.'[31] That is, the subject needs to be abolished *qua* subject.[32]

In the opening section of *Music for Porn*, this primary shame also carries a political character. The speaker is 'hailed', an act of authority that instils in

26 Tomšič 2021, p. 54.
27 Ibid., p. 87.
28 Žižek 1997, p. 175.
29 Lacan 2001, p. 88.
30 Ibid., p. 94.
31 Tomšič 2021, p. 126.
32 Lacan 2001, p. 95. This is what Tomšič sees as the unified pursuit of Lacanian psychoanalysis and Marxist communism: Tomšič 2021, pp. 247–9.

the subject the sudden awareness of being *complete*. This completion, however, is immediately 'hideous': it causes in him the forfeiture of the illusion that he could ever be fully complete. As the father reveals the fantasy of the masculinised authority of fathers through his appearance in the scene of sacrifice, through his presence in the eradication of himself, the American subject as presented by Halpern accordingly descends into a ruinous incompletion through the demand to be complete.

Turning up at the scene of a generalised demand, the perverse ceremonies of collective individuation that form the basic rituals of American life, the speaker is given over to a demand for 'justice in excess of any legible demand.' In this social scene of hailing, the assembly of his desire reaches the point of excess, but this vision is suddenly violated by the brutalising erasure of desire in excess of the commodified subject-form: prison house, abattoir, social waste. He sees only death, only ubiquitous ruin. This is the crucial volta that recurs throughout the collection with explosively depressing force.

Following this violated turn, the speaker resigns himself to enjoying the conditions of this brutality:

> The way they burn the bodies, on certain days, when there's a gentle breeze coming from the north, what sweet odors move me. If y're quiet, you might hear the war moving thru every sound I make. Like his cremains, unidentifiable chips of bone ground to a fine powder for making the paste.[33]

His reaction to the erasure of sentience is to feign a nonchalant pride, to assume a nihilistic expansionism, forcing the world to become exactly what he cannot bear, which is, of course, himself and his own illusion of independence. If the subject cannot exist, neither will anything else.

The subject of Halpern's poetry, I am suggesting, is a synecdoche for the nation as subject. The speaker is America. The question remains, though, of what has caused this collapse of the primary relation of one to one's surroundings? What has given the speaking subject over already to these speculations on a metonymic genealogy of destruction, the father-destroying son following the world-destroying father? Why is Halpern's ultra-American subject so incapable of recognising his constitution in the impossible optics of others? What makes him so simultaneously reliant on others and unable to accept this reliance?

---

33 Halpern 2012, p. 111.

3 Poeticising Crisis

In *Music for Porn*, the agonism of a possible ethical relation is held in the limitless projection of the subject's desire. Desire here, though, is not a possible ethics of exposing one's impossible subjective independence to the constitutive other, but rather an archetypally aggressive projection of the penis. The speaker of the poems is forever horny, always pursuing the consumption of the other. Everything slips into thoughts of sex: while meditating on the role of poetry 'a string of phonemes fills my mouth like his dirty ejaculate';[34] the 'body at war' becomes 'open to risk without tenderness, penetration without pleasure';[35] in the pursuit of '[a]nything for more soldier fuck,' the speaker '[dashes] into a desert hut to filch a flask of fuel. I conceal every sign of my arousal.'[36] There is something essentially American about this painfully insatiable desire.

The *Wertkritik* tendency – the value-critical tradition of Marxists who publish the journal *Exit!*, infamous for their contradictory mix of communism and Zionism[37] – is concerned with this connecting point between the national, the economic, and the social. As Robert Kurz writes, the military dominance of the US economy places the production of value in an aporetic industry: the production of military equipment occurs largely outside the wage-relation, through often unpaid prisoners' labour and a non-competitive state company, and therefore without the consumption of commodified labour-power by capitalists, which is the sole source of new surplus-value.[38] How can the expansion of this commodity lead to increased profits? This is where the crucial and hidden difference between surplus-value and profit comes into play, and its difficult entanglement in desire.

The classic capitalist wage relation represents the positions of someone who buys time (capitalist) and someone who sells time (worker). The wage is not so much a direct – if always partial – remuneration for labour-time as it is the minimum requirement for the worker's survival and continued dependence on this relation. This relation is valorised later in exchange, when the use-value of the commodity is purchased from the capitalist in exchange for money. While value is created by the consumption of the cooperative labour of production, then, that labour is only valorised as a means of facilitating the totality of the system: surplus-value is reliant on the circulation of commodities and commodified

---

34 Ibid., p. 4.
35 Ibid., p. 57.
36 Ibid., p. 99.
37 Leslie 2014.
38 Kurz 2014b. Best 2024, p. 23.

services, but its value is created in production.[39] In the contemporary US economy, however, productive labour assumes a reduced role in production, and production a reduced role in the economy generally, giving rise to the question of how the production of surplus-value is maintained.

In the US economy, the ratio of unproductive to productive labour has vastly increased since the end of World War II. In 1983, value-form theorist Fred Moseley studied the organisation of labour from 1947 to 1977. In that period, the number of productive workers (those whose labour, when consumed by a capitalist, produces surplus-value[40]) increased by 35% while the number of unproductive workers (those whose labour, though remunerated in wages, does not produce surplus-value) increased by 143%.[41] Unproductive labour increased at over quadruple the rate of productive labour, which resulted in a reduction in the surplus-value available for accumulation, and led, Moseley concludes, to the severe economic crisis at his time of writing in the early 1980s.[42]

As Moseley notes, Marx's theory of the laws of motion of capitalism, including the tendential fall in the rate of profit, does not include a comparative study of productive and unproductive labour; Marx's reading focuses only on the fall in the profit-rate of productive labour.[43] In a text published in 1991, Moseley seeks to take a step further than Marx by assessing the causes of the relative rise in unproductive labour in the US economy.

At first, it may seem that the primary cause of this shift is the outsourcing of production to other countries, with many US industries displacing production to China and elsewhere while developing separate but connected logistics industries to bring the commodities back to the US for consumption. However, this accounts for only a small portion of the change in labour.[44] Moseley divides unproductive labour into two main types: circulation labour (i.e. the exchange of existing value, including insurance, accounting, banking, and real estate) and supervisory labour (i.e., the management of production workers). The former made up 80% of the mass of unproductive labour between 1950 and 1980.[45]

In the twenty-first-century US economy, it is necessary to add a third category of unproductive labour: care work, which has increased enormously

39 Best 2024, p. 27.
40 See: Marx 1990, p. 270 f.
41 Moseley 1983, p. 182.
42 Ibid., p. 185.
43 Moseley 1991, p. 123.
44 Ibid., pp. 123–4.
45 Ibid.

since the time of Moseley's study.[46] In 2006–7, care work formed up to 22 % of the paid labour force in Massachusetts.[47] This increase in low-waged care work, alongside a rise in high-paid financial and tech jobs, has resulted in an increasingly polarised economy, with very little growth in mid-wage jobs.[48] Both the lowest paid care jobs and the highest paid speculative financial jobs, however, are largely unproductive: they only redistribute existing value. To compensate for this loss of productive labour, governments withdraw state services, which results in an increased need to commodify all care work. Since, in capitalism, unproductive labour is reliant on the redistribution of the surplus-value created in production, with a falling mass of surplus-value, unproductive labour becomes increasingly unable to redistribute sufficient surplus-value to keep workers alive and the economy functioning.[49] People are unable to reproduce their conditions of survival without constant and ubiquitous sources of minor income: instead of living in their home, people sublet every available space as a holiday rental; instead of caring for oneself and one's social life, people take cash-in-hand extra jobs; instead of taking time off to productively consume, people take up temporary jobs in the gig economy. All time becomes unproductive labour-time, and the economy becomes formed of endlessly occupied and depleted but unproductive workers.

'Next to the facilitation of an upward redistribution of wealth,' as Nat Raha writes, neoliberalising governments have enforced 'a disinvestment in social security' since the 2007–8 financial crash, especially focused on cuts to social and welfare services.[50] The responsibility of reproductive care is displaced from public organisation to the family, which entrenches the ideological privacy of the family as the basic unit of social formation.

These conditions affirm an increasingly close connection between the ideological production of subjects, the private form of the hetero- or homonormative family, military operations, the aggressive defence of (national or corporeal, global or personal) borders, the expansion of commodified care work, and the reduction in the possibility of social practices of care without the mediation of commodification. As Lisa Duggan writes, 'we get marriage and the military, then we go home and cook dinner, forever.'[51] The ideological militar-

46 Moseley has continued to study the relative proportions of unproductive labour but without a specific focus on the contemporary US economy: see Moseley 2016, p. 72.

47 Duffy et al. 2013.

48 Dwyer 2013.

49 Roberts emphasises the 'dependence' of unproductive labours on productive labours: Roberts 2014, p. 337.

50 Raha 2021, p. 92.

51 Duggan 2003, p. 62.

isation of American subjects is entrenched by the crisis of surplus-value and the desperate proliferation of unproductive labour in the service and care sectors that attempt to redistribute a dwindling mass of value. The crisis here is global, economic, and imperial as much as it is personal, subjective, and ideological.

The rise in care work has occurred alongside the expansion of another industry in the wake of neoliberal reforms since the late 1970s. While largely replaced by the expansion of care and service work in the twenty-first century, the general displacement of US production to the Global South in the final decades of the twentieth century caused unprecedented levels of unemployment in the USA, especially among black and working-class Americans, which, as Jaron Browne writes, occurred at the same time as the rise of the US's staggering rates of incarceration.

> It may surprise some people that as the number of people without jobs increases, the number of working people actually increases – they become prison labourers. Everyone inside has a job. There are currently [in 2007] over 70 factories in California's 33 prisons alone.[52]

Nowadays, two thirds of the US's almost 2 million prisoners are forced to work while incarcerated. Many additionally choose to work.[53]

The close links between the state's requirement for a divided labour force, whose internally competitive pursuit of few resources restricts unified action, and mass incarceration goes back to the very beginning of prisons in the US. As Browne notes, the prison system began in earnest after the 1865 ratification of the 13th Amendment. Slavery was abolished, 'except as a punishment for crime,' but a reformulated legal structure, called the Black Codes, was set up to maintain the racialising control of those who had been enslaved. In the case of the Angola Prison in Louisiana, the conversion from plantation economy to prison economy was direct and literal: the state purchased a private plantation and opened it as a prison. 'Slave quarters became cell units.'[54]

After the abolition of the Black Codes, the regulation of black life inherent in the operation of American policing continues unharmed. Black and Hispanic people especially are removed from civic life and placed under an injunction

52 Browne 2007, p. 42.

53 ACLU no date.

54 Brown 2007, p. 43. See also: Wilson Gilmore 2007.

to labour for free or far below minimum wage – an average of 13 to 52 cents per hour for prison maintenance jobs[55] – without choice.[56]

Bourgeois economists have long been concerned not with the ethics of encaging people and forcing them to work for free, but with the impact prison labour has on market competition. Non-incarcerated artisans and businesses cannot produce commodities as cheaply as the prison labour system can, since it has very little or no expenditure on variable capital, so they cannot compete with the state on the competitive capitalist market.[57] In 1934, the government responded to these concerns by setting up Federal Prison Industries (FPI), a state-owned company that sells the products of incarcerated labour almost exclusively to federal agencies, limiting its role on the competitive market. The company, trading as UNICOR since 1977, presents itself as 'the largest inmate training program' in the country, claiming on its website – under a photograph of incarcerated workers sewing military uniforms – that the commodities produced 'are merely by-products' of 'inmate release preparation.'[58] However, as shown on the company's website, the equipment of the US military is made by these incarcerated workers, which not only bases American neoimperialism on a necessary foundation of mass incarceration, but also removes American military pursuits from the standard competitive operation of the capitalist market.[59]

While the circulation of commodities produced in prisons is in fact not sufficiently widespread to impact private market competition, as bourgeois economists worry,[60] the circulation of enforced labour certainly carries a social, historical, and semantic weight in the operation of US imperialism. Kim Gilmore plainly summarises the problem: 'as the punishment industry becomes a leading employer and producer for the U.S. "state," and as private prison and "security" corporations bargain to control the profits of this traffic in human unfreedom, the analogies between slavery and prison abound.'[61] The performance of the permanent war that has upheld the global imperial ideology of the USA for the last half century is subtended by a system of unpaid

55 Mercer 2022.
56 For more on this, see: Alexander 2010.
57 See: Derrick et al. 2004.
58 Federal Bureau of Prisons no date.
59 See: Alexander 2010, p. 219. Also see the Department of Justice's 2016 report into defective production of military helmets by UNICOR incarcerated workers: https://oig.justice.gov/reports/2016/i1608.pdf.
60 See: Derrick et al. 2004, pp. 78–80.
61 Gilmore 2000, p. 195. It should be emphasised, though, that it is only an *analogy* that connects enslaved and prison labour; they are in fact very distinct, as I argue below.

incarcerated labour, undermining the imperatives of the free market that supposedly govern this imperial-capitalist expansionism.

4 The Masquerade of Profit

The entanglement of incarceration, enslavement, military expansion, and the production of value is the sociopolitical background of *Music for Porn*, while its subjective background is the aggressive desire of a subject who cannot bear his constitutive social vulnerability. The speaker of the collection is dumbfounded by the fact that this overwhelming brutality can continue to reproduce itself with only minor and occasional disruptions. Reproducibility, for this nihilist speaker, becomes confounding, nestling into every semantic link of reproduction: sex becomes indistinguishable from military violence.

The collection is split between verse and prose sections, with the former tending to throw together the overwhelming experiences of war and desire and the latter tending to investigate, in language that strikingly resembles academic Marxism, the national and global causes of this suffering, while also relating these broad temporalities to the poem itself.

In one of the prose sections, the speaker is '[b]oarding a bus to tour the devastation,' when 'a spontaneous surge of meaning irrupts inside the grid.'[62] The grid, however, is not the spatial form of globality, or the vast network of global relations of production. It is, instead, the body itself, entangled between citizen and soldier, between named subject and anonymous flesh. 'A blackening corpuscle, an indecipherable glyph, ruin lurks deep in the bowels, my poem's stupid plan, a wasting syndrome, this place without history.'[63] The tour of devastation is a general condition, and what arises when it is observed closely enough is the hieroglyphs of determination worn deep in the foundations of the body, expressed alternately as racialisation, sexuation, nationalisation, and exploitation.

The emergence of this foundation of violence is not in any sense new to the speaker. 'Yesterday, the situation arrived at its crisis, and tomorrow it will arrive again. Our current state being one of permanent interruption, this account appeals to a timeless suspension of the monetary form, already dissociated from its social base.'[64] The repetition of brutality occasions a perplexing temporality. The brutality recurs without end, and that recurrence produces

62 Halpern 2012, p. 101.
63 Ibid.
64 Ibid., p. 103.

the experience of permanence, both as a 'state' of being and as the 'state' that organises military expansion and prison labour. The timelessness of this repetition, though, cannot eradicate the embodied presence of the speakers; someone remains as the observer of imposed infinity. He has access to the specific temporal referents of *yesterday* and *tomorrow*, even if they do not specify where in history he is. He is nonetheless stuck in a *today*, a today that is interrupted without end by the intrusion of the unborn future and the accumulated ghosts of the dead past.

For Halpern's speaker, there is only life in the universalisation of horror, since the only life he can recognise is death in the commodified form of value. 'Having grown accustomed to the abrogation of such acts *freedom of movement, freedom to farm* I imagine a compensatory access to withdrawn life, the way money traces suppressed flows until motion comes to a standstill, the whole order arriving at equilibrium in dead labor.'[65] A certain synonymy across history is imagined here, but the synonymy does not arise from history's own indistinct reproduction of itself. It comes rather from the expansion of now, the bloating death of labour as the eradication of a sentient present, a sensible presence.

This subtle claim on the totalisation of an empty present marks a difference in the historical forms of labour that have defined the USA. Both incarcerated and enslaved labour are removed from the wage relation in which variable capital is a principal capitalist expenditure (even if capitalists do not distinguish between expenditures on variable and fixed capital). However, what appears as 'equilibrium in dead labor' is in fact a differential accumulation of living labour.

On top of the regulations that limit its impact on the 'free' competitive market, prison labour emblematises a contemporary shift in the US economy from production to consumption and conquest. In the eighteenth and nineteenth centuries, the US was reliant on slavery to maintain its economic expansion, and today that remains the case for incarcerated labour, with many politicians explicitly refusing reductions in the number of prisoners nationwide lest the incarcerated workforce also diminish.[66]

Incarcerated workers are not commodities, but their freedom to enter into the wage relation is still removed, often permanently, which decommodifies their labour-power. Labour-power can only be a productive commodity when it is exchanged as a necessarily exploitative relation between capitalist and worker. This reduction of labour-power through incarcerated labour, then, must reduce the production of surplus-value.

65 Ibid.
66 ACLU, 'Captive Labor', section II.

Labour productivity is in relative decline in the US, resulting in a cumulative loss in national output of well over $10 trillion since 2005.[67] Productivity has grown at an average rate of 1.4% since 2005, significantly less than the 2.2% average of the 1990s boom.[68] Consumption of commodities, however – despite a drastic fall in material retail during the COVID-19 pandemic – increases continually, with physical shopping growing by 8% in the year to March 2022, and online shopping by 27%.[69]

This is the crisis that subtends the aggressive misery of Halpern's speaker. The crisis of value and the collapse of profit are explicitly the reason and justification for the militarisation of the soldier's body: 'Appearance and value are rent asunder in his beauty *this chasm in sense, an emptiness that's killing me*. Having cut himself loose from the social relations that make him what he is, his figure stands in for universal profit.'[70] As the ideological appearance of a form in freefall, the soldier is under an anxious injunction to maintain a perfect facade, to be independent and separated from social life. This beauty, though, slips straight away into murderous nonsense. The speaker is killed by the duplicity of appearances, witnessing instead the fatal collapse at the core of this crisis. 'Sensing its own decay, value clings with fierce tenacity to the very things *bodies* that will be sacrificed for it. Just as he disavows the debauchery of capital *whose servant he is* my soldier becomes evermore debauched *sinks below the hemisphere of sense, as I might sink my nose in his ass* down along the precipitous fault of old imperialisms.'[71] The despair of the system has invaded the body he longs for; his desire is contaminated with crisis. This despair determines every moment of intimacy, withdrawing the possibility of sex and pleasure from their only sense in social life. The debauched servant of capital does not even enjoy his servitude, instead disavowing what he already has become. The crisis of value, for Halpern, is the crisis of the most immediate experience of our own bodies.

The economic cause of the crisis is a topic of heated debate in value-critical Marxisms.[72] While it remains a mystery to bourgeois economists, who see no difference between surplus-value and profit, the dramatically expanding gap between production and consumption in the US economy reveals the core

67 U.S. Bureau of Labor Statistics 2021.
68 McKinsey Global Institute 2023.
69 McKinsey Global Institute 2022.
70 Halpern 2012, pp. 152–3.
71 Ibid., p. 153.
72 For a relatively clear overview of Marx's long and extremely complex discussion of crisis, see: Best 2021, pp. 902–3.

of capital's constitutive contradiction, which is the focus of crisis theory.[73] Massimiliano Tomba provides a distinctive overview of crisis:

> The falling rate of profit provides the measure of the obsolescence of capital in terms of an increase in the constant part of capital. If, indeed, the falling rate of profit is given by the ratio of surplus-value as the numerator, and the sum of variable capital (wages) and constant capital (machines and raw materials) as the denominator, by increasing investments (and, at the same time, assuming that labourers are being paid the bare minimum necessary for survival, so that almost all labour-time is surplus-labour), the denominator tends to increase, leading to a decline in the rate of profit.[74]

Value is produced through the consumption of labour-power in the production process, which generates new value in commodities. This value, as Michael Heinrich notes, is not determined by the value of labour-power – it is not the quantity of labour that produces new value – but rather by 'the extent to which the labor expended counts as value-producing, abstract labor.'[75] It is the formal arrangement of this labour as abstract that counts.

All capitalists want to reduce the costs of production, which they generally attempt by lowering wages or extending the working day while keeping wages constant, resulting in more *profit*. This reveals the fundamental difference between profit and surplus-value. The latter is a category that appears through the study of value, calculated analytically by the rates of constant capital and variable capital alongside newly added value. This, however, is of no concern to capitalists: they are not students or analysts of capital, but rather capital personified. They are only concerned, necessarily, with *profit*, which is the difference between a commodity's value at the point of sale and its cost of production, rather than the specific characteristic of surplus-value, which is the consumption of labour-power.[76] In their pursuit of higher profit, capit-

73 This originally arises from Marx 1991, pp. 317–75. However, the current tendency largely follows the so-called 'Fragment on Machines' from notebooks VI and VII of the *Grundrisse*: Marx 1993, p. 690 f. While it has been very important for many Marxists over the last few decades, especially the Italian autonomists, *Potere Operaio*, and the contemporary left accelerationists, Marx's way of thinking in the fragment is largely absent in *Capital*, written in the decade following the *Grundrisse*. For a detailed discussion of this, see: Saito 2022, pp. 136–59.

74 Tomba 2013a, p. 77.

75 Heinrich 2004, p. 101.

76 Best 2024, pp. 15–50.

alists lower the costs of production, reducing the variable capital expended in the product, and thereby unwittingly reducing surplus-value.

Heinrich points out that this reduction of surplus-value occurs foremost when the value of the mass of surplus-value falls quicker than that of the advanced capital. It is also possible, however, that advanced capital could fall quicker than surplus-value, resulting in an increase in profit. Heinrich, in the tradition of the *Neue Marx-Lektüre*, sees the tendency of the rate of profit to fall not as a law – as *Wertkritik* understands it – but rather as one possibility of capitalism. For Heinrich, capital is able to adapt to sustaining itself – even if not in the long term – on profit rather than surplus-value.[77]

For the theorists of *Wertkritik*, the law of the tendential fall in the rate of profit is what defines the inevitable crisis of capitalism. As Norbert Trenkle summarises,

> since the 1970s, as a result of the worldwide, absolute displacement of living labor power from the process of valorization, capital has reached the historical limits of its power to expand, and thus also of its capacity to exist. In other words, modern commodity production has entered a fundamental process of crisis, which can only result in its downfall.[78]

As the ratio of necessary labour to surplus labour is decreased by the increasing productivity of labour – this reduction in the quantity of labour-power required for each commodity is what Marx calls relative surplus-value – capitalism loses its mechanism of valorisation, displacing its sole purpose into the mysticism that shrouds capitalists from knowledge of their absolute reliance on living labour.

The resulting crises manifest first as bubbles of expanding profit, which drive the market's representatives to even further speculative expansion, but this profit is empty, no longer based on living labour. Capitalism is a system of organising social relations, turning people's *a priori* impulse to gather in exchange into the private accumulation of people's living time, rendering lifetime as abstract labour. Once this crucial organisation of social life has been released from the circulation of capital, valorisation occurs at a critically low rate. The market becomes sustained by an entirely illusory structure that is neither able to extract new living labour as surplus-value nor to sustain the conditions of workers' self-reproduction.

---

77 Heinrich 2004, pp. 151–3.
78 Trenkle 2014b, p. 13.

These crises can, as Kurz writes in his monumental magnum opus, *Das Schwarzbuch Kapitalismus* (*The Black Book of Capitalism*), at times take 'eine kleine Pause [a little break]' in moments of cohesion between the political staging of stability and the belief in profit over surplus-value.[79] However, the result of this forced suspension of crisis is even greater impoverishment for many, and even deeper ideological confusion for the economy's representatives. In the collapse of *die kleinen Pausen*, finance capital desperately attempts to cover the failure of valorisation by throwing even more capital extracted from as-yet-unrealised future labour into speculation and market betting, while the state increases public borrowing. These manic actions of capital personified appear as the cause of crisis once the economy's masquerade of stability is broken but are in fact *responses to* the ongoing and constant crisis of capital's valorisation.[80]

At a national economic level, then, the necessary impulse of capitalists as capital personified to pursue greater rates of profit above all other considerations results in a fall in surplus-value. At a subjective level, this always-suspended crisis manifests as a fundamental vacuousness, a constitutive abyss in the form of subjectivity. What is pursued – surplus-value – is not conscious; everything is computed by a phantasmatic future, and economic agents are subjected to the programmed determinacy of subjectivity.

The centrifugal construction of subjects around this limitless need for increased production opens a psychoanalytic drama in the operation of subjectivity. The abstraction of value-relations empties out the social grounding of the subject in this militarised expression of desire. It is this abyssal psychoanalytic drama that Halpern reveals as the core of capital's maintenance despite its imminent crisis. What upholds the remnants of the edifice of value and keeps it in expansion is its constitutive interplay *as* the subjects of capitalism, who ceaselessly strive to become the perfect synecdoche of America, of the nation-state constructed on the principle of value's valorisation.

5 Constant Interruption

The painful trauma brought out in *Music for Porn* is the fact that it does not even matter if one learns of one's form-determination, one's production as a subject of capital. Halpern's speaker is aware of the constitutive abyss that displaces his entire affective capacity; his nose is right in the asshole of value's debaucherous

79 Kurz 1999, p. 243.
80 Larsen et al. 2014, p. xvi.

colonisation of his soldier-lover's body. Halpern's anarchic American subject knows that commodities are speaking for him, that all his expended body-energies are accumulated as the perpetual condition of his own critical collapse. He is bound to the affectless creation of his own suicidal crisis, the crisis of capital. He is in love with a man literally dressed in the produce of incarceration, clad in a military uniform probably sewn in prisons, withdrawing these commodities of punishment from the market and placing them instead in the ideological optics of the American Empire. The soldier acts as the simultaneous animation of incarcerated commodities and imperial ideology, enacting economic politics internationally as the imperative to kill and be killed. At home, removed from this perverse and narcissistic murder cult, Halpern's speaker is reduced to insatiable nihilism.

At certain moments, the speaker is – like Halpern himself – a critical intellectual who has studied the forms of his own determination and wants to show the reader the satirical cynicism of the knowing, if miserable, author:

> To negate the soldier, then, by restoring the body to unthinkable relation *rematerialize a dematerialized sensuousness* to return the immune to community, to render the body as site of common refusal: refusal of transcendent property (identity, enclosures, contracts); refusal of self-preservation (the death drive in disguise); refusal of hardened borders (the uneven distribution of vulnerability).[81]

The speaker is desperately attempting to purge himself of his own constitutive violence, manically chasing the eradication of the conditions of his eradication.

This attempt is conducted in broken language, with the psychotic disturbance of other sentences entering in italics with increasing regularity. In the above section, the italicised interjection '*rematerialize a dematerialized sensuousness*' bursts into the otherwise roman narrative. In the collection's final section, 'Whither Porn?, Or the Soldier as Allegory', these interjections are constant: 'That work concludes with a blank bar [–] *placeholder for all we can't perceive haunting all we can* like the mark of something withdrawn from sense', 'a floating caesura separating visible and invisible *logic of porn* audible and inaudible *aesthetic of state secrets*', 'issues from this fault of perception *constant interruption* were seeking *groping* a figure'.[82]

81 Halpern 2012, pp. 58–9.
82 Ibid., p. 149. Original brackets.

In the expected order of the section in roman, a recognition of the limitations of speech and subjectivity is critically proposed: 'That work concludes with a blank bar … like the mark of something withdrawn from sense'. The speaker is aware of an absence but cannot account for its peculiar presence that nonetheless survives in his sentence. The section in italics, however, throws the disjunctive awareness of absence into the presence of speech. What cannot be said is suddenly apparent, but cannot be spoken as standard text: '*placeholder for all we can't perceive haunting all we can*'. In this example, the logic of the italicised section explains its own disjunction; it is the distorted space that carries the unbearable awareness of another kind of presence, a haunted absence, which exposes the finitude of the surrounding sense.

The sentence itself is in crisis. The order of speech has been punctured and an excess of sense bursts in. The subject is no longer subjected to the norms of subjection; a terrifying, unspeakable disruption has broken through. The italicised interruptions reveal something of the cause of this crisis, with each interjection turning a sentient experience into a commodified form, abstract and inaccessible to the speaker, from the '*logic of porn*' to '*aesthetic of state secrets*'. The commodification that produces and determines the speaker's subjection has permeated his ability to speak of himself, and the crisis of crisis is exposed.

As Beverley Best writes, 'capital's crisis tendency' can be defined as follows:

> capital drives to expand by augmenting productivity across all spheres of production through the introduction of new productive technologies or the rational reorganization of the labor process. By increasing productivity, capital is able to expel, in an increasing ratio to the value-magnitude of the social product, value invested in labor-power (i.e., workers!) from the production process. … If the portion of value invested on wages shrinks in relation to the size of the social product, consumer demand shrinks proportionally – a further, internal obstacle to capital's ongoing reproduction.[83]

Social reproduction increasingly has to happen without the mediation of the wage. People have to find ways of surviving without the remuneration of their labour-power, by, for example, turning to food banks, finding an empty plot of land to plant some crops, organising communal forms of childcare without paid daycare centres, and sharing goods through community gift economies.

83 Best 2021, p. 902.

'The more the work of social reproduction is unwaged,' as Best writes, 'the more it participates in propelling capital toward the crisis of its own reproduction.'[84] In crisis, people become both more precarious, making them less able to return as productive labour-power, and potentially less reliant on the system of value-production, turning instead to social means of survival.

Crisis, then, both constitutes and deconstitutes subjectivity, producing both its possibility and its impossibility. Halpern's speaker is cast into this confusion, with a part of his speech still clearly formed of expected units of sense, but with a disjunctive remnant of uncontrolled social life pushing through. He lingers at the border of total collapse, the crisis economy constituting the limits of his subjection. In the increasing crisis of contemporary capital, a profound instability opens, destabilising both those subjected and the authority of subjection.

In addition to severing the stability of social reproduction, crisis emphasises the antagonism between capitalists: rentiers, or landlords, are reliant on the population receiving a sufficiently stable income for social reproduction to continue in order for them to receive rent, while value-productive capitalists seek a reduction in expenditure on variable capital, bringing down wages and transferring production to constant capital (through technological development).[85] The crisis, then, increases not only *inter*-class competition, with workers desperately seeking more remuneration from capitalists and capitalists frantically looking for ways to reduce variable capital expenditure, but also *intra*-class competition, with rentiers and value-productive capitalists undermining each other's project and workers competing for ever fewer resources.

In addition to the possibility of capitalist authorities simply doubling down on their violence and turning to all-out genocide and ecocide (as we are already witnessing), two radical possibilities arise from this crisis of reproduction. On the one hand, there could be a total collapse of the value-form and its production of subjectivity, leaving capitalists vying for an ever-diminishing mass of surplus-value, with the workforce fatally incapable of self-reproduction and labour-power unable to return to productive exploitation; speculative assets are withdrawn and the promised increase of value disintegrates, with the entire temporality of capital as a promise of future expansion falling into ruins. It is this collapse that *Wertkritik* awaits as the possibility of overthrowing the dom-

84 Ibid., p. 901.

85 This antagonism between capitalists is the focus of 'political Marxism'. See: Moreno Zacarés 2021.

inance of capital, turning everyone against its hegemonic temporality once its attendant production and determination of subjects is in freefall.

On the other hand, a more psychoanalytic possibility opens, one in which the crisis exposes a potential ethics of vulnerability. Crisis here begins with the acknowledgement of mutual recognition: both the authority of subjection (generalised as capitalists, or embodied capital) and subjected subjects (generalised as workers, whose only commodity is their own commodified, potentially value-productive time) require each other to survive *as subjects*. The subjective order of capital only functions if capitalists keep remunerating labour-power with sufficient variable capital to survive, for which they need workers (as producers, consumers, and tenants), and workers keep productively expending their labour-power. The way in which this exchange is organised has undergone many historical and cultural shifts, but the fundamental necessity of commodified labour-power and its remuneration by the purchasers of labour-power is constant.

When crisis reaches such a scale as to make this exchange impossible, the mutual reliance of subjects collapses. Capitalism, as Nancy Fraser writes, 'is not an economy but a *social system of class domination*'; the collapse of value-production is the collapse of social reproduction, and the collapse of social reproduction is the collapse of value-production.[86] While capital certainly has more violent means of ensuring the continued production of value – given its unceasing involvement in expropriation, appropriation, dispossession, colonisation, imperialism, and genocide[87] – the normative production of subjects as mutually reliant sellers and buyers of labour-power is jeopardised, and total crisis is drawn from a suspended future to the very brink of the present.

In this crisis, however, the impossibility of mutual subjective recognition is not simply *produced*. The mutual recognition of subjects did not function perfectly before the eruption of crisis. Instead, as Judith Butler writes in their reading of Lacan, the recognition of *subjects* is never focused on *the content* of singular persons, but rather on *the subject as a symbolic position*. 'The symbolic is secured precisely through an evacuation or negation of the living person,' Butler writes; 'thus a symbolic position is never commensurate with any individual who happens to occupy it; it assumes its status as symbolic precisely as a function of that incommensurability.'[88] The symbolic role of the subject is disrupted by the failure of recognition, which exposes the persistence of something else.

86 Fraser 2016, p. 165. Original emphasis.
87 Ibid., pp. 166–72.
88 Butler 2000, p. 14.

As Butler writes of Sophocles' archetypal tragic heroine, through her refusal of the symbolic order of subject positions, Antigone 'exposes the socially contingent character of kinship', which is to say, she exposes both her own and the system's vulnerability.[89]

Suddenly, in the crisis of recognition, the finitude of the symbolic form of subjects is itself exposed, and the antagonistic content of that symbolic form emerges. Those productive modalities of being that limit life to the exchanges of subjects become vulnerable to a sociality that exceeds them. The content of that sociality cannot be fully formatted by the normative form of production and exchange. 'The frame never quite determined what it is we see, think, recognize, and apprehend,' as Butler writes. 'Something exceeds the frame that troubles our sense of reality'.[90] This *trouble* has long been the focus of Butler's work, from the very beginning of *Gender Trouble*, in which they argue that, despite what feminists up to then had understood as the possible *trouble* brought to feminism by the indeterminacy of gender, *the trouble of gender* is precisely the aim of feminism: to make trouble by troubling the limits of gender.[91] For Butler, the radical project is to locate those points of excess and actualise them as a social means of making trouble.[92]

In Halpern's constant interruptions, the order of the production of spoken sense is not simply refused through confusion. Neither is it only a persistent *desire* that is exposed. When 'seeking' is replaced with a burst of italicised '*groping*' and the 'visible and invisible' is broken by '*logic of porn*', the permanent impossibility of 'seeking' and the ongoing instability of the 'visible and invisible' is exposed. In the excess of these appearances, Halpern's speaker encounters commodified violence; not sex or passion or contact, but the groping logic of porn. The finitude of the production of subjects is revealed here, bringing out a suggestion of fugitive excess, which Halpern, in his aggressively fatalist poetry, turns into another layer of social determination, another opportunity for violence. But in that exposure another imaginary is possible. As we will see in Part 2 of *Poetics of Value*, uncapturable social modalities can also be found in this exposure of excess, where the mutual reproduction of the conditions of crisis cannot reach.

89 Ibid., p. 6, p. 10.

90 Butler 2016, p. 9.

91 Butler 2007, p. xxix.

92 Butler 2016, pp. 170–1. However, Butler unfortunately understands the ethics of vulnerability as a *social ontology* (2016, p. 3), thereby reducing a possible project of differential survival – in which the fugitive temporalities of other ways of being survive against and despite the homogenising temporality of capital and its crisis – to a new form that claims

Through these constant interruptions, Halpern's speaker uncovers the pervasive totality of commodification, determining his necessary refusal of affect and vulnerability. His narcissism and his aggression are fused, forming the impossibility of the subject's escape from subjection. His attempt at love and his uncontrollable hate have become a single form, foreclosing access to his vulnerability to the social. Lacan's neologism for this condition is *hainamoration*, incommensurably formed of 'hate' (*haine*) and 'in love' (*enamouré*).[93]

At other moments, when unbroken by psychotic italicised interruptions, the speaker is vulnerable and out of control. His perplexity at the violence he lives in is too overwhelming to allow him to act. The constant semantic noise of the italicised sections has burst the sense of his otherwise roman prose. Instead, the speaker pursues his own erasure as the only response to immanent and constitutive crisis, a crisis that literally cancels his capacity to speak, to move, to feel:

> My body, a public feeling, a floating intensity no one can claim. You can put anything inside me, I want to say, anything to amplify these feelings of pity and shame, whatever it takes to get me off. More refined techniques generate impressive indices of the war's most delicate pleasures. Take that Arab boy as an example, the one they reported dead in a ditch just outside a village whose name I can't pronounce. Beauty is a detour, like his tongue in my ass, a moment of grave remove, reflex of a system in love with its own reform.[94]

This passage epitomises the subject's impossible engagement with the horror forming him at the level of national subjectivity. In the optics of permanent war, in the entanglement of everything within the violent mania of value-production, his singular body is a public vessel exposed for cultural distraction and vilification. The soldier's body – racialised, removed from personal context in an unspeakable village, nameless – is the most grotesquely embodied form of this endless ideological war, which seizes even domestic, civilian bodies.

The security of home is no security at all anymore. The pervasiveness of surveillance as the constant threat of this permanent military expansion extends back to the home territory as much as to the space of conquest. The poem's

hegemonic stability, imposing itself as a universal through ontologisation. See: Mulaj 2024. For other criticisms of this position, see: Mason and Moro 2025.

93 Chiesa 2007, p. 20.

94 Halpern 2012, p. 104.

speaker cannot bear witness to the presence of his own body without it assuming the monstrous form of an abstraction, a 'floating intensity' which, again, roots itself in a nihilistic drive for eradication: 'put anything inside me' for the advance of 'pity and shame.'

At the core of this nihilism is an absence of material meaning: the symbolic form of the subject has erased the content of social life and its sexual desire with and for others. As the totemic son pursues the murder of his father, his only possible realisation is that the father is not 'Father' at all; he is a projected image of the necessity of eradication. He is only a vapid emblem of what must be destroyed for the fantasy of the son's own masculinity to survive. The impulse of value and the sexed subject are brought together as synonyms of passionate violence in Halpern's poetry.

Music for Porn displays the afterlife of subjectivity, the animated residue of dead labour in the economy once all social life has been suspended by the crisis of value. Nothing is produced, only the unending expansion of the illusion that profit will redeem the inevitability of collapse.

6 The Subject's Patiency

In his essay 'Becoming a Patient of History', Halpern investigates the war trauma of the poet George Oppen. Following the disappointment of radical action in his involvement with the US Communist Party, his immersion in death in the trenches of WWII, and his exile in Mexico, 'Oppen becomes a patient of history.'[95] The condition that captures him is 'patiency[:] agency's inverse and compliment.'[96] The characteristic feature of this patiency is not necessarily subversive action, which so often in Oppen's life resulted in political failure; it is, rather, becoming open to the absence that exists already in one's grounding constitution. In patiency, one finds within oneself the wounds of vulnerability, the openings into incompleteness. One disregards the illusion that one was ever whole. Patiency is 'to will a suspension of an agency that has been already historically suspended.'[97] It is the refusal of what has been refused. What this comes down to, for Halpern, is the abandonment of the complete and individualised body, presented as both an (internal) ethical imperative and an (external) obligation of the military-capitalist order.

95 Halpern 2013, p. 57.
96 Ibid., p. 56.
97 Ibid.

In his own poetry, Halpern develops this ethics of 'patiency' as the state of the body whose vulnerability has become its weakness in relation to permanent militarised violence:

> Despite whatever delusion of mastery, the soldier's body is a *patient* body, informed equally by what it can do and by what can be done to it: at once the agent of dispossession and the patient of an expropriated common. Given over to the reigning sense of public good *security money carnage* the soldier's body materializes a fundamental ambivalence, its militarized agency *prosthetic of state power* being paradoxically a function of that body's *patiency*.[98]

This passage marks the philosophical weight of Halpern's poetry, despite its difficult aesthetics of violent sex and war. Ultimately, it is attempting to speak the psychotic, affectless impossibility of the contemporary American subject.

Alongside his poeticisation of his own patiency is another layer in which the poet *knows* of his patiency. He is communicating his awareness of the paralysis of total determination, within a political project that works in the melancholy wounding of the book's perversely broken subject. This is poeticised through the patiency that Halpern finds in Oppen's work, despite the decisively fatalist rumination at the beginning of *Music for Porn*:

> Maybe this is what Oppen means by 'vivaporous,' being forever fucked by the thing we're wedged too deep inside to even posit as an object of our own sensation, there being no 'out there' anymore determinate force having made no mensch of me.[99]

In his essay on Oppen, what Halpern learns from the Objectivist poet is the assumption of political responsibility, the obligation not only to resolve this fundamental severed relation of America's capitalist dominance but also to reconstitute oneself constantly in the knowledge of one's failure to have abolished the agency that suspends the ethical relation. The obligation Halpern imposes on himself in his poetry is the unbearable shame of not yet having overthrown the violence that constitutes himself and his social life. As Halpern writes, 'To write about this world, for Oppen, is always also to write about a world he failed to make, the other world that haunts this world.'[100]

98 Halpern 2012, p. 51.
99 Ibid., p. 6.
100 Halpern 2013, p. 60.

At the beginning of *Music for Porn*, the book's prominent theme of shame seems to be the result of a conservative prohibition on queer desire, and an enforced separation between the masculinised authority of the military and the queer – implicitly emasculated – longing for a soldier, especially given the political disagreement inhering in this desire from a Leftist poet to a representative of the US military. As the long book develops, however, and even more so in response to his essay on Oppen, Halpern's shame emerges as a confrontation with his own failure to have done anything to end these conditions.

The soldier acts on his principles, even if those principles are maintaining the violent status quo of permanent war for the sake of suspending capital's ultimate crisis. The poet, meanwhile, does poetry. As Kurz's critique builds a critical universe around 'the helplessness of critique,' Halpern's poetry is the poetics of poetry's helplessness.[101] Patiency is a constitutive condition for both the poem and the poet.

The effects of the crisis of value create Halpern's subject. He reveals, in a sort of hipster accelerationism that turns up the volume of the depressed subject's determining forces, the totalising interplay of the production of value with every manifestation of the aesthetics, culture, (anti)sociality, and governmentality of capital as a global system. With aggressive aesthetics and dizzying linguistic force, Halpern brings out the necessary causal connection between the means of production and the body. In his essay 'Realism and Utopia', Halpern follows this same line of thinking in Walter Benjamin's *Illuminations*:

> Benjamin grasps the inseparability of the somatic and the social, comprehending a whole corpus ravaged not only by war, but by new apparatuses of social mediation – *communication* – whereby the individual body becomes increasingly abstract. Under such conditions, the fate of storytelling is wedded to the fate of the throat, the mouth, the tongue, the teeth, and all of the organs through which speech must pass in order to live.[102]

In *Music for Porn*, the immediate materiality of bodies is obscured by the project of visuality, or the bourgeois mode of objective observation, which makes all markers of difference incalculable to the only available future, which is the

101 Kurz 2014c.
102 Halpern 2011, p. 87.

realisation of value. The speaker, longing for a soldier's body, is aware of the violence of his position, but in the style of hipster morality, this awareness only heightens his craving for the exoticised other. He knows that he is engaging in violence and reproducing a regime that he hates, but his immersion has reached such a point that nihilistic despair and destructive acceptance is his only impulse now. Acknowledging his own ruin within a ruined empire, he pursues one last climax to end the world on:

> Faking our most sensual relations with wage-slaves around the globe, then harvesting their earnings for warmth. Jerking-off onsite, I imagine a hot day laborer using my shirt to wipe his jizz, then my hand to wipe his ass. Producing appetite thru forced withdrawal, I marvel at the thing's capacity, a magnitude of failing grip.[103]

Recognition of his own collective moral duplicity turns immediately into sexual fantasy. No thought can be maintained, no criticism carried through into action.

This brutal fatalism forms what could be seen as his poetry's ethics. In the heavily theoretical prose sections of the collection, Halpern's sentences often contain two separable parts. In the above section, there is the recognition of a general Euro-American bourgeois moral hypocrisy, in which sympathy with the globally exploited and abused is explicitly faked. Sympathy is nothing but a ploy. Then, there is the sexual fantasy of being used, of being exploited, of having his clothes dirtied without care. The fantasy inheres in its callousness, in its repetition of the fake morality of comfortable Americans. In this way, the two parts of the sentence are intimately connected, one providing the social conditions for its sexual ransacking in the other: (*1*) *look at how fecklessly duplicitous we are in this violent mode of ideological, military, and economic production;* (2) *the only response possible is aggressive sexualised nihilism.*

It is also possible to read the two parts of the sentence in another way, one in which each provides an escape from the other.

> I heard Verizon is going to refund data charges on my phone, and for a moment I'm feeling sort of happy about that, but if only we could explain the survival of the working day as an accepted unit of economic measure, well, then we might be getting somewhere.[104]

103 Halpern 2012, p. 7.
104 Ibid., p. 6.

In this sentence, the first part fetishises the quotidian sensuousness of consumption. Attaining money without work, instead by refund, offers the subject a semblance of a feeling. In the paradise of purchase, alienated subjects achieve the only pleasure available in American capitalism: free money, or consumption without production. This semblance of pleasure, however, causes an accidental slippage, a Lacanian erasure of sense: suddenly a Marxist understanding of the working day impinges on this paradise.

In these moments of Marxist theory, the logic of the rest of the sentences is brought out. Psychoanalytically, the meaning of the first sentence above ('Faking our most sensual relations ...') now takes on a distinct form: the speaker's recognition of his nation's collective moral duplicity produces such depletion of his desire to live that all he can imagine is being carelessly used. The abyssal horror of his situation causes an expansive need for acute meaninglessness to be projected onto everything, everywhere, without restraint. Meaninglessness becomes a tool to attack any threat of meaning. This universalisation of abyssal pain constitutes his act of global love: he turns the world into himself. And then, when his careless violence is enacted back onto himself, his own careless violence will be justified.

This narrative is recounted in the lines that follow:

> From somewhere deep, waste returns, my constant theme, this decay of sound, a wall of pure significance, the way capital flickers in an Afghani's wound, hedging our implausible intimacies, materializing my love. Identity being at once realized and negated in the soldier I sing of, whatever hope remains remains mediated by the same defiled corpses.[105]

The condition of America's military economy is here psychoanalysed as the deep return of the constant theme of waste, a waste it projects as the empty relations determined by value onto every mediated interaction in the world. The economic principle that is the USA is the expansion of the moment in which it collectively recognises its own constitutive immorality. The possible ethics of shame, realised through the subject's opening to his own vulnerability which in turn abolishes his being *qua* subject, is constantly and obsessively suspended, returned again to the reactive animation of aggressivity. The contemporary subject's uniquely militarised American determination is the foreclosure of any ethical opening that might result in the self-abolition of the subject. This foreclosure, however, is never total. There is always a fugitive remnant of surviving sociality.

105 Ibid., p. 7.

7 The Limits of Freedom

Standing in the face of his own erasure, witnessing the disappearance of the other in whom he finds his social grounding, the poem's speaker lives as the embodiment of his own loss. This loss, as Elena Louisa Lange emphasises, begins as an appearance produced through the value-form, but becomes instantiated in material social lives through the subject's performative reaction: the subject lives *as if* loss were its constitutive condition, moving the abstraction of value into the determination of material social relations.[106] Any ethical opening, however, is suspended at the level of the economic and its determination of the social:

> I'm evoking the soldier as neither a thing nor an idea, but rather
> a relation *like capital like value* visible and measurable only in the
> effects it achieves and the affects it arouses.[107]

This passage highlights the uniquely affective economic criticism of *Music for Porn*, placing it at the threshold of Marxist value-criticism and psychoanalytic ethics.

In Halpern's poetry, violence against the body is essentially an economic problem. In the obligation of valorisation in the social form of exchange, what the *Wertkritisch* theorist Ernst Lohoff calls the 'asocial sociality [*ungesellschaftliche Gesellschaftlichkeit*]'[108] of capitalism is the mediator of relations. Contact with others passes necessarily through the determinate stage of potential valorisation; gathering occurs only as the given format of competition for accumulation. That gathering, of course, is formed of living bodies. The form the body can assume is determined by national-scale economic closures and accumulations, a determination which works back onto the living bodies of production.

This cross-scale determination is revealed by Halpern in the explicit destruction of the body as a complete and bordered form. Body parts are blasted out of the independent frame of the fully homeostatic human. In Halpern's poetry, it is the asshole as much as the mouth that speaks: 'Bullet hole, foxhole, asshole: openings thru which our common product enters and exits *like my mouth*',[109]

106 Lange 2021, p. 4.

107 Halpern 2012, p. 51.

108 Lohoff 2014, p. 155. This phrase ultimately comes from Kant ('*ungesellige Geselligkeit*') and was subsequently taken up by both Hegel and Marx. See: Kant 1784. See also: Battersby 2021, p. 110.

109 Halpern 2012, p. 58.

and later: 'my poem keeps / – *singing of shit*.'[110] The mouth or the asshole is shitting in and out, excreting the refuse of processed meaning, and, privately, opening up for reception.[111] In psychoanalytic theory, the oral and anal phases constitute the primary means of communicating with the world in early childhood. To speak, to shit, to fuck, all bound up in the operation of opening and closing, in the ethics and the shame of privacy and exposure.

In this gasping in and out of space, the contraction and expansion of history is produced in the subject. As Kurz dramatically writes,

> *Homo economicus* lives almost in the time horizon [*Zeithorizont*] of a small child; namely, in an eternal present of market actions, all seeming to take place on the same timeless plane. If the conservative spirit invokes history to falsify it in the name of authority, the economic-liberal spirit [*wirtschaftsliberale Geist*] sells off history like underpants, fighter bombers, ready-made soups, and other market goods into which the sensually experienced world [*erfahrbare Welt*] indiscriminately transforms.[112]

The temporality of the sensual subject is closed as the finitude of capitalism's promise of freedom. One becomes a free subject once one has foreclosed the infinity of the past to one's perception: history must be exchangeable, reproducible, simple and sudden like the production of underpants and missiles. Halpern's subject accumulates within himself the infinity of pasts and functions as a mechanism for processing them, rendering them instead as solitary shit. He consumes valueless social life and regurgitates it as waste.

This reading of Halpern's work opens a difficult border binding psychoanalysis and politics. The painful considerations of one's ethical relation to the Other, in *Music for Porn*, are always undergirded by explosive political and economic ruptures that destabilise any grounding for an ethical relation.

Lorenzo Chiesa is concerned precisely with this question of a potential psychoanalytic politics. For Chiesa, the limitation of the Lacanian project is not its finitude but its 'failure to universalize infinity … as the production of active indeterminacy.'[113] This is the political *limitation* of Lacanian psychoanalysis, the limit of its designation of an opening in the species-being after the resolution

---

110 Ibid., p. 93.

111 Uncannily summarising this anal poetics, Paul Preciado calls the mouth the 'public extension' of the anus: Preciado 2018, p. 30.

112 Kurz 1999, p. 4.

113 Chiesa 2016, p. 113.

of the Oedipus complex (i.e., one's inherent incestuous fantasies for primary caregiving others).[114] The unfolding of a future, that is to say, stops precisely at the point at which one is relieved of the constitutive egoistic fantasies of incest, after which psychoanalysis abandons its subject. But at the same time, this limitation forms the non-political movement of psychoanalysis: 'There is no Lacanian politics insofar as Lacanian psychoanalysis does not thematize the infinite deployment of subjective indeterminacy as *universal* production (of the species-being).'[115]

Chiesa is a dedicated Lacanian – he even has the same hairdo as Lacan – but where he parts from his teacher is in the precise meaning of determination. Lacan finds no freedom in the way of being *qua* subject, in the wake of subjectivation, but neither does he posit an eventual redeeming freedom in the process of psychoanalysis. Therapy is not a process of absolution. Instead, the subject of psychoanalysis can reposition themself within the structuring order of the Law of the Father, or the given form of authority generally. Lacan sees this as a *re*-determination of one's relation to authority, which carries within it a certain semblance of differential unfreedom, if not of *freedom*.

Chiesa, however, adds a significant point: what is pursued in the differential unfreedom of psychoanalysis is not a *re*-determination of one's position regarding authority, but rather the *indeterminacy* of this position. For Chiesa, the psychoanalytic project's radical disruption of subjection is that, through the self-abolishing work of confronting one's constitutive fantasies and contradictions, one does not *change* one's freedom, or lack of freedom, but becomes *indeterminate* in relation to freedom.

In Halpern's poetry, history itself has no agency and no objective validity. The subject is 'writing something history can't write about itself.'[116] The speaking subject, though, does not create history by speaking on its behalf, since the subject is already positioned within the authoritative relations of the historical form of power, psychanalytically summarised as the Law of the Father. 'No origin obtains in the forms we create, but when we emerge from the mud we all have names.'[117] Those names determine our capacity to imagine the possibility of *re*-determination. Halpern's speaker may be acutely aware of the historical lines of power and violence that intersect at the core of his body, but he never relinquishes his guiding desire for that history, embodied in *Music for Porn* as the soldier's body.

---

114 On this resolution, see: Chiesa 2007, p. 6 f.
115 Chiesa 2016, p. 112.
116 Halpern 2012, p. 26.
117 Ibid.

In *The Coming Community*, Giorgio Agamben brings together the hopeless patiency of Halpern's speaker and the potential indeterminacy of Chiesa's post-analysed subject. For Agamben there is only ethics because there is *not predetermination*: 'The fact that must constitute the point of departure for any discourse on ethics is that there is no essence, no historical or spiritual vocation, no biological destiny that humans must enact or realize.'[118] Whatever condition of patiency obtains, it must contain within its performance a residue of indeterminacy, otherwise there would be nothing to determine. The ethical duty is to expose 'one's own amorphousness and in every act one's own inactuality.'[119] One must not so much *enact* one's own potential not-being as displace the presupposed completion of one's being. One must expose oneself as incomplete.

As Halpern shows throughout *Music for Porn*, however, this incompleteness is certainly not entirely to be celebrated. As Agamben continues,

> Since the being most proper to humankind is being one's own possibility or potentiality, then and only for this reason ... humans have and feel a debt. Humans, in their potentiality to be and to not-be, are, in other words, always already in debt; they always already have a bad conscience without having to commit any blameworthy act.[120]

At the core of the subject, something is carried through from a constitutive sociality in excess of the obligation of being properly formed. That excess – that moment of immeasurability within the form of being – simultaneously pushes the subject out of the purview of Oedipal power and traps that same subject forever in the shame of having eluded full determination. It is *feeling shame* that opens the ethics of being human, because shame is a response to the incompleteness of the potentiality not-to.

In Chiesa's Lacanian model, the ethics of psychoanalysis disbands its deployment of the praxis of living well at the point of politics: ethics is always *before politics*.[121] This pre-ontological ethics, however, still carries a certain conciliatory *Aufhebung* (sublation) in that the dominant ontology determines both the subject who perceives the world *and* the world that is perceived. That is to say, capitalist ontology determines also the environment that forms the experiential opening of the species-being.

118 Agamben 2007, p. 42.
119 Ibid., p. 43.
120 Ibid., pp. 42–3.
121 This is similar to Emmanuel Levinas' influential temporality in which *ethics precedes*

Chiesa's Lacanian response is that the point at which freedom stops – the freedom to recognise one's impotential freedom, or one's inability to find meaning in such a value-determined promise as freedom – is not the ontological but *the political*. In entering the political without a subject form-determined as potential freedom, which is to say in entering politics after psychoanalysis, one enters indeterminately, without foreclosure from the promise of freedom. As Chiesa writes, 'freedom is a fantasy par excellence,' but the possible 'liberating effect' of this is that fantasies 'can be traversed.'[122] There is no psychoanalytic politics as such. What there is, for Chiesa, is the possibility of disbanding the promise that confines the subject to competitive independence, which, as Halpern shows in those rare moments of vulnerability in his poetry, can result in an opening to the social.

Chiesa's project for subjectivity is rooted in a necessarily *impossible* pursuit of infinity, limited by the finitude of its own impossibility, through which its production of the universal can never be fully attained, since this ethical subjectivity is grounded in no possible resolution, no ultimate *Aufhebung*. Instead, infinity finds itself ethically bound in *indeterminacy*.

Where Chiesa stands back from Lacan is in the psychoanalyst's insufficient fathoming of indeterminacy. The subject is only ethical once it pursues infinity not as eternity but as the possibility of indetermination. The process of ethical becoming is the process of endlessly escaping the form-determination of productive subjectivity, of living in and as what Matthew Omelsky calls 'fugitive time'.[123] Reading this temporality of indeterminate subjectivity through Leonard Cohen's rendition of the French resistance song 'The Partisan', Chiesa writes:

> the humanism of the partisan is a humanism of impossibility – as it answers to the temporary suspension of the faithful subject in a time of disaster ... – and a humanism of infinity as repeated concentration of the naming of the new ... in a historically specific period of time that does not partake of any kind of eternity.[124]

Where *Wertkritik*'s general tendency is toward an impossible infinity of capitalist eternity – the endless expansion of empty desire, desire for nothing but the

---

ontology, which has often been cited and discussed in English translation as 'ethics as first philosophy'. See: Levinas 1989, pp. 75–87.

122 Chiesa 2016, p. 46.

123 Omelsky 2023. The book's introduction (pp. 1–32) contains some specific though implicit links between 'fugitive time' and Marxist psychoanalytic theory.

124 Chiesa 2016, p. 114.

growth of desire, is the perverse necessity of capital – Chiesa locates a possible excess to this infinity. That excess is the ethics of indeterminate social openings, of relations without determination.

As Halpern writes, value is 'visible and measurable only in the effects it achieves and the affects it arouses',[125] but the subject lamenting this totalising form-determination is nonetheless impelled to poetry because of a relation that exceeds the aroused affect of value: his desire is not for desire itself but for the lost object of his affection, which, despite his profound melancholia, is real. The love object really was there and really is gone. As Omelsky writes, fugitive time 'begin[s] with the materiality of the body. The surge toward an otherwise existence is initiated in the body's phenomenological flight from trauma'.[126] The limitation of the body is its fundamental reliance on others, its primary sociality; one's ethical move out of the determining historical and political structures that impose continuous trauma is the move towards these constitutive others, a move that reaffirms the limitations of the body. Freedom here is not the attainment of unconditional flight, but the vulnerable opening to those others on whom one's fugitive flight is reliant.

In Chiesa's psychoanalytic ethics, a subtle inversion occurs on the temporal plane: the infinity that refuses eternity is relinquished from determination at the point of abandoning its hope of infinity. The infinite promise of this ethics is its own finitude, which is its indeterminacy: the fact that it cannot be fully determined by this expansive, extractive desire is its finitude.

As a practice, psychoanalysis gives up on its subjects precisely at the moment in which they speak openly of their constitutive Oedipal trauma: *I will never be able to be fully me because I will always have been separated from the one who I wanted (to be), i.e. Mother* (as any primary caregiver rather than necessarily the birth-giving person). At the moment the patient enters psychoanalytic theory, they are dismissed from its practice. As soon as one realises oneself as not one, (not-)one is released back into the plurality of social life. They have overcome the power that overthrew their claim to being infinite. They have finally found their indeterminacy, the impossibility of their infinity. The virtual point of freedom has been encountered.

At a talk at *Svenska psykoanalytiska föreningen* (the Swedish Psychoanalytic Institute) in January 2023, I asked Chiesa about this limit-point of freedom. In his response, he could not stress enough that there is no freedom outside

125 Halpern 2012, p. 51.
126 Omelsky 2023, p. 9.

the environment of the species-being, beyond the givenness of our human finitude. Our environment is accessed as a resolution of our temporal finitude, our distance from eternity. But that is all a biological ruse from the perspective of politics. There is no freedom because there is no access to a way of understanding freedom that evades the format of subjectivity; there is no freedom from the determining relations of society.

Despite this foreclosure, though, something survives in the excess of our finitude, something that cannot be fully explained by the partisan who ethically partakes of no eternity. This survival is the faint hope displayed in Halpern's poetry of generalised brutality.

> To make the other sky this
> Sky being a thing we've failed
> To do having survived our own
>
> Survival of the one failing sky
> The dead this time will bury
> Themselves & their graves
>
> – *will look like my house*[127]

The speaker cannot escape from the aesthetic and ontological determination already instantiated in the very form of his being: the shape of his house, the structure of his life in society, the primary possession he functions through as militarised capital personified. He has, indeed, already failed any aesthetic project. But despite all this failure, all this brutal determination, all this mimetic constitution in death, he survives, and not only as himself, implicitly as a speaker in the form of poetry – every poem is textual testament to the deformed survival of poets – but as a general *we*, a *we* without referent. The speaker has erased himself as his act of resistance to the project of self-erasure. The speaker, finally, is indeterminate, unable to claim himself as 'I', a property-owning subject; instead he is just some failed *us*, in a house that accumulates the unbearable loss of a failed and failing past.

We are brought back here to what Kurz calls the '*Zeithorizont* of a small child' in which *homo economicus* lives, partitioning history for the market like ready meals. History itself, *Weltgeschichte*, is produced as the universal expansion of a single form, an ampliative desire wholly empty of content.[128]

127 Halpern 2012, p. 38.

128 There is a vast literature on the temporalities of capital's global expansion in Marxism. This

Capital is the production of universal history, a cultureless expanse of time that subsumes the difference of space.[129]

Halpern's poetry erases the spatial and cultural difference otherwise separating the US military from the local contexts into which it exerts its anxious and empty desire, desiring nothing but its own universalisation (it is archetypally unpsychoanalysed). In *Music for Porn*, there is only militarised culture, only cultural spaces form-determined by value. Violent expansionism is the only animating impulse of every relation.

At rare moments of vulnerable exposure, emerging in the gaps of the nihilistic force of an otherwise aggressive sexual lexicon, the subject offers a tiny opening into an alternate plane of being, a way of relating in *patiency*. He is open to his wounding, to the originary condition of his having been wounded. Instead of turning this wound into a weapon that pursues the infinite expansion of his abyssal desire, he opens it as a site of grief. He grieves the loss of himself as a subject, the loss of the possibility of infinity, and, by doing so, turns this impossible infinity from a refusal of finitude into the vulnerable exposure of a social opening.

Halpern's subject is released, although ambivalently, from the illusion of being an independent subject. He was only ever a determined form of capital personified, animated by the requirements of its anxious postponement of crisis. In giving himself over to the unknowable and unbearable face (or asshole, or mouth) of others, Halpern's desperate subject disbands the animating infinity that drives him toward constant expansion and constant consumption. The freedom that forms the shame of the subject's fantasies of infinity is abandoned through a poetics of grief, opening the sentient site of value's calculating accumulation to an ethics of loss.

My intention in this chapter has been to situate the Marxist study of subjectivity from the previous chapter in the precise conditions of the US economy and its production of a violently expansive narcissism, captured both by the crisis of value and the infinite growth of desire, with its abyssal realisation in capitalist consumption. Halpern provides a uniquely value-theoretical insight into the subject's tragedy: the computation of America's defining desire for infinite freedom. Meanwhile, he allows moments of access to a world after the crisis of value. Halpern's shocking collection *Music for Porn* is a burlesque siren song for American capitalism, drawing in the armed subjects of an unending military regime and poeticising their abandonment of the constitutive illusion

---

chapter, however, is specifically focused on the way *the subject* experiences this expansion, rather than this expansion itself. See: Tomba 2013a; Harootunian 2015.

129 Marx 1993, p. 524.

of freedom. Freedom must be abandoned for sociality to be exposed; the illusory basis of the individual must be overthrown.

Freedom for the post-Oedipal subject is found in the abandonment of the desire for freedom, which is to say that psychoanalytic ethics becomes apparent as a way of life in the abyss that opens after psychoanalysis. One's unspeakable sexual urges and inherent incestuous fantasies are the constitutive logistics of one's primary understanding of social relations. In the horror of our contemporary economy, these relations are suspended as a performative refusal to accept the crisis that subsumes and consumes the possibility of a future. Every movement seems already to be exchanged as an illusory promise, offering freedom to subjects wholly emptied of content.

> We were once ourselves, but now, traversing the trench, a fault between dim pockets of damaged life, I'm beginning to feel something, a mind without sex, a shudder with no reference, yr breathtaking crevasse, a loss I can't mourn and which I've hastily mapped onto this making of waste. These words extend the body in accord with natural rhythms, and the false immediacy of that. *Exposed before the others* I write, dreaming of belief, crying faith in deadly light. So now there's nothing, the shadow of a name having melted to my cock, their skin, my urethane veneer.[130]

In the undoing of the sense of oneself, patiency overcomes the apocalypse of the economy. We are not only what we appear to be. In the ethical obligation that severs the promised endlessness of desire, people emerge as a social song against the totalising freedom of the subject, as a common poetics of indeterminate grief against the long ballad of *Music for Porn*.

Halpern's freedom inheres in giving up on freedom: his radical act is to abandon the subject already produced and determined by the ruinous crisis of America. What remains a mystery, however, is which exact form compels and constructs the constricting freedom that constitutes form-determined subjectivity. What form enacts the subject, and what formless, material life survives despite subjection? These are the questions I confront in Part 2.

---

130 Halpern 2012, p. 11.

PART 2

Socialities of Value

Introduction to Part 2

In the previous three chapters, I have presented my general thesis of how value's form-determination of subjectivity in capitalism produces the (anti-)social modality in which relations are already computed by the speculative temporality of productivity, which assigns *differential* potential productivity to subject groups by way of the *undifferentiated* expenditure of their labour-power.

Marxist-feminists and social reproduction theorists have studied capital's requirement that a minimum level of social life survives so that the labour force can continue to reproduce itself, as I studied in the introduction and chapter one. They do not tend to question, however, the precisely *differential* survival of forms of life within and despite their *undifferentiated* expression as labour-power. In Part 2, I am concerned with the differential form in which survival is given. I pursue this question in the radical modality of black studies, which studies the ways in which the fundamental difference of blackness antagonises and exceeds capitalism's racialising project.

In the transatlantic slave trade, Euro-American enslavers specifically grouped enslaved Africans in incompatible cultural groups, placing people together who did not speak the same language or have the same traditions, thereby prohibiting the possibility of assembled dissent. Through the disjuncture of difference, enslavers sought to homogenise black life, producing a racialised population in which, as Cedric J. Robinson writes, '*all are equally incomplete*.'[1] This incompletion, however, was assumed by the enslaved as the fugitive sociality of black life, giving way to the constant uprisings and escapes that the enslaved practiced.

The imposition of incompletion exposed a sociality that exceeded the reach of this imposition, a sociality that was expressed as the survival of black life *qua* blackness despite its obsessive erasure by enslavement. Enslavement attempted to *produce* and *determine* black lives as slaves, but in doing so it unwittingly exposed a survival that exceeds its productive logic. This foundational moment of the USA set up the dialectics of fugitivity and raciality that continue to define its sociopolitical tension. As Laura Harris writes,

> Blackness, in this sense, manifests itself in what is perceived as the unruly creativity and disorderly sociality that the subject, in its commitment to the idea of its own freedom as self-determination, as the self-conscious

1 Robinson 1980, p. 199. Original emphasis.

> exercise of pure individual will, secured by self-possession, must at all costs defend itself against, however violent its defensive maneuvers may be as it confronts the impossibility of this "freedom."[2]

The impossibility of the 'freedom' of black lives exposes a form of fugitive survival that persists in the excess of both freedom and self-possession as the definitional logics of capital's subjective regime. In the three chapters in Part 2, I am concerned with locating this fugitive sociality in poetry. To do so, I return to the 'primacy of insurgency' that I posed as my principal temporal proposition in the introduction.

The question is: what survives in and as the primacy of insurgency? There is a world in which subjects and authority interact. In that world, for Marxists, class struggle is the defining force that pushes history on. Within that ongoing struggle, a very difficult question is nestled: what is the temporality of social insurgency in relation to oppressive authority? At what point do networks of power and assemblies of struggle meet as the antagonism of history?

What these questions come down to is the possibility of insurgency against the power of capital. This possibility has very distinct coordinates depending on how the temporality of struggle is understood. Broadly, there are three dominant critical theses regarding this temporality.

(1) If power permanently precedes the struggle and those who struggle, then any revolutionary act is bound foremost to the destruction of the world as it is. Everything must be destroyed because, in the world as it is, power assumes ontological primacy, and there is no way back into the social life which precedes that totalising power. As I explored in chapter one, this is the position generally theorised throughout value-critical Marxisms, in which subjects are fully produced by the requirements of capital. The form-determination of subjectivity, for value-critical Marxists, is totalising, and there is no remnant of undetermined social life that can be recuperated or accessed by anticapitalist praxis. The revolutionary possibility of release from this determined form of being is withheld in the future, which will be actualised by the total abolition of value in the present. My contention with this temporal imaginary is that it is equivalent to that of capital itself, which posits *the expansion of value* as withheld in a permanently postponed future that we must work towards in order to realise the full potential productivity of our self-possessed freedom.

(2) If, however, power precedes the struggle but in an unstable and symbiotic relation, in which power requires the constant formation and subsumption of

2 Harris 2018, p. 3.

subjects for its own survival, then there is no way of imagining a total revolutionary rupture in this world. The world, then, is the permanent grounding of an unstable relation between the law (of the father; of value; of the state) and its subjects, each of whom requires the other and is equally bound to this repressive requirement. In this formulation, only an internal repositioning of the subject is possible, recalculating one's relation to power without abolishing that power, since it is also required for the subject to survive *qua* subject. This is what I summarise as the political-psychoanalytic approach, exemplified by the work of Judith Butler.

(3) If power is in fact the productive ideological narration of its own permanence, retroactively establishing the illusion of its necessity in the moment of its violent seizure of ongoing social lives, then the revolutionary act required to rid people of power is not the enactment of a new future, but rather a (re)turn to a surviving way of being that has been muted by the historical, material, and ideological expansion of power. In this understanding of the temporality of struggle, people are already existent in and as social life, but that life is severed by the subsumptive arrival of power, which redefines the requirements of production to such an extent that its system seems necessary and natural. However, that system is reliant on the survival of sociality and its nonproductive rituals of sharing and care, which it cannot itself provide, so it maintains social life in a suppressed form. People continue to share, talk, love, offer, give away, invite others in, and produce social meaning, despite the ubiquity of power's co-option of living body-energies. The struggle, here, is primary, but surrendered to power's form-determining force. The revolutionary focus of this movement is into an obscure beside, into a surviving alternative past, or the excess of the present, in which social life without power (i.e. anarchy) survives. This radical project *returns* to something already existent, already surviving, but in doing so it changes and disrupts that survival to the extent that what is *returned to* is not the same as before its form-determination: it is rendered instead as *insurgency*; it antagonises the homogeneity of the temporal present. I therefore employ the somewhat outmoded stylisation '(re)turn' to describe this movement of turning back to a modality that is no longer what it was. I categorise this third approach as that of black optimism, exemplified by the work of Fred Moten, often in collaboration with Stefano Harney.

These approaches constitute the theoretical groundwork of chapters four and five, centred on the poetry of Rowan Ricardo Phillips and Fred Moten respectively. Having discussed the first approach to the temporality of sociality and subjection at length in Part 1, especially chapter one, in chapter five I study the second and third approaches and attempt to stage a dialogue between them. In chapter four, however, I take this temporality of struggle back to the beginnings of modernity's inaugural refusal: to Kant's moral order and its rejection of an experience that precedes morality.

In his moral texts, Kant is adamant that the *form* precedes the *content* of any moral obligation. One must act according to the categorical imperative because it is the categorical imperative, not because of its particular reasoning. The example Kant constantly turns to is friendship. For him, one knows what friendship is, as a form, before one has ever experienced the content of friendship, as a particular friend. However, both in his own life – which was spent surrounded by good friends – and in certain texts, Kant reveals the fear that undergirds the desire to maintain friendship as a form: the fear of *losing friends* makes one act according to a set of moral guidelines that ensures the survival of friendship. In order to fear the loss of those friends, however, one must have experienced their presence; one fears losing not only what one has but what constitutes one's sense of being.

Through Rowan Ricardo Phillips's poetry collection *Living Weapon*, I look for moments of poetic access to this material life of friends that precedes and exceeds the moral form of friendship, exposing Kant to a persistent sociality that provides the condition for his moral law. What I am in pursuit of here is the residue of a sociality that survives in a fugitive temporality beside, before, and in the excess of the present, as I explored in chapter one.

In chapter five, I read Fred Moten's work as a poetic proposition for this surviving temporality: this is what I call above the black optimist approach, in which insurgency, sociality, and struggle are primary. I read Moten alongside Judith Butler, who is usually read in a more Levinasian vein as proposing that the ethical relation between I and Other is primary, but in whom I also find a remarkably Foucauldian temporality of power, in which there is no escape from the totalising reach of the Law, an approach also closely tied to that of the Lacanian philosopher Lorenzo Chiesa, as I discussed in chapter three.[3] This is most apparent in Butler's earlier works, but continues to occur in subtler forms – despite their proclamations against their prior over-Foucauldianism – in later works. I stage this temporality of struggle through the scene that Louis Althusser provides in his well-known 1970 essay 'Ideology and Ideological State Apparatuses', in which an officer of the state turns an individual into a subject by interpellating – or hailing – them on the street, calling out, 'Hey, you there!'. Butler's reading of this scene has been criticised – by Maya Rivera, alongside Martín Alcoff, for example – as stifling the possibility of alternative subjectivit-

3 I discuss the Levinasian and Foucauldian influences on Butler's understanding of power in my contribution to Mason and Moro 2025.

ies, and instead, like Althusser, closing the subject entirely within the oppressive function of the interpellating authority.[4]

For Butler, subjectivation is the total epistemological generation of subjectivity, leaving subjects with no access to a way of being in the world or knowing the world that precedes this violent subsumption. They nonetheless celebrate the forms of performative rebuttal that exceed the subjectivating function of authority. How exactly this performativity functions, however, is difficult to pinpoint; it changes radically from text to text in Butler's vast corpus.

For Moten, crucially, the street is the prior and surviving public setting of social assembly. The street, primarily, is the incomplete arena of assembly, which Moten, in describing the spatiality of friendship, calls 'an off square, a failed cube and plaza.'[5] The space of assembly is always incomplete, for Moten, since it can never contain the gathering of social life that precedes its formation.

In chapter six, I take inspiration from Marina Vishmidt's experiments in appropriating *speculation* as a mode of exposing alternative futures, against the accumulative withdrawal of the future into the present as undertaken by financial speculation.[6] In this experimental chapter – more of a speculative application of the preceding theoretical apparatus than a concluding statement – I posit two pages of architectural art, from Darell Wayne Fields' 2000 monograph *Architecture in Black: Theory, Space, and Appearance*, as the excess of poetry itself, exposing a textual poetics of fugitive sociality surviving within the page.

---

4 Rivera 2015, p. 148.
5 Moten and Tsang 2016, p. 7.
6 Vishmidt 2018a.

CHAPTER 4

Rowan Ricardo Phillips and the Form of Friendship

1 Moving Bodies

Rowan Ricardo Phillips is a contemporary Enlightenment poet, in the same breath singing verses for birdsong and against police brutality. In his poetry, he responds to the traditionally fundamental questions of being human, with an emphasis on formless social lives that slips out of the classic binary of form and content. His content is a challenge to his form; his form a living weapon.

A Catalan translator and highly regarded poet, he is also a tennis expert and keen sportsman. His second nonfiction book, *The Circuit: A Tennis Odyssey*, introduces the experience of 2017 through its tennis tournaments, almost as if addressed to someone not from Earth. While their contents have no connection, this critical style of presenting a particular experience through everything that surrounds it also occurs in his first book of essays, *When Blackness Rhymes with Blackness*, which, if it can be said to be about anything as such, is about poetry and race.

What these nonfiction books display is Phillips's concern with form: the form of bodies and the form of texts; the way they move, and the way they are prohibited from moving. His books, above all, are experiments in the possibilities of form. Phillips's poetry follows a similar pattern. In direct and everyday language, his poetry usually unfolds in one particular scene with an easily recognisable narrative structure. A character does something, and the description of that act constitutes the poem. His poetry is also remarkably consistent in its themes. Throughout his corpus, there are five principal thematic concerns that recur as the structuring semantics of almost every poem: being black, music, the city (Barcelona and New York specifically), religion, and what poems are.

These concerns are structured across two perceptual forms: (1) the spatial plan, dealing with how things can move, where they move, and (2) the ontic plan, dealing with whether things can move, whether they are alive enough to move. What I call the ontic plan is matter; it is the experience of proximate bodies, and deals with the physical feeling of relations, equivalent in Marxist terms to the commodity's 'natural form'. What I call the spatial plan is the multi-temporal, retroactive, and constitutive force of those relations themselves; it is both the appearance of these relations – the form in which they present themselves – and the undergirding motivation to sustain this system of movements and interactions, equivalent to the commodity's 'value-form', or value *as* form.[1]

In this chapter, I attempt to situate these two plans in relation to the history of form, which, given its vast reach in every part of discourse, I reduce to two polar ends of its possibility: Kantian morality as the fundamental form of human relations, and Phillips's poetry as a direct antagonism to the survival of Enlightenment form.

In *Objections*, Sven Lütticken brings out the labyrinthine semantics of form. Value, as a relation of exchange, is a form. It is also expressed via a material object, a useable thing that is touched, distributed, and consumed by human bodies. It forms the life surrounding it.[2] A form can be a prescriptive format, a reproducible code for copying objects infinitely: you must fill in the form in the correct form, black ink and capital letters. But *form* is also the irreducible singularity of an object's movement. The value-form of a commodity is a unique expression of desire in which, ultimately, human bodies come together to pursue the ends of their needs and wishes. I gather at the store of all the things I want in order to achieve my possession of them. But the very formality of that form also withdraws from the uniqueness of each scene of exchange, calculating the value of exchanges on a standardised and general scale. The labour valorised through exchange is not the tangible toil of a sentient body; it is standardised abstract labour, and the form of value is the 'becoming-concrete' of this abstraction itself.[3] As a real abstraction, through the spatial plan, value is formed as a material relation *per se*, assuming the form of an ontic plan.

In this chapter I study the moments when form trips over itself, exposing a material sociality in the fault lines of the subject's ideal abstractions. In a grand historical gesture, positing Kant as the archetype of the theoretical refusal of the body's fleshy presence, I use Phillips's poetry as a tool for pulling apart the formal surface of Kantian philosophy. In the shreds of form, I hope to find a precarious and vulnerable object, a material thing that precedes and exceeds the forms constructed on it. I will call that material thing, quite simply, a friend.

Marxist theorists – such as Alfred Sohn-Rethel, Frederick Harry Pitts, Sven Lütticken, and Christian Lotz – have often focused on Kant's ontology (the transcendental ideality of spacetime) in order to provide a value-theoretical critique of the human subject's production of forms. In this chapter, I focus on

---

1 Marx 1990, p. 138 f.

2 Lütticken 2023, p. 138.

3 Lütticken 2023, p. 238.

Kant's moral philosophy, and particularly his thinking on friendship, which I read through Adriana Cavarero's critique of rectitude. Here, however, I am not very interested in *critiquing* Kant, but rather in making friends with him and Phillips. I take up Denise Ferreira da Silva's injunction to move beyond critique '[f]or the simple reason that, due to its Kantian origins, critique cannot but restate (usually by the back door of redress) the premises of modern thought.'[4] I try to operate in the excess of critique – that is to say, in a logic that is beyond any means of measurement[5] – by inclining towards Kant, listening closely to what he says about his friends, and studying how his words disrupt and are disrupted by the strange formality of Phillips's poetry.

I want to ask what embodied forms of ethical sociality survive not in the outright disbandment of Kant, but within his own system of rational rectitude. What plan does Kant offer in excess of his own awareness? What proximity to an ethical plan does he skirt around despite what he – and his long wake in philosophy – understands as proper reason? Kant may just be the opening into an anti-Kantian antagonism in the project of ordered sense. As Fred Moten says, what makes Kant so radical is his 'perhaps inadvertent openness to the irrational condition of possibility of rationality.'[6] Kant's moral order is reliant on the existence of synthetic judgment *a priori*, which I will try to reveal, as Moten always says after Nathaniel Mackey, as an insistent perviousness that precedes and pervades each and every natal occasion.[7]

To beckon forth this friendly antagonism, I begin by discussing Kant's obsession with the upright, independent, and autonomous man, which I read as imitated in Phillips's poem '1776', from his 2020 collection *Living Weapon*. I then counter this moral rectitude through Adriana Cavarero's ethics of inclination, which posits the presence of a social disruption in every attempt at autonomous independence. I read this inclination in Phillips's poem 'The Golden Hour', which acts as the B-side of '1776', suddenly confronting the poem's subject with the impossibility of his solitude; instead, he must incline towards his friends. I then take this study of friendship to the shortest poem in *Living Weapon*, 'Tradition and the Individual Talent', which I read as Phillips's ultimate refusal of the illusory rectitude of humanity, additionally expressed in 'Mortality Ode'. In the final section, reading between Phillips's more recent poem 'Child of Nature' and Kant's moral texts, alongside a wine goblet given to the philo-

4 Silva 2018b, p. 25.
5 Ibid., p. 31.
6 Moten 2003, p. 245.
7 Moten repeats variations of this phrase throughout his works. Its fullest explanation is given in Moten 2003, pp. 251–4.

sopher by his friends that Christine Battersby finds in Kant's archives, I look for an internal dehiscence in Kant, and the ways in which a study of Phillips's poetry can reveal Kant as primarily a friend who failed, like all of us, at standing upright.

2 Rectifying Inclinations

Throughout his 2020 collection *Living Weapon*, Rowan Ricardo Phillips follows the movements of a character called Rowan. In his first collection, 2013's *The Ground*, the character and the poet inhabit the same body and speak in unison: 'Hi, I'm Rowan. We likely haven't met. / And if we have or have not I love you', he plainly says in 'To the Reader'.[8] By *Living Weapon*, these beings have separated. Now the poet Phillips speaks of the character Rowan as a disconnected and unruly assemblage: 'The Good Rowan; wake good Rowan up – / And tell him that the poet he hears trapped / In the ivory made it out, and lives.'[9] Beneath the being as presented in authorship or in text, a riotous form of life survives, a trapped anarchic residue of other times.

The primary concern of both collections is New York City and the way a singular body positions itself in relation to this vast accumulation of history. While there is a certain Romantic spirituality and idealism in how Phillips imagines a human body's relation to its surroundings – musings on art and music give him access to the materiality of the city – the scenes described in the four poems I focus on in this chapter are fully material: the One World Trade Center skyscraper, a meeting between two strangers, a police shooting, and waiting for a repair in a phone store.

At the heart of *Living Weapon*'s concerns is the form-determination of the body. For Phillips, the human body is at once a spiritual accumulation of poetic history – with snippets of centuries of verse guiding the movements of Rowan – and a profoundly viscous singularity, a vulnerable object positioned in the centre of modernity's structuring orders: the body is a racialised, exploited, gendered, and muted mass of animated loss.

With extreme attention to detail, Phillips investigates the spatial boundaries of bodies, and the possibility of a single body's movements out of the determining forces of the city. Does poetry have any effect on bullets? Can a poetics of somatic exposure collapse the historical forces that place certain

8 Phillips 2013, p. 18.

9 Phillips 2021, p. 45.

bodies in the firing line? If Phillips can produce a poem that disrupts the accumulated history of the body, bringing out its primary vulnerability to sociality, then he can collapse a long and dominant tradition in racialising philosophy.

These questions that antagonise corporeal unity are present in all of Phillips's poetry collections. In *The Ground*, which describes post-9/11 New York, vulnerable bodies are situated in relation to the dispensation of death through the World Trade Center attacks, the colonisation of the Americas, and the logistics of distribution.[10] In his second collection, *Heaven*, Paradise's own abstract uniqueness is ruptured, attempting instead to construct itself as a city on Earth.[11] It is in *Living Weapon*, though, that these deeply philosophical concerns are placed in direct relation to their opening Enlightenment formulation: the Kantian morality of the upright body.

In the first poem of the book proper, after a prelude elegising the death of Phillips's grandmother during the COVID-19 pandemic, Rowan flies up to the top of One World Trade Center in Manhattan, the skyscraper that marks the absence of the Twin Towers and celebrates the resurgence of the USA. It stands 1776 feet high.

The speaker, Rowan, is invisible, removed from the space of the city:

> … I've put my faith in being
> unseen now among the low iron clouds.[12]

Rather than space upholding him, there is the sound of winds, which 'work their way up the tower's panes of glass like / fingers on the fret board of a guitar.'[13] This overwhelming sound removes the sight of the city, removes its site, and opens into time.

> Hovering here, I thought for once to try to remember it all;
> I thought this would be a remarkable moment …
> but do I sound remarkable to you?[14]

Two levels of urban living are split in this scene: (1) the spatial plan, which, though dominant at the quotidian level of the street, is meaningless and invis-

10 Phillips 2013, p. 3, p. 13, p. 33.
11 Phillips 2015, p. 37.
12 Phillips 2021, p. 3.
13 Ibid.
14 Ibid., p. 4.

ible at this height, and (2) the ontic plan, which assumes dominance once the subject is made only of music, spinning back through a time unbound by the constraints of space.

At the top of the monument of accumulated national trauma, with the visuality of the archetypal expansive capitalist authority structured in protected and policed steel beneath him, a very peculiar erasure is enacted on this poetic subject: he is both individuated from his surrounding social life, withdrawn into the loneliness of clouds, and simultaneously forced into a nonspecific and subjectless wound that collectively defines the nation. In the gigantic, solid sign of the nation's grieving hubris, Rowan melts into air. There is a struggle ongoing between the spatial plan (what one sees) and the ontic plan (what one feels), a struggle situated precisely in Rowan's body.

The main effect of this struggle is the loss of the illusion of free will:

> All things this high up in the air have a living quality to
> them, how they move oh so slightly in the upper atmosphere
> as though breathing or, at the very least, being breathed into.[15]
>
> ... for the first time
> that I can remember, I felt hysteria lap my blood. I flapped
> all of me – arms, legs, wings – I flapped all of me like a feral
> animal. My mother says this is how I came into the world.[16]

Like in Alli Warren's poetry, as I wrote in chapter two, the principal relation here occurs between a non-human commodity – a skyscraper, in this case – and a person wholly determined by this relation. The wind and the terrifying height at the top of the tower have destabilised the subject's ability to control his body.

Rowan is accustomed to this dizziness. The summer morning when '1776' takes place is not the first time he has engaged in this divine movement in history:

> I've done 1776 before. I've even been higher than that. Oh, I've been much higher than that. Once, I reached the end of the lowest ring of the Earth's atmosphere. ... I flew so high up that the sky itself ended.[17]

---

15 Ibid., p. 3.
16 Ibid., p. 6.
17 Ibid., p. 5.

He is not particularly shocked to be here – this was, after all, how he came into this world, with wings[18] – but still the erasure of space takes away any recognition of himself. He cannot find a position that is *himself* without the coordinates of space. The test at this atmospheric height is to assume a form of movement that is not determined by the recognisable marks of cartography.

Eventually, he does this by making music. He waves his wings and a song is produced. The song and the flight carry him through the years of American history: 1868 (14th Amendment), 1865 (end of the Civil War), 1787 (signing of the Constitution and establishment of the first US government), 1776 (Declaration of Independence). These markers trace the historical monuments of modern liberalism, accompanied by its most obvious spatial marker in the One tower.

The motivation of the flying subject in this poem is difficult to ascertain. He does this regularly and it comes naturally to him, but he does not particularly enjoy it. His extensive rectitude pushes him all the way up above the city, out of its sociality.

> The first blue aspects of the sky at this hour are unreason –
> ably beautiful, like the color of that color in a cube of ice.
> ...   ... but seven seconds
> into that feeling and the achingly early morning traffic has
> already begun to seep through the solitude.[19]

At these heights, the rationality of his perception remains, calculating every sight he encounters, but the rationality of space itself has disappeared. The unreasonable beauty of the sky confounds what he expects as a coherence between his consciousness and its objects, or the phenomenal and noumenal scenes. Even the unreasonableness of the word 'unreasonably' itself has split, falling off onto another line, parted by poetic space.

3 Upright Reasons

Every part of Kant's transcendental idealism and moral law is followed in '1776': in order to have consciousness of being determined in time, Kant writes in the *Critique of Pure Reason*, there must be '*something permanent*' in relation to which one defines oneself, but that thing cannot be inside oneself since then

18 Ibid., p. 8.
19 Ibid., p. 8.

there would be no transcendental relation.[20] My existence is knowable to me on the condition of the existence of objects in space; it is the temporal continuity of myself in relation to those objects that provides proof of my own consciousness. Phillips affirms this necessary transcendental proof by overemphasising the subject's rectitude, flying straight up out of the city, past the sky, to the point at which any experience of time fades. The most secretly Kantian moment of all of this is that once Rowan's perception of space-time is withdrawn, the possibility of knowing *other people* collapses.

This erasure of sociality highlights the binding impulses of Kant's philosophies of perception (in the Three Critiques) and morality (in the metaphysics of morals). For Kant, space is a projection of human perception. The projected perception is received in the human mind from external objects themselves, but since those objects are unknowable according to their own terms, in their own forms, it is the form of human minds that renders them spatial, projecting this gridded cartographic logic onto what we come to understand as the objective order of the world. As Lütticken notes, for Kant these projected thought-forms arise from an already formed mind; the 'preforming Kantian mind appears to arrive on the scene fully formed; it is *itself* preformed.'[21] However, following Alfred Sohn-Rethel, Lütticken emphasises that this mind must be understood as arising out of social relations. The mental projection of perception is itself produced in relation to a social life in which the perceivable form is value; the object accumulated into the mind and rendered perceivable is an object of exchange, an object already mediated by relations of production and circulation. As Lütticken writes, 'the exchange process is marked by an abstraction from all material and sensual qualities that prefigures and informs the operations of the Kantian mind.'[22]

Kant's philosophy of perception, then, is a historically discreet capitalist form of relation, which reifies existing material social relations, abstracting perceived objects as value-forms bearing no trace of their living residue. 'The specifically *capitalist* value-form,' Lütticken continues, 'is the autonomized expression of labor-time. Commodity fetishism is a type of formalism: it occludes the role of labor to suggest that value is actually determined by being realized on the market.'[23] The Kantian mind perceives only what follows the mediation of form; it grasps only that which is already rendered perceivable. This temporality in which the form is projected as the groundwork of the material relation

20 Kant 1998, B274, p. 195.
21 Lütticken 2023, p. 156. Original emphasis.
22 Ibid., p. 159.
23 Ibid.

itself – a projection that obscures the antecedence of that material relation – is reproduced in Kant's moral philosophy.

In his moral writings, Kant is responding to the increasingly absolute authority of the church in his lifetime, by which 'religion makes itself lord over morals, and statutory religion becomes an instrument of state authority (politics) under religious despots.'[24] In this scenario, morality is authorised after the act. First, one acts, and then the authority of moral law determines the value of that act. This action can never be moral, for Kant, because it is guided by its end rather than by morality itself. One must act according to what one *should in every circumstance* do, regardless of the particular end of this or that action.[25]

For Kant, one must be simultaneously impelled by an *a priori* Good, but also be always independent, deciding one's own acts and making sure they are good. What means does one have, though, for acting according to an implicit moral order that produces and affirms the autonomy and independence of the subject? This is the question Kant confronts in his two great moral texts: *Groundwork of the Metaphysics of Morals* (1785) and *The Metaphysics of Morals* (1797). The former is the preparatory exploration for the latter and gives a general overview of proper morality. The latter supplies further examples and tries to deal with the problems that arose in response to the earlier book.

At its core, Kant's moral philosophy relies on the existence of synthetic judgments *a priori*. At the very beginning of the *Groundwork*, he makes the case for their necessity. First, there is the distinction between synthetic and analytic judgments. An analytic judgment contains only as much information as is in the object itself, while a synthetic judgment provides more knowledge than is contained in the object. Analytic judgments are true by definition, while synthetic judgments inform us about the world. Second, there is the distinction between *a priori* and *a posteriori*. *A posteriori* judgments follow from experience; we know them because we have experienced them. *A priori* judgments are independent of experience; we know them already, as part of our being.

Our experiences always teach us about the world – something is revealed by experiencing things – so *a posteriori* knowledge can never be analytic; it is always synthetic. Two types of knowledge are immediately clear, then: synthetic *a posteriori* (I know my name is Kant because I have heard people calling me by my name: my experience *informs* me of the name I carry and its coded

---

24 Kant 2006, pp. 332–3.

25 See: Kant 1997, 4:441, pp. 47–8. In these citations I refer to the standard Kantian text positions, followed by the page number.

genealogy), and analytic *a priori* (I know that things have names without needing to experience this fact; things having names is inherent in the logic of naming and of language).

The final form of judgment is Kant's focus: synthetic *a priori*. These judgments guide us in the world, informing us of new possibilities of knowledge, but are not produced by experience. Very importantly, the first example Kant gives of this judgment is friendship. Friendship is not a definition; it certainly reveals something new about the world and the possibility of relations. But, according to Kant, it is not known through experience. One knows already what the form of friendship is: 'pure sincerity in friendship can be no less required of everyone even if up to now there may never have been a sincere friend, because this duty – as duty in general – lies, prior to all experience, in the idea of a reason determining the will by means of *a priori* grounds.'[26] Friendship is synthetic *a priori*. We know already what friendship should be – even if it never meets that fantasy – and it informs us about the world, providing new information.

The subject's ideal independence and autonomy is developed through the precise employment of synthetic judgments *a priori*. The fundamental imperative of this form of knowledge is that it precedes and exceeds all action: regardless of what one is doing, what one's aims are, what the uses of the activity are, one must always act in accordance with the moral principle that lies universally before all action. This is summarised in the famous categorical imperative, which, for Kant, is universal and absolute: '*act only in accordance with that maxim through which you can at the same time will that it become a universal law*.'[27] Universality is the condition of morality.[28] One *must* act morally and never incline towards one's subjective fantasies: 'the will is a capacity to choose *only that* which reason independently of inclination cognizes as practically necessary, that is, as good.'[29]

The physical form of the moral actor here is crucial. Following the classic gendered geometry of the masculine as vertical and the feminine as horizontal, Kant firmly situates morality in the upright body. This vertical stance – a rectitude at once moral and ontological – is the critical focus of Adriana Cavarero's monograph *Inclinations*, which notices that serious philosophers always stand upright and erect, resisting any inclination towards others: 'in

26 Kant 1997, 4:408, p. 20.

27 Ibid., 4:421, p. 31. Original emphasis.

28 A lot has been written about the duplicity of this 'universality', which of course refers only to white, European, cis-hetero, property-owning, able-bodied men. A few suggestions among many important texts: Eze 1997; Moten 2018a; Lloyd 2019; Yountae and Craig 2021.

29 Kant 1997, 4:412, p. 24. Original emphasis.

the theatre of modern philosophy, center stage is occupied by an I whose position is straight and vertical.'[30] What Cavarero poses as the ethical alternative to rectitude is inclination. Fundamentally, inclining objects meet at a certain point, reaching over to each other, and can never assume the independence of an upright posture. 'An inclined I, leaning toward the outside,' as Cavarero writes, 'is no longer straight.' Unbalanced by inclination, it cannot be 'an autonomous and independent subject.'[31]

The assumption that synthetic judgments *a priori* are possible, that they form the basis of moral conduct through their necessity and that they are carried as the projective perception of the properly upright body, has had an enormous influence on modernity's general imaginary of moral activity. This is why, despite Judith Butler's warning against generalising the conditions of something as imprecise as 'modernity',[32] I maintain a certain dedication to a continuous current that pushes from Kant to our contemporary, which is sustained exactly by our rigid belief in Kantian morality. Cavarero goes so far as to define the eighteenth century to now as 'the Kantian era,' a time 'of straightening and rectifying: from pedagogy to military discipline, passing through medicine, orthopedics, and gymnastics, we find a series of technologies aimed at producing a postural rectitude, whether on the physical plane or that of ethics, politics, and society.'[33]

This universalising moral conduct is what Phillips counters with delicate, subtle force in *Living Weapon*, by exposing the sociality that provides the possibility of individuated rectitude.

4 Inclining Rectitude

Two-thirds of the way through *Living Weapon*, in 'The Golden Hour', Rowan returns to his flight from '1776'. Having been an indelible Kantian character during his historical journey, Rowan now finds himself stunted by the appearance of an other.

> Wait. So you're new? Great.
> I've always wanted to show someone around.[34]

30 Cavarero 2016, p. 6.
31 Ibid.
32 Butler 2016, p. 108.
33 Cavarero 2021a, p. 38.
34 Phillips 2021, p. 41.

This other does not arrive as such; rather, Rowan notices that an other always had to be there. The other is, indeed, 'new', but also causes a simultaneous break and continuation: 'Wait', i.e. stop, and 'So', i.e. continue this conversation. No answer is given. The other never speaks. Instead, everything is already understood. The form of the other's arrival – the very language of address that conditions the speaker's relation to the world – traumatically breaks the independence of the poem, revealing a permanent condition of social life, since the speaker, so lonesome in '1776', *always* wanted this other to arrive.

The title, in this sense, is crucial. In photography, the golden hour is the time around dawn and dusk, when sunlight is soft and bloodred at the horizon. In medicine, however, the golden hour is the time (traditionally conceived as an hour) between a traumatic injury and certain death without medical help. In a short period of time after the heart and respiration stop and bleeding continues, one's chances of survival fall to zero. The golden hour is the time in which survival is urgently pursued; the time in which one most immediately needs help. By gradually inclining towards death, one calls on the inclinations of others.

The traumatic exposure of the poem's speaker to an other has a peculiarly anti-Kantian effect on Rowan. For Kant, reason is an *author*, the scribe of one's actions, demarcating one's position in the world by existing as a logistical object, a distributor of one's will: 'Reason must regard itself as the author of its principles independently of alien influences; consequently, as practical reason or as the will of a rational being it must be regarded of itself as free.'[35] Confronted suddenly by an other, though, Rowan loses his authority. His words become muddled, and the mostly standard, simple prose of '1776' becomes a panicked jumble of free verse (which is rare in Phillips's poetry).

The speaker begins by positioning himself in relation to his silent interlocutor:

> Here: If you look straight up you'll see
> The tops of skyscrapers
> Staring straight down[36]

The flyers are now on the ground, in the familiar American urban position of looking up at skyscrapers in awe. But as the line lengths extend, the depiction of the city loses its sense:

---

35 Kant 1997, 4:448, p. 54.

36 Phillips 2021, p. 41.

And the sidewalks you thought you were walking on
Are actually way up there in the high distance.[37]

Both the streets and the tops of buildings are above these newly joined voyageurs. The characters are, in fact, beneath everything, stuck under the whole city. The structuring order of the world has given in to the material site at which two people meet. The sudden entrance of a body into the discourse of ideal flight through history unhooks the whole historical architecture that kept the subject in his fantasy of soaring independence. In 'The Golden Hour', friendship breaks the form of reason.

Focusing on friends has recently had an unexpectedly ruinous effect on morality in Kantian scholarship. In a 2021 essay, Christine Battersby contends with Cavarero's critique of Kant by arguing that it enacts its own Kantian universalisation: Cavarero projects a universal Kant. In the archives of his friends, Battersby pursues another Kant, a silenced comrade behind the moral philosophy of rectitude. The main object she focuses on is a wine goblet, given to Kant by his friends on 30th August 1763, when the philosopher was 39, long before he wrote his most important texts.

In addition to rebutting Cavarero's conflation of Cartesian and Kantian ontology and affirming the intense friendships Kant had – his daily siestas with Joseph Green are particularly memorable, the friend with whom he discussed every single sentence of the *Critique of Pure Reason* – Battersby importantly notes the continuity of theories of friendship throughout Kant's corpus. 'Underlying Kant's disquisition on friendship in [*The Metaphysics of Morals*] is his insistence that a "human being is a being meant for society",'[38] making friends want to reveal themselves to each other, while also fearing what the revelation of secrets could threaten. The exposure of friend to friend works only on the condition that it is mutual and esoteric, meant for these friends only.

For Cavarero, this gives far too much credit to Kant, who established modernity's refusal of the maternal ethics of inclination, an ethical stance that recognises a universally – if differential – constitutive vulnerability that invites and demands practices of care. Kant's refusal of this inclining ethics has established a pursuit of autonomous rectitude that pervades every modern institution.[39]

The point for Cavarero is not to try and redeem Kant by forcing an inclining social life into him. Instead, she writes, the ethics of inclination intends

37 Ibid.
38 Battersby 2021, p. 115, citing Kant 1999, pp. 602–3.
39 Cavarero 2016, p. 34.

> to think relation itself as originary and constitutive, as an essential dimension of the human, which – far from limiting itself to putting free and autonomous individuals in relation to each other, as the doctrine of the social pact prescribes – calls into question our being creatures who are materially vulnerable and, often in greatly unbalanced circumstances, consigned to one another.[40]

For Cavarero, the ethical opening of inclination is not the introduction of a new practice as such, but rather the realisation that we are already constituted by a vulnerability that dispossesses our claims to independence and autonomy. We are already inclined towards others, reliant on their support, and can never fully claim the upright balance of the Kantian *I*. There is no *other* ontology in which inclination is prescribed. Rather, ontology itself is undermined by its internal inclination, its constitutive erasure of the individuality of each *I* by vulnerable reliance on others, as Butler emphasises.[41]

For Kant, on the other hand, the problem with inclination is that it assigns only 'conditional worth' to its objects, rather than the 'objective end' of the categorical imperative.[42] Its objects are used as a means, which determines action by subjective desire, and for Kant that can never be moral. The way of assessing whether an object is worthy of being an objective end is already set in nature. 'Rational beings,' also called '*persons*,' cannot be determined by the desire of an action because they themselves have their own will, so they are necessarily treated as ends in themselves. Those without reason, or '*things*,' are instead treated as a means towards the rational being's goals, leaving them open '*to be*[*ing*] *acquired*' by reason.[43] For Kant, these categories are absolute. The borders of reason designate certain beings as absolutely rational and others as absolutely irrational.

The logic of the reason that *acquires* as opposed to *being acquired* is precisely the activity of the subject, the one who enacts the presupposition of subjective will onto the world by appropriating the world into human reason. That is, the material activity of the subject consists in *forming* a world chartered according to the form of rational thought. The world is made as the world of subjects by subjects perceiving the world. This is the dialectical operation that is undermined in 'The Golden Hour', when a friend arrives to break the ideality of flight in '1776'.

40 Ibid., p. 13.
41 Butler 2021b.
42 Kant 1997, 4:428, p. 37. Original emphasis.
43 Ibid. See also: ibid., 4:438, p. 45. Original emphasis.

In the first poem, it appeared to Rowan that he could fly anywhere, back to any time, and, even if dull and repetitive, it was freeing. The world fit the form he projected. In 'The Golden Hour', in the face of an other, the impossibility of his solitary flight is traumatically exposed. Before the form of reason, there is the fleshy presence of a friend.

When flying alone in '1776', he believes himself to be above and beyond history, but is in fact wholly determined by its ideological frames, by the military macho self-confidence of the USA, proudly emblazoning its survival on the sky in the One World Trade Center tower. Rowan, in his temporal voyage upwards, believes himself to be the determined result of this imperial history. Once the destabilising encounter with the other occurs, all his confidence is erased; it is rendered suddenly impossible through the demand that the other necessarily places on oneself: to realise that homeostasis is always illusory, that one cannot determine oneself within the individuated fantasies of nation, of capital, or, most of all, of one's individual, sovereign body.

In 'The Golden Hour', the material and relational conditions of history emerge, and Rowan realises, in his ethical confusion, that he was in fact never flying upwards anyway:

> … Touch me.
> Oh, that's right. You have no hands.
> Imagine touching me. It's much better that way
> anyway. Anyway …
> Yeah. No. It doesn't rain anymore. But
> There's the sun up there maybe perhaps.
> And every golden hour (I don't know what that is),
> Like clockwork (I mean, right?), they
> Have their people shake their trash cans
> Out their windows
> And the coins that make it down here
> They feel kind of a little bit like rain.
> They call it watering the money tree.
> I'm just happy to be in the way.[44]

This subject, perversely convinced of his independence and self-constitution, realises that he was bred at the bottom of a well, caught beneath an illusory money tree, showered in coins at the golden hour (either as the aesthetics of

44 Phillips 2021, pp. 41–2.

dusk or the moment of possible survival before death). At so many levels, the individual flight of the self-constituting man in the first poem is revealed as a farce. The tragedy of this farce reveals that before the form of the subject-world, there was a material opening, a constitutive vulnerability found in friends – not friendship as a form, or a moral order, but friends as proximate, singular bodies.

This primary materiality of friends opens a problem with the fixity of Kant's categorical border that separates *rational beings* and *irrational things*. The question is: what does the friendly goblet mean? Kant was given a wine glass by his friends, which he kept for the rest of his life. He drank and laughed and shared in joyous social life. But what is the *objective end* of friendship? If 'reason entirely by itself determines conduct' and 'it must necessarily do so *a priori*,'[45] which rational principle has determined the motive towards friendship? Why does Kant need his friends? Why are they not open to being acquired by his reason, and why is he so acquirable in the desire of their generous gifts?

The 'autonomy of the will' arises categorically from the production of moral law *within* the rational subject, so that each moral act is never imposed on the actor but rather emerges as a function of that actor's own *a priori* moral reason.[46] That subject, though, is also a friend, also determined by the desires of social life. Another force, with no end or reason to speak of, disrupts the moral function of this generative will. Maybe this simple, silly wine glass that Kant's friends made for each other reveals a rupture in the borders of reason.

5 Friends before Form

Denise Ferreira da Silva's principal reason for dismissing critical philosophy's attempts at disrupting the subject with 'truth' (à la Alain Badiou) or 'objectivity' (à la Bruno Latour) is that they 'do not even pretend to contemplate the instances in which the *human* itself emerges as an "object," as registered by raciality, sexuality, and other modern concepts.'[47] These critical traditions cannot address a being without the coordinates of the subject.

Silva maintains that the form of address critical philosophy relies on in theorising the liberation of subjects is rooted *formally* in the Cartesian address that survives in Kant. The principal subjective movement of this address is

45 Kant 1997, 4:427, p. 36. I have modified the translation throughout this chapter by returning 'a priori' to the italics in which Kant writes it in German, instead of the upright roman in the English translation. That is, I have, like Kant, inclined the priority of the *a priori*.

46 Ibid., 4:433, p. 41.

47 Silva 2018b, p. 21. Original emphasis.

the positioning of oneself as the coordinating and regulating logic of external space. One marks the world as the form in which one's subjectivity fits, positing a temporal break at the beginning of one's subject-form: before one's perception of the world, nothing has yet been determined. It is *the human mind* that determines the world, and the mind arrives already determining. This projective address is deployed throughout modern thought in numerous forms: as 'the one that knows (Descartes), judges (Kant), recognises (Hegel), and measures (science).'[48] Against this address, Silva seeks to 'undermine the Kantian forms of the subject, that is, the implicit and explicit positions of enunciation – in particular, the loci of decision or judgement or determination – this subject occupies.'[49]

For Silva, it is the *form* of the subject that carries the violence of the Kantian address into our contemporary, surviving in the presupposed antecedence of morality *qua* abstract reason to the material social life of friends: 'it is the *formal* (both as abstraction and shape/ figure) element of patriarchal authority, which remains in the image of the proper ethico-juridical thing, namely the *citizen*, and anchors *his right* to decide, to control, and to kill.'[50] Kant's positioning of the *form* of being in the abyss before the emergence of material social lives allows the establishment of an ontological map that provides the calculating grounding of all social experience: by the time one experiences the tangibility of social life – by the time of being among others – one must already have fit into the prescriptive reason of the map. One must have accounted for oneself in relation to the world and to others. In order to become a subject, then, a mute object that correlates with the projective reason of the subject must already be understood to exist.

In the demand to be a subject, in the act of addressing oneself to the world as subject – and if that address correlates with the pre-formatted map of subjects acting on the world, then this address presupposes whiteness and cismasculinity as the speaking form – an object is required. One must address oneself *to an other*, an other whose muteness in the face of this address places them/it as an object on the map of speaking subjects. 'What is troubling is not that (in actuality) a cisman will occupy the position of the subject, but that the gender-sexual feature – referent of the patriarchal-form – requests both positions (a subject and an object).'[51] The object *qua* object is an effect of the subject's address.

48 Ibid., p. 27.
49 Silva 2018a, p. 1.
50 Silva 2018b, p. 23. Original emphasis.
51 Silva 2018b, p. 25.

Across '1776' and 'The Golden Hour', Phillips disrupts this dialectic of nation- and world-formation by suspending the subject's emergence in relation to an object. The inanimate object, for Silva, is the blueprint for the other as interlocutor. Critical theorists who attempt to recover a certain latent objectivity in both the other and the subject, Silva argues, fail to account for the presupposition of an object dominated by the expansive subject in any understanding of intersubjective activity. These projects are constrained by 'Thought' as the 'seat of the universal.' What Silva proposes instead, in her black feminist poethics, is 'existing,' which 'chases away the dominant fantasies of a kind of knowing that can only determine itself if with iron hinges of universal reason.'[52]

In the operation of Thought, one calculates oneself as the source of reason in relation to the nonsense of the object, an object that makes no sense without the order of the subject's self-address. In speaking to the other, one brings sense to the world as the interaction of rational speakers. In 'The Golden Hour', *existing* – or what I call here *the ontic plan* – breaks the sense of this order, or *the spatial plan*. The speaking subject attempts to guide the mute other, but his discourse falls apart. The world he seems to have known is not in fact knowable.

Even the language with which the speaker describes the world is removed from inscription. Welcoming the other to 'The First Light', he implores his co-flyer to

> ... Enjoy
> The feeling while it lasts.
> Because soon this will all be normal to you
> And you will feel as normal as *&#%
> And believe me that will #$*!&^@ suck. ...[53]

Rowan cannot properly authorise the authority of his speech; it comes out instead as prohibiting symbols, crucially barring the most material, animal actions of the poem: the words disguised by random symbols are, surely, 'shit' and 'fucking' – the somatic functions prohibited by the ideal morality of form, since they are functions that cause the body to incline, to lean into itself and to others.

The body *as form*, as the prescription of Thought, accesses a modality of reason that is disconnected from the mortality and finitude of the body, but Phillips's speaker brings the subject back to traumatically face what has been

52 Silva 2014, p. 86.
53 Phillips 2021, p. 41.

removed from his materiality: his own body. Through a friend, a physical site of primary sociality, the speaker's body no longer speaks but instead exposes the viscous presence of his entanglement in the social life of bodies that shit and fuck, that interact with the world. The body as the ontic plan has uprooted the form of the world as the spatial plan.

In opening his lonesome flight to an other, the fantasy of an object-world that provides the inanimate foundation for the subject's wandering is erased. The world will no longer conform to the speaker's reason. By inclining into the other, Phillips locates the impossibility of the subject's upright maintenance. Instead, he leans in, physically and materially, undoing himself through an opening into the formless presence of friends.

Inclination is revealed even in Kant himself. In the archetypally erect subject, the upstanding moral actor, an anxious resistance to inclination is already presupposed, an anxiety that reveals a recognition of its precarity. Behind every standing object is a network of support, an often elided but constitutive social life of sharing. As Butler writes in response to Cavarero, '[t]he upright figure, no matter how self-standing it claims to be, is implicitly in the process of warding off an infrastructural disaster.'[54] The infrastructural disaster for Rowan is the eradication of the illusion of flight, a disaster that occurs at the hands of an unnamed friend. For Kant, the disaster is a wine goblet. This token of friendship is the ruin of his autonomy.

Is Kant subject to the laws of friendship? The inscription on the wine goblet reads (in English), 'Secrecy in love and sincerity in Friendship, all Happy together notwithstanding what happend in the world [*sic*]' (referring to a global banking crash the same month).[55] Has this sincerity not determined Kant's conduct? As Derrida knows so well, generosity is not a one-way act. Receiving a gift is replete with duty and pressure. Inheritance of any kind is at once a gift and a burden, a ghost to carry as the afterlife of generosity and loss.[56] Someone has lost something, and it is the receiver's duty to generate the worthiness of that loss, to make it meaningful by animating the ghost of giving.

Kant cannot dismiss determination while he lives in the social life of friends; his friends unmake the obsessive independence of his philosophy, leaving him undetermined by his own will to autonomy. Instead, he lives indeterminately. At certain moments, on certain evenings while slumped on a divan, drink-

54 Butler 2021b, p. 48.
55 Battersby 2021, p. 114.
56 See: Derrida and Dufourmantelle 2000; Derrida 1994.

ing wine with his friends, the philosopher of reason renounces autonomy, and underneath that illusive independence, in its excess, he finds the sincerity of friendship.

Uncovered within the logic of rectitude is a surviving inclination that constitutes the possibility of imagining oneself as autonomous. Or, as Rowan knows in his flights through time, eventually you reach a point at which there is nowhere to go but down, nothing to do but fall, and then you need a friend. Which is to say: and then you need to disband your fantasies of upright moral autonomy and give yourself away to a constitutive sociality that reveals the foundational vulnerability that has always formed the core of what kept you standing.

6 Plans for Survival

In the shortest poem of *Living Weapon*, Phillips gives his fullest rumination on the complexity of form. In only two lines, this poem dispossesses form of its primary formality, saturating itself so profoundly with form that the disjunctive survival of a singular body becomes a world-ending event. The poem in full, titled 'Tradition and the Individual Talent', is:

> I wandered through each chartered street
> Till I was shot by the police.[57]

This poem holds within it the history of poetry. The title is taken from an essay by T.S. Eliot, the first line from William Blake's 1794 poem 'London', the length from one of Ezra Pound's early Imagist poems, 'In a Station at the Metro', the iambic tetrameter from Alfred Tennyson's 'In Memoriam', and the scene is shared with so many other contemporary critical poems.

The form of the poem is itself the poem's scene. It plays out within the structure of Tennyson, under the title of Eliot, in direct mimesis of Blake. Everything is determined by a form that precedes the subject who speaks: the form of address has already prescribed the poem's content, structure, and capacity to speak. The form of the poem as a mode of address is fully determined by the history it accumulates. Any expression of itself as a poem is relinquished to this accumulation, displaying only the marks of its determining forces rather than speaking as an independent *I*.

57 Phillips 2021, p. 27.

In this short poem, the body is placed in a street whose code is already established. It has been affirmed by a charter. The spatial plan of the city produces a code that distinguishes the body from the street, the woundable from the chartered. This spatial plan is carried through to an ontic plan that enacts an absolute cut – a dehiscence, as Fred Moten loves to say – in time: the *I* can walk in the city, until the *I* cannot, stopped by a bullet, which was fired by the chartering authority. The spatial plan cuts across the performance of the ontic plan.

But after this absolute cut, the body survives. It is still speaking of the scene in which it is erased. 'If certain lives do not qualify as lives,' as Butler writes, 'or are, from the start, not conceivable as lives within certain epistemological frames, then these lives are never lived nor lost in the full sense.'[58] In the frame of war, the logic that retroactively eradicates the fullness of life and its grievability is made explicit, but the spatial plan maintains this erasure in the civilian city. The *I* of 'Tradition and the Individual Talent' is not fully dead because he was not fully alive, but he was only not fully alive as he wandered each chartered street because that stroll resulted in erasure from the state. The spatial plan works back in time and tampers with the archives of the ontic plan, brushing off the bloodstains.

Grief is expressed already in the spatial plan of the poem itself, in its metre. Iambic tetrameter is used throughout Blake's 'London', an elegy for a miserable city. Wandering through each chartered street, Blake encounters a loss so profound that it steals the final iambic foot of his stanzas:

> And mark in every face I meet
> Marks of weakness, marks of woe.[59]

The wake of grief lives on in its own monstrous stain: everything is grievable because everything is grief, a world of constant movement reduced to a static image of despair.

This metric scheme is universalised as the rhythm of grief by Alfred Tennyson's 'In Memoriam', perhaps the most famous elegy in the history of English poetry. This long 1850 poem, in which the poet reflects on the death of a friend, is entirely in iambic tetrameter. The formal reverberation of this spatial plan emphasises Phillips's poem as an elegy, despite its lack of any sign of mourning. The object of Blake's poem is grief itself, the general condition of

58 Butler 2016, p. 1.
59 Blake 1794.

mourning that pervades the polluted smog of the labouring city. The object of Tennyson's poem is grievable to the extent that he is fully treated as a subject: Tennyson's friend is worth ruminating on at length, and the grief that follows his passing is a public event, spread universally by 'In Memoriam'.

Phillips's *I*, however, has no one to grieve for him; he speaks only of himself. No friend arrives to write the elegy of the *I* who was shot by the police. Instead, he survives, perversely signalling himself as an *I* who was shot but who continues to speak. The problem of agency here is unresolvable. The *I* is shot, absented, and speaks only as the accumulation of the authorities of his genre, literally taking them into his own body like bullets and presenting himself as the animating voices of prior power. And yet he is the speaker of the poem. Given the refusal of originality in the *content* of the poem, the complication Phillips is shooting into subjectivity operates at the level of the poem's *form*.

In the second line, the first and third feet ('Till I' and 'by the') are naturally pronounced as trochees: *Till* I / was *shot* / *by* the / po*lice*. The iambs are turned around, the pressure of their second syllable pushed back to the first.

The two inverted iambs refer to the agency of the scene: who was shot, and who shot. The narrative subjects here are 'I' and 'police'. According to the spatial plan, the architectonics of the spectacle, the one who shoots is the subject, this uncountable force called *the police*, and the one who is shot is the object, the receiver of action. In the ontic plan, the linguistic script that undergirds the positioning of these relations, though, the subject is the speaker, the one who claims the protagonist primacy of *I*, while the object is both that which is spoken about and that which assumes no full human force: *the police*, unnamed, incalculable, unembodied; a ubiquitous force that expands to fill space.

The *I*'s formation of agency is undermined by the trochaic inversion of the second line. Both 'Till I' and 'by the' do not fit the iambic continuity of the poem's literary references, the cradling rhythm of Tennyson and Blake. The emphasis instead is placed on opposite parts of the foot in each trochaic instance: in the first, the subject is unstressed, left silent after the temporal marker (**till** I), while in the second the agency of the subject is stressed (**by** the). It is *the agency of the object* in the spatial plan of the scene that does not fit the scene's material relations. *I*, in the spatial plan, is the object, the one who was shot, but his own referent to himself as 'I' is removed by the trochaic twist: I is $_{\text{I}}$, minute and silenced, the wounded body, wandering and shot, lost and lost, unmapped and unlifed. 'I' was always lost already, wandering the city streets in search of an ontic plan that would survive, that would make this moving loss finally grievable.

The police, meanwhile, is the expansive institution of the street, the formless accumulation of power that cuts one's wandering, one's being-lost, and turns it into loss, into the ungrievable absence of life. In the ontic plan (what we hear), once again, the police is the *object*, the one not speaking, but in the spatial plan (what we see), the police is the *subject*, the one acting. Within the very mechanics of the ontic plan, the spatial dominates: the police has assumed the position of agency by the stressed syllable *by* over and against the unstressed *the*: *by* affords emphatic primacy to those who shoot.

And yet the ontic plan somehow survives. Which reminds me: despite a resolute projection of rectitude, of proper philosophy performed alone in a serious position, Kant's joyous goblet of friendship and love survives in the archives. And *I* survives as poetry despite his erasure from the primacy of syllabic stress.

7 A Moving Abstraction in Blue

The question left, then, is why this wandering *I* was shot by the police, which ultimately – since we must ask *in which present* the speaker survives and in which he does not – will come down to a question of the form of presence, the form assumed by the present. In the eponymous essay 'Tradition and the Individual Talent', a hundred years older than Phillips's poem, T.S. Eliot argues that poetry should properly be an impersonal reflection on history. It is the poet's mature reflection on history that removes the personal from poetry. One past – 'the mind of Europe' – operates in one present, a present that, in its singular sacrifice, folds back into that singular past as its animating differentiation.[60] This whole present and whole past affect each other, but the possibility of alternative contemporaneous presents is unimaginable.

The subject of Eliot's essay is the proper conduct of a poem, the official charter of verse, decreeing how a poem should walk. If the poet is shot, the poem should not stumble. The past in which the poet was walking is not aware of the present in which a shooting occurs, and it would be unfaithful of the poet to fall over while his upright past is so intent on proper rectitude: 'the difference between the present and the past is that the conscious present is an awareness of the past in a way and to an extent which the past's awareness of itself cannot show.'[61] Which means: don't fall over; don't incline the way the bullet pulls you.

60 Eliot 2001, p. 1094.
61 Ibid.

So why does Rowan incline? Why does he fall when he is shot? Something like a reason occurs to Rowan a few pages earlier, in 'Mortality Ode', which by the by is perhaps my favourite ever poem. In this incredibly simple and impossibly complex scene, Rowan goes into a phone store to get his phone repaired. Two police cars pull up and four officers follow him into the shop, not to follow him, but to fix their phones. Rowan sits and waits, watching the officers who wait. And that is it.

The officers are part of the nature of this quotidian urban scene. One of them 'leans / Forward, like a dark blue crane' – like a bird with a long neck, or the hoisting machines that punctuate the skyline of the city?[62] This leaning in that the officer performs seems semantically a little like inclination, but its possible ethics is immediately refuted in an astounding encyclopaedia of the mechanics of power:

> … The person at the front
> Of the line, over whose shoulder he makes concrete
> The coarse abstraction of his presence, doesn't turn.
> The woman behind the counter asks the officer for his name, which
> begins
> With Officer, she tells him he's now in the system,
> She'll call him when it's his turn, to make himself
> Comfortable. …

This is a scene, archetypally, of interpellation, of being called into being by and as authority. The strange twist of the subject position in the clause beginning 'over whose shoulder' emphasises the porousness of power's instantiation of subjects in this scene. The shoulder belongs to someone (the person at the front of the line? The officer?) and, through that belonging, regardless of to whom it belongs, affirms the ubiquity of possession as the logic upholding these relations in the act of exchange. This ubiquity eradicates the individual meaning of *whose* possession any object is, an indistinction emphasised in the grammar of the poem by its consecutive clauses parted only by commas, despite the semantically distinct sentences. As possessions, objects are mystified into a continuous, indistinguishable form.

Qua power, the officer exists as the embodiment of a name, a universal and anonymous name that is not less name-like because of that but rather universalises itself as the authority of naming. His name *begins* with Officer and then

62 Phillips 2021, p. 14.

disappears, the rest redacted. He is not so much *a name* as *naming* itself. This being-as-authority is, by this fact, exposed as not quite a concrete moment in the scene. Instead he is labelled incomparably as a 'coarse abstraction', which Marx would have said in the exact same way if he was a poet in 21st century New York.

A threat is posed by the officer leaning into others, casting a shadow of authority that poses the imminent possibility of erasure. The person at the front of the queue could be erased, and the officer instead placed at the front of the queue. The core of the possible duplicity of inclination is the existence of Officer, of the official discourse of authority.

As the officers stand around pretending to be busy, everyone else seated and silent in the shop, Rowan wonders what affords these officers their authority:

> ... like all of them
> Unbalanced but propped up by strange gravity now visible,
> A monochrome, unearned elegance.
> He orbits us, curious for a moment about
> His future, about what will be in his hand when
> It's not reaching into a holster, when he checks the weather
> And wonders what in the world to wear.[63]

The possibility of imagining himself without a uniform – unofficered – denudes this officer, throwing him from the position of authority into a lack of balance whose gravity is visible. That dark blue mask he wears is what keeps him fixed in position, in the duplicity of the aggressive incline, the lean-in that demands to break through, rather than exposing itself in vulnerability to the other.

This vulgar exposure – this moment of visible gravity, the trick revealed, the strings holding up the puppet accidentally caught in the light – forces the officer to attempt a confirmation of his authority. 'He leans forward the way his partner did as though he is / Learning something or remembering something / Or being someone learning something or / Remembering something'.[64] The imitative, empty performance of power emerges, and Rowan understands the terrible lie of this inclination: the officers, all along, were erect, standing upright, only miming someone who is leaning in.

63 Ibid., pp. 14–15.
64 Ibid.

The manipulative mimesis of power begins the violence that will condition the rest of *Living Weapon*. Although it is a mostly subtle and discursive violence, it will break everything. All along, Rowan now knows, officers were appropriating the inclination of social life as the abyssal surface of their murderous performance, but behind it, always, in the formal structure of their power, they were standing high and upright, never able to understand what their leaning bodies meant.

Suddenly the store worker comes out of the back room and gives Rowan his repaired phone.

> I turn the phone on: the black screen ignites, singing
> A single, held passionate note, a pretense
> Of life, then stops, revealing my home
> Screen. Everything I had before looks up at me now
> From the sleek mirage of short-lived newness,
> Short-lived lightness, but it's pretty, though.[65]

Two presents are thrown forth by this poem's understanding of history: one is the value-form, by means of which commodities, including labour-power, are valorised; the other is the living past of Rowan's memories, his photos and the phone numbers of his friends and all the messages of love and longing he sent and received, his shared memory of social life awakening again as a fugitive moment of survival. Beside the present of commodity exchange and in the excess of the present of Officer's deadly official authority, a formless presence survives.

This present, this brilliant other-present poeticised as the fugitive survival of (black[66]) social life, is shared with the phone store worker:

> The guy who's been helping me, without looking up
> From his monitor, his hands still resting on
> His keyboard like hands holding the end of a net,
> Asks me – his voice quick as a Camaro –
> If I think I'll want protection for that
> Because you never know: you never ever know.[67]

65 Ibid.

66 Phillips is rarely explicit about the movements of raciality in his poetry. In this poem, the speaker's immediate discomfort around the officers seems to arise as a function of his unspoken race (Phillips is black). This shared moment with the store worker is also a feature of blackness: he is referred to as 'the brother'.

67 Phillips 2021, p. 16.

The impending erasure of his presence that will occur in 'Tradition and the Individual Talent' is staged in this intimate, shared moment of vulnerability.

In order to situate one's 'private' mind in a 'much more important mind,'[68] a mind that is 'among the dead' of poets past,[69] as Eliot writes, one must first imagine oneself as stably alive in the present, as inhabiting an invulnerable present that is not at risk of collapsing through the dead past at any moment. One must be able to imagine oneself, like the officers in the phone store, as bearing the capacity to lean in without opening oneself to the other, without collapsing one's illusory autonomy as a finite body in the absolute and universal present.

Across four poems – '1776', 'Mortality Ode', 'Tradition and the Individual Talent', and 'The Golden Hour' – Phillips forges an irreparable wound in the authoritative subjectivity of modernity and its presupposition of the body as the moral form of rectitude that can be upheld in the invulnerable singularity of the present. Phillips gives us instead an experience of another present, a time unimaginable to Kant or Eliot, a time of fugitive survival in which inclination is the ethical practice of shared vulnerability, and in which the experience of sociality precedes the form of its moral authority.

In our wandering, we have arrived back at the street where Kant walks. Some call him the ultimate upright man, while others observe a sneaky incline. Somehow I am inclined to think that this ambivalent ground between rectitude and inclination will open an ethics that disrupts the rhythm of subjectivity, positioning its politics as the mediation of love and rage, of standing up and leaning in.

8 Citing Friends

If Kant loves drinking with his friends, if they make funny goblets for each other, if he is kind and warm and sociable, then what happens to philosophy? The spatial plan of ontology and morality is fully chartered, every movement demarcated by the script of possibility. The whole city is built already, and renovations do not fundamentally disrupt the position of streets and buildings. Bodies might experience a certain kind of agency in choosing which street to take, but the possibility of not taking *a street* or, more importantly, of *not going somewhere* is absolutely unavailable to them. One must abide by the charter of the streets, whichever way one goes.

---

68 Eliot 2001, p. 1094.

69 Ibid., p. 1093.

But maybe Kant, in the end, was never Kantian. I was speaking to the literary theorist Duncan M. Yoon at a bar in Stockholm and he said, 'There is no need to resolve the contradictions of Kant, no need to destroy his entire legacy or try to excuse his racism.' The poet Judith Kiros, a friend of mine who was also present, said, 'Exactly. Politics is a messy combination of love and fury.'

Kant never quotes his friends, hiding them from his readers. He never wrote about the goblet of his loving comrades. What does it mean to erase the presence of one's social life from the mark one leaves on literature? What is involved in the decision to neatly delineate the parameters of serious study, with friends permanently excluded from the institutional charter of the published text? Friends are not reliable sources. Kant is a reliable source. But Kant has friends, scandalously. I might even say, if you'll let me, friends:

> He wandered through each chartered street
> Till he was cited by his friends.

Citing him places him in their sights, as a site that is seeable, which is all very Kantian (*citation needed*). But what it also does is place him in the failure of citation, the slip and spill that always results from attempts at mimesis. A twisted remnant of an ontic plan survives despite the domination of the spatial, an ontic plan whose life has an unmappable plan for this uncitable city of friends. Before the moral-form of friendship, there is the material experience of friends.

Kant's main moral proposition is this: I know what I ought to do before I have any experience of this obligation, and what I ought to do produces the world I experience; but it only produces a moral world if it is, precisely, experienced as an *obligation*, not a desire. I do what I ought to do because I *have* to, not because I *want* to.

In Kantian friendship, there is no *will* to be a friend, no inclination toward another through the allure of desire, the experience of laughter. There is only upright, rational, and objective duty. As my friend Jens Eriksson says, Kant's theory of friendship sounds strangely like the theory of someone who has no friends, and no experience of friendship. So what about Kant's friends? In the closing section of this chapter, I attempt a dismissal of Kant's denial of friendship, offering him instead a friendly invitation into the ethics of inclination.

9 Planning Plans

Once the ontic plan – as what (a) being is – is revealed as simultaneously disrupted by and an internal disruption within the spatial plan – as where (a) being goes and *can* go – then a contention opens in Kantian ethics: synthetic judgment *a priori* is not possible, because it is not fully *a priori*.

Presupposed in Kant's category of the *a priori* is recognition of liveability. The subject who accesses a form of knowledge that precedes experience must be recognised *a posteriori* as a subject. This recognition occurs after the experience of knowledge. But before *one*'s experience, there is the experience of sociality. In the Second Critique, Kant gives the example of friends who resist deceiving each other because they fear already the *absence of the experience of friendship*, which reveals them as given over already to an *experience* of friendship.[70] Before the rational duty not to deceive, there is the experience of friendship and its loss through deceit.

For Kant, judgments are moral because of their form rather than their content, or their spatial plan rather than their ontic plan. It does not matter which act the judgment contains, nor its purpose. It only matters that it reveals something about the world in a form that precedes experience, that is knowable to everyone, and that can be universally practiced.

The long-standing critique of Kant's categorical imperative is that the universality it relies on (which Kant is very adamant about) is never truly universal. That is, the *content* of the categorical imperative is false. However, while I certainly agree with this long history of anti-Kantian critique, Phillips's poetry – as the surviving disruption of the ontic in the spatial plan – gives us a feeling for the falsity of its *form*, which is where it hurts for Kant. It is, it seems, not *a priori*, and therefore there is no synthetic *a priori*, and therefore there is no moral law. Which really means: there is no Kant as a philosopher, that upright man who marks his spatial plan as the expansive proposition of proper sense, but only Kant as a friend, that ontic singularity who shares wine mugs with the ones he loves.

When Kant is given a goblet by his friends and that goblet survives, hidden in the archives of the history of philosophy, Kant has relinquished the presupposed autonomy of his actions. His afterlife has been determined by his friends. His capacity to act upon the world is not free of outside influence, imposed by rational moral law on his surroundings. Kant is redetermined by the social life of his friends. When I say 'Kant' and I think of him with his friends, drinking wine from a pretty cup, I make a synthetic judgment *a posteriori*, a judgment that follows from the cause of experience. And that is to say, as I will elaborate on in the coming chapter: before the imposition of power as the command of Reason, there is social life, a social life that is indeterminable in the calculations of power.

---

70 Kant 1999, p. 210.

Kant's happy determination by his friends, though, is not disruptive of his project *per se*, since he does not pose reason as existing in the world of appearances but rather in the human mind, or the world of understanding, as a function of how we regard ourselves. This way of regarding ourselves, as Kant finally studies at the end of the *Groundwork*, is determined by the world of things in themselves, a world our reason is separate from. Here a problem opens.

Our reason is not autonomous, since the world in itself is at least partially autonomous and determines what is available to us as reason. So Kant provides an excuse. The noumenal world is in fact partially created by our own imposing reason: our acts, guided by our rational subjectivity, affect the world, a world which then contains our effects, so when in its turn it affects us, we are partially affecting ourselves.[71] Through this operation, for Kant, we come to understand the cohesion between the world of understanding and the world of sense, which is bound in the (rational) human mind by *reason*, by which we intuit that we ought to act on the proposition that coheres, 'and this *categorical* ought represents a synthetic proposition *a priori*.'[72]

But what is actually happening in this excuse? As free and autonomous rational beings, free from 'inclinations and impulses,'[73] we are also members of the world of sense; we are caught in the interplay of things in themselves and our apprehension of them in our rational faculties. Dialectically, these objects determine each other, and each determining agency carries something of its 'ought' into the other, conditioning the autonomous object with a moral will that proves its morality through this determination. The world of sense, that is, reaches into what Kant adamantly regards as his uninclined, autonomous consciousness, and leaves a residue of sensuality, of its feelings in the world. Carrying that emotional duty, Kant finds himself enlightened by an *a priori* awareness of what friendship is, a synthetic knowledge of the world of pleasurable relations. But what gave to him this knowledge of the joy of loved ones? Without an ontic plan – an antecedent feeling of being-loved – the spatial plan of transcendental perception would be merely mechanical and therefore not productive of moral sense.

As Kant has already said early in the *Groundwork*, ideal friendship is the duty of every friend, even if one will never truly experience ideal friendship because as a duty it exists 'prior to all experience, in the idea of a reason determining the will by means of *a priori* grounds.'[74] The faculty of reason knows friendship, and

71 Kant 1997, 4:453–4, pp. 57–9.
72 Ibid., 4:454, p. 58.
73 Ibid., 4:454, p. 59.
74 Ibid., 4:408, p. 20.

gives that knowledge to the will, before any experience of friendship. But our reason, as Kant acknowledges, is determined by nature and by our experience of the effect of our own actions, which have in their turn affected nature. In the dialectics of experience, what we understand as reason *before* experience folds back into a material experience that grounds the possibility of reason.

It is to the example of friendship that Kant returns again and again throughout his texts. In the *Critique of Practical Reason*, as I noted above, he writes that 'every even moderately honorable man' has been in the position where it would be easy to deceive a friend for his own gain, but he chooses not to, solely 'not to have to despise himself secretly in his own eyes.'[75] Even his moderate honour stops him from deceiving a friend. But why? This moderately good friend *knows*, somehow, somewhere inside his moral capacity, that his friend would be hurt by this act of deceit and would probably stop being his friend. He has experienced the deceit of friends, and knows of its possibility because deceit, of course, exists in the world. This knowledge of the experience of friendship, and the possibility of the loss of this experience, prohibits him from deceiving his friend. That is, *before* the *a priori* reason of moral duty, there has already been an *experience* of friends and the possibility of the loss of that experience.

Before the autonomous freedom of the subject, then, there is the experience of friendship. Before reason's investment in the possibility of experience in the world of sense, something of that world has already left its friendly rhythm on the internal world of understanding, which then inscribes itself back into the objects themselves, claiming to have made them all on its own. But friendship was there first, underlying the individual order of reason.

The suspended grief of friendlessness, the sad possibility of losing social life, has already given rise to the possibility of imagining one's own animating reason, which – if this is indeed the case – undermines the entire formal apparatus of Kantian morality.

Kant freely recognises the illusion of freedom that he proposes. His will to freedom is determined already by the laws of nature, so we must think of the subject as split between one side that is free and another that is determined, otherwise philosophy would fall into a ruinous contradiction.[76] Kant is friendly enough to offer us the secret of his impossibility, even if at the very end of the book. He does not lie to his friends; he is an upstanding incliner, a moral actor of contradictions.

---

75 Kant 1999, p. 210.

76 Kant 1997, 4:456, p. 60. Also: ibid., 4:459, p. 63.

Before the form called Kant, there is a friend called Immanuel, holding out a wine glass. Which is, really, all I want to say about Kant, and all that Phillips gives us to understand about the conditions of subject-production in this capitalist post-Enlightenment. Whatever illusory object we name as 'reason' is the residue of the social life of friends that survives in excess of our individuated will.

In his poem 'Child of Nature', Phillips provides a response to Kant's friendly contradictions:

> What forms
> First: a thing or its form? The I or me?
> The maker or the thinker? A bird's-eye
> View of the life, what Arnold called the din
> Of strife, a little like Floyd's "Us and Them,"
> Soothed the doom of numb Zoom rooms. But what sweet
> Prison's not still a prison? What kind heart
> Isn't bathed in blood? What mind doesn't mind
> Being the mind's second act? …[77]

The real contention of Phillips's Phillis Wheatley-esque neoclassical musings is not clear until the end of the verse, an architectural biography that finds the antecedent condition of the poet:

> … My soul
> Has grown from a Bronx tenement's power.
> My Old Testament: a corner store's joy
> At being part of the life of things.[78]

Phillips says to Kant: *you were made by the goblet, my friend, and so were your friends; the glass itself was made by an experience that precedes the form that makes you, and that experience is friends.*

For Kant, the form of judgment must precede its content. There must be a universal judgment accessible to any experience of the world, entering as a synthetic *a priori* before individual experience. But, as Phillips writes in this recent poem, that form is already part of the life of things, things that assume the form of a building, a tenement, a structured spatial plan for life, but way before that,

77 Phillips 2023. Later published in Phillips 2024, pp. 43–8.
78 Ibid.

everywhere the spatial plan cannot reach, is the ontic plan of things. In the world of sense, the social life of friends has its own plan, and that plan – as Kant knows without knowing it – extends its animating survival into the bordered spatial plan of reason.

The point for Kant is that to be moral we must not *feel* for others, or *feel* others at all. We must, instead, be guided only by disinterested duty.[79] The antagonism I want to throw into this moral order is the seemingly simple question: what happens, then, when we feel duty? Feeling is against duty in the Kantian schema, a schema that has given rise to the ideal disinterestedness of the apparently free market and its competitive, possessive subject.

Neither our disinterested removal from moral concern nor our concerned moral empathy are neutral, as Butler writes. Rather, the conditions of power create 'this differential at the level of affective and moral responsiveness,'[80] which, for Butler, is a responsibility held in the fact that one's own feeling for the world is never separated from that world; the differential worthiness of feeling afforded to certain subjects imposes on everyone a duty to be *interested*, a universal obligation of concern for this ruinous differential computation, arising from the fact that it is from social life that feeling emerges. 'Our affect is never merely our own; affect is, from the start, communicated from elsewhere.'[81]

For Butler, indeed, it is not only the *presence* of this differentially wounded social life that opens and obliges ethics, but its absence also. 'Affect depends upon social supports for feeling: we come to feel only in relation to perceivable loss, one that depends on social structures of perception.'[82] In recognising others as formed by the possibility of *loss*, of grieving and being grieved, of being constituted in the obscure experience of sociality that gives the possibility of subjective moral experience, what is recognised is precisely the indeterminacy of ethical social life. As Phillips goes on in 'Child of Nature',

> … heathen
> Sunday mornings, and phosphorescent grief.
> No one is ever alone with their thoughts.
> Alone on a cliff or here beside me,
> We are crowded by presence …[83]

---

79 Kant 1997, 4:399, p. 13.
80 Butler 2016, p. 50.
81 Ibid.
82 Ibid.
83 Phillips 2023.

Grief precedes and overrides the false aloneness of our thoughts. Phillips's approach here works alongside Butler's strongly anti-Kantian theory of the body, its vulnerability and differential grievability. Both, in the ethics of their grief, incline towards obscure others, toward the fundamental primacy of friends. 'If I survive,' as Butler writes, 'it is only because my life is nothing without the life that exceeds me, that refers to some indexical you, without whom I cannot be.'[84]

If there is no synthetic *a priori* and the experience of social life undergirds the form of the subject, then there is no universal morality; there is no command that initiates the psychic solitude of a single mind's solid walls. The subject is already porous and exposed to sociality, the 'I' already a Bronx tenement and the excess of its power in the life of things.

In this staging of the city, the simultaneously quotidian and esoterically poetic portraits of life in Phillips's poetry, the interests of modernity are held and given over to an inclination towards primary sociality that topples the mystifying rectitude of form. Phillips offers us the experience of primary social life, which Kant, despite everything he ever said, knew all about through the gift economy of his drunken friends. Phillips and Kant, in the end, are comrades in their anti-Kantian communism.

What I have attempted to show in this chapter is the formal structure that undergirds and upholds the temporality of the subject. In the first of the three temporalities of subjection that I posited in the overview of Part 2, value-form theorists understand the subject as a total form produced by the requirements of value, which form-determines the possibility of relations. There are many disagreements regarding the extent of this determination – whether *all* conduct is commodified by the value-form, including nonproductive moments of social sharing such as cooking for friends or caring for loved-ones, or whether there is a necessary excess of social reproduction that cannot be fully determined by value[85] – but throughout value-critical Marxisms, the temporality in which *social life historically and logically follows value-production* remains consistent, as I studied in chapter one.

My general contention in *Poetics of Value* is that social life in fact *precedes* the production of subjects and *exceeds* its form-determination by value. In chapters two and three, I attempted to study the relations and constitutive subjective contradictions that expose a prior social life. In this chapter, I have attempted to posit this social life as *surviving* in the material presence of

84 Butler 2016, p. 44.

85 For an overview of these debates, see: Rey-Araújo 2024.

friends, a surviving materiality that exceeds the full determination of friendship as a form, which I have read through the archetypal formal temporality posited by Kant at the very beginnings of industrial capitalism.

Having now exposed a social life that precedes the production of subjects, and found that social life to be a surviving material presence in the present, in chapter five I turn to the *insurgency* of this survival, studying the ways this fugitive persistence of sociality antagonises the totalising temporal present of form-determined subjects. In order to bring out the *insurgency* of the primacy of friends, I turn to Fred Moten's poetry, which I read with and against Judith Butler's work on the temporality of subjection.

CHAPTER 5

Fred Moten and the Primary Antagonism

1 Assembling a Friendship

Throughout his corpus, as I have mentioned various times already in previous chapters, Fred Moten emphasises a temporality of struggle that situates sociality as primary. This temporality arises also in other critical traditions, but Moten is particularly concerned with its necessity to radical struggles.[1] In a 2020 interview, Moten's longtime collaborator Stefano Harney makes this temporal primacy clear:

> Insurgency is primary. Rebellion comes first. We don't rebel against the police because there's police. The police come after us if we show ourselves as that primary antagonism. … What does it mean to show ourselves? Well, what it *doesn't* mean is that somebody who is an individual is walking along and gets killed by the cops. That's what we see once we've moved into the frame of visualization. … There is something that called those cops out *before* that person. … There's this general antagonism which blurs the distinction of any individual person. [The narrative of critiques of the police is] 'you've failed to see the individual', but that's because *you actually are the maker of the individual*, as a cop. … The police are there to separate us from our social wealth … and yet it is at the same time the most obvious failure of the police to actually make this stick.[2]

The stakes of the primary antagonism of sociality are here affirmed theoretically: the police as archetype of authority arrive to individuate the assembly of sociality, which exists already in and as insurgency. In what precise form, though, does insurgency survive before the individuating authorities of the state and the police? How does sociality live before the emergence of named individuals marked in the codes of authority? Is this temporality of individuation singular, operating at the scale of each person's life, or sociohistorical, operating through broader political movements?

---

1 See: 'Introduction', above.

2 Moten and Harney 2020a, minutes 15–17. Original spoken emphasis.

Practical political answers to these questions are difficult to locate in Moten's work. While, as he consistently proclaims in interviews, Moten is certainly dedicated to radical struggles, the range of his objects and areas of study and the performative play of his writing make any tangible political project seem lost in poetic abstractions. Both the primacy of sociality he continuously attends to and the poetic routes he takes to describing it are the basis of many criticisms of Moten, which see his work as obscuring a materialist plan for struggle.

In this chapter, I am interested in bringing Moten's theoretical and poetic works into conversation with another radical theorist who has long been dismissed for their idealism and lack of historical materialist critique: Judith Butler. My contention is that bringing these theorists together can expose the material and radical politics of a temporality they share: sociality comes before individuation. Where they differ is on the relation of this sociality to constitutive authority. For Moten, as Harney lays out above, power arrives after the insurgency of sociality. For Butler, meanwhile, power and sociality are historically tangled in a process of continuous mutual constitution, through which each remains forever reliant on the other.

In what follows, I closely read the corpuses of Moten and Butler to bring out the political meaning and matter of this temporality of struggle. I begin by looking at the precise position of each theorist. I then test the validity of their temporalities by placing them in relation to a famous theoretical scene of power and individuation: Louis Althusser's scene of interpellation, when a police officer produces a subject by calling upon an individual with the refrain, 'Hey, you there!' In the final section, with a turn to Gramscian hegemony, I propose a politics of the primacy of sociality.

2 Listening to B

Throughout Moten's work, there is a remarkable erasure of the borders of genre, to the extent that often there is little to distinguish his books published as poetry and as philosophy. Very little, though, has been written about his poetry, despite its deeply theoretical grounding. In this section, I bring out the temporality of struggle in Moten's corpus by focusing on his third collection of poetry, *B Jenkins* (2010).

In *B Jenkins*, a direct act of social interpellation opens every poem, with the title summoning a famous singer and/or theorist: 'billie holiday/roland barthes'; 'alexander weheliye, lygia clark, ed roberson'. The whole collection is named after Moten's mother, B Bernese Moten, known as B Jenkins, who worked as a schoolteacher.[3] The collection is a mourning ritual, calling on the social life that produced a lost and loved mother.

The constitutive social life of Moten's poetry arises from his mother's pedagogy. As Moten says, discussing his mother's pedagogical relationship with her own mother, B Jenkins's pedagogy comes

> under the rubric of respect: to not interrupt, pay attention, don't ask questions, if you pay attention you will figure it out, if you don't pay attention you won't, and if you ask questions, that's not paying attention. So just sit there and watch. … Ain't nobody *teaching* you, … but we will let you watch. … After being on the earth together as cooks for fifty years, my mother … and my grandmother … might *eventually* have a conversation about cornbread, and it'd be deep, and it'd be theoretically rigorous.[4]

This pedagogy relinquishes the duty on the other to accurately assume the performance of the teacher. The disciple-other remains outside the practice of the master-I, relieved of the expectation to conform to a singular set of practices determined by the master-I. Instead, an opening is provided, an opening that exposes an already ongoing practice.

This maternal pedagogy brings out not only a method of learning, but also an artistic practice, which Moten understands specifically as the mode of black performance. 'What I love about black performance is that it is a zone in which the distinction between audience and performer breaks down,' Moten says.[5] In both pedagogical and artistic relations, there is no position of mastery, since the master does not function as a repository for the impossible fantasies of the disciple's individuation, and the disciple is not suspended at the unbearable threshold of needing to become and yet never being able to become the master. What occurs instead in this black performance of pedagogy is the maintenance of the distinction between master-I and disciple-other, setting up an ethical relation without the rubrics of determination. The disciple is opened to a social life that exceeds the format of their pedagogical relation; outside it and before it, the master is already involved in a social process, which is then opened for the disciple to access.

In the opening poem of *B Jenkins*, also titled 'b jenkins', Moten's mother is named through a complex of metonyms that intersects at both the specific life of B Jenkins and the broader history of black America.

---

3 White 2021.

4 Abdurraqib and Moten 2021, 20–2.

5 Ibid., 19.

> Her territory sunflower, insurgent floor time in real time in the field museum – bertha lee and her lyric ways and her urban plan. up and down[6]

The Delta blues singer Bertha Lee assumes the position of a master without mastery, a teacher who allows her student to sit and listen in a 'field museum' that spans the semantic topographies of *fields* where cotton grows, plantations, the archetypal American spectacle of racist mastery, and of *museums*, where the enclosure of survival is displayed. This is both a territory – the privatisation of space, the restriction of movement to the possessive grasp of ownership – and a sunflower, which always finds a way to look toward its source of life, scouting out the sun.

In the moment of dancing to Bertha Lee's swinging blues, there is no temporal positioning of the past; it is not suspended in a discrete place that is no longer accessible. It is, instead, the 'insurgent floor time' of 'real time', and it is real because it is experienced as the organisation of social life, as the urban plan. This movement between Moten, Jenkins, and Lee, across the whole of the twentieth century, is the way poetry speaks 'one more time about the theory of who we are',[7] which breaks the text into a right-justified bridge:

> In the names away in blocks
> with double names to interrupt and
> gather, kept dancing in tight circles
> between break and secret, ...[8]

The 'theory of who we are' is separated from the act of naming. Names are 'away in blocks', doubled somehow in a gathering of dances that encloses another secret. In the break between the movements of this dance, there is a way of knowing one another beyond the relation to power presupposed in the fact of naming. Both the named people in the poem, indeed, use a name that is not quite their own: Lee's birth name was Bertha Lee Pate, and she later added her common-law husband's surname, Patton; and B Jenkins was a nickname for Miss Moten.[9]

In the third poetic paragraph, returning to prose but indented slightly more than the first paragraph, a 'you' emerges from the confusion of 'who we are'.

6 Moten 2010, p. 1.
7 Ibid.
8 Ibid.
9 See: White 2021.

'You' as a referent from the poet to themself is a familiar trope, but in Moten it assumes a particularly arbitrary referent. Nothing is called into being by this 'you' but the activity of past reflection itself: the rumination on this act of listening, of learning from and mourning the afterlives of Lee and Jenkins, is a practice in which people gather to hear the song, in which the dance is the movement bringing the past into now as much as it throws the present into the living past of Lee and Jenkins.

> Now the cold new reckoning is tired and you've been
> waiting for a preferential song. the multiplex should be in the
> frame like bodies in a house way back in the woods ...[10]

Within the tangle of identities that places Moten and a universal 'you' at the feet of the singer (Lee) and the listener (Jenkins), himself a secondary listener learning to listen, in this passage an ethical obligation arises: the multiplex *should* be in the frame. The semantic complexity here is typical of Moten's work. A multiplex has both a visual and sonic referent. It is, in one sense, a cinema that shows various movies on different screens, a significantly American visual technology. In another sense, multiplex communication occurs when many signals are combined into one: various vibrations cohere as one sound, as an intelligible rhythm. A multiplex is the mode of bringing multiple sounds into harmony. It is the technology of making music.

The formation of music is the ethics of sociality: relinquish the illusion of one's solo, and instead sit and listen to others, knowing, foremost, that you only ever picked up that instrument because the band was already playing. '[T]he multiplex should be in the frame' becomes a reformulation of the arch-ethical question for Judith Butler: 'How ought I to treat you?'[11] The *ought* of ethics, in Moten, becomes a way of dismissing entirely the ethical presupposition of a break between *one* and *other*: one must learn how to act without the illusory independence of subjectivity, instead with the ethics of having been shared, realising that one is given to the sound that others, long before us, have already made.

In the collection's next poem, 'gayl jones', Moten brings this musical concern with insurgency as the erasure of interpersonal ethics to a personal scale. After discussing memories of childhood and his family, Moten writes:

---

10 Moten 2010, p. 1.

11 Butler 2005, p. 25. Years later, Butler significantly removes the other (the mysterious 'you') from 'the basic ethical and political question,' becoming 'how ought I to act[?]' Butler 2015a, p. 23.

… cried sometimes in the same
broke off the same piece left each other

the last piece practiced the same piece
got warm on the same. however,
I'm so full this morning I have
to try and make you understand[12]

Sustenance is shared between the players in the poem, breaking off the same piece. This sharing opens an ambivalent scene: they both *left each other* a piece of what was broken off, sharing a single substance, and *left each other* to realise the impossibility of their mutual singularity, since to be shared with one another presupposes a separation that itself constitutes ethics: 'How ought I to try treat you?' is at once an ethical demand and a recognition of the other's fundamental otherness.

This sharing is a condition of life, as the 'last piece' must be shared, but it is also the condition for the coming together of those who share, as a piece of music or of dance practiced together. From this intense sociality, rooted in an ethical ambivalence that desires the other while requiring a fundamental separation that maintains the other's place outside the I, then comes the ethical demand on oneself: the I is full, stuffed with meaning, warm from the dance of practicing the piece, and overflowing with the sociality of sharing, so much so that only a demand is left: 'I have / to try and make you understand'.

This poem itself is given a semantic code in the obligations of ethics. It *must* teach you, but not by teaching you. Rather, by speaking while you listen, by inviting you into the ritual site where knowing is already taking place; the reader's invitation into the ongoing life of learning, the circle of sharers that is already gathered, is the pedagogical obligation poeticised in the frame of ethics.

The sociality to which Moten appeals in his poetry refuses the presumption of individuation – as authorship and as singular poetic speaker – on textual and paratextual planes. In a more recent collection, *All That Beauty*, each poem is written explicitly with a list of others, including friends and colleagues like R.A. Judy, Denise Ferreira da Silva, Elizabeth Povinelli, and Stefano Harney, artists and collaborators like Arthur Jafa and Wu Tsang, and family members like Laura Harris (Moten's partner) and Lorenzo Moten (their son). The precedents and friends who surround Moten's poetry and theory are present in

12 Moten 2010, p. 2.

the assembly that exceeds the textual form presented to any reader. Instead of *producing* a text for a reader, Moten exposes the reader to a conversation that has always been happening. His poetry is not an interpersonal exchange in the symbolic order of power, but the social life that has been shared in the excess of being as one in relation to an other.

In this sense, Moten's poetry has a peculiar way of gathering as poetry. What is on the page is a minor expression of the poem's poetry. In *B Jenkins*, jazz singers intersect with Moten's parents and friends; American history merges with the temporality of personal memory. The poetry is a practice of feeling history, of mourning those who cannot be mourned, most fundamentally *with* those whose mourning is both ongoing and impossible. In the present of the poem, social life has been foreclosed, and Moten's poetic act is to fugitively break out into the ongoing past in which that sociality survives. As far as I understand it, this is the primacy of social insurgency in his poetry.

Moten follows the living residue of foreclosed social life in the excess of its violent erasure. This functions as an attempt to refute power's function as the subsumption of the struggle to the point that power itself appears as the *a priori* grounding of struggle. When moments of struggle erupt on the street, it seems as if any insurgency occurs in retaliation to power, directly countering police aggression or destructive governmental policies. But that is exactly the ideological intention of power's erasure of the struggle's antecedence.[13]

Instead, for Moten (and Harney), the struggle is always ongoing, but has been hidden. The mark of people's constitution is worn as social life, but is perceivable in the normative function of power only as competition and further individuation.[14] Despite the requirements of white supremacist modernity that demand the constant submission of racialised populations to the productive mechanisms of racist capitalism, black *life* survives in a gathering of sociality that exceeds the temporality in which black *lives* are killed. 'Even though they kill every one of us,' as Moten says, 'they can't kill us all.'[15]

This primacy, however, can appear as a simple state of nature, an apolitical *a priori* ontology in which social life exists without threat or insurgency. Kevin Ochieng Okoth argues that Moten's dedication to a social life that is *already* fugitive, already at an ontological level living separately from the totalising violence of capital and its raciality, necessarily forecloses organised political struggle against the authorities of violence.[16] For Okoth, Moten's 'Black radic-

13 Moten 2018b, p. 44.
14 See: Moten 2018a, p. 76.
15 Moten and Harney 2020a, minute 21.
16 Okoth 2023.

alism always-already *is*.'[17] Antiracist resistance, then, is not a constitutive part of politics, but rather exists in a given social context that necessarily exceeds politics. This social focus on blackness 'precludes Black people's participation in radical politics by confining resistance to spaces outside of the political sphere.'[18]

Annie Olaloku-Teriba similarly argues that Moten is a 'comfortable antagonist' for Afropessimism.[19] While Okoth is heavily reliant on Olaloku-Teriba for his criticism of Afropessimism, there is a confusion in their approaches: both argue that Moten's project is reducible to Afropessimism since he is grounded in the same premise that posits the world and its ontology since the transatlantic slave trade as the totalising enactment of antiblackness, as I discussed in chapter one. Okoth argues that the specific problem with Moten's 'black optimism'[20] is that he situates the insurgency of blackness *prior to* the racialising regime of slavery and ontology, while Olaloku-Teriba's contention is that Moten does not 'attempt to elaborate the meaning of Blackness beyond the assumption of a coherence between Africa and her slave diasporas.'[21] On the one hand, then, Moten is attentive solely to a prior and surviving insurgency that exceeds the frame of politics, grounding blackness in a social life that precedes and exceeds its enslavement, while on the other, Moten provides no means of understanding blackness without, before, or beside enslavement.

These criticisms of Moten's temporality of struggle importantly highlight the difficulty of locating a precise radical program for the primacy of insurgency. While Moten's poetic style certainly has a theoretical use in itself as an antagonism in the expectations of academic discourse, as a political theorist in these times of crisis it is nonetheless crucial to be able to retrieve a plan – even if not, of course, strictly political as a manifesto or in the name of a particular party – for radical assembly and action from his corpus. What I think these criticisms miss, however, is an attentiveness to the actual stakes of primary insurgency: what does it mean for politics, ontology, and radical action that insurgency is primary, emerging always before and in excess of its foreclosure?[22]

---

17 Ibid., p. 40.
18 Ibid., p. 34.
19 Olaloku-Teriba 2018, p. 101.
20 Moten 2008.
21 Olaloku-Teriba 2018, p. 101.
22 The criticisms of Moten I discuss here ask this question backwards, ultimately withdrawing the stakes of Moten's fugitive primacy of insurgency by locating his theoretical beginning in Afropessimism, which is, quite adamantly, a program without politics. What might be more interesting to study is how Moten takes this initial supposition in a completely different direction to Afropessimists.

Before tackling this question, I turn to Judith Butler and their theorisation of the temporality of struggle. I then bring these temporalities together in an attempt at formulating a politics of primary insurgency.

3 Opening to Others

For Judith Butler, fundamentally, people gather on the streets in rebellion *in response to power*. As is typical in Butler's work, this analysis of power is structured across two parallel temporalities: one psychoanalytic, one political. Throughout their mid-career works – especially *The Psychic Life of Power* and *Precarious Life*, but also *Giving an Account of Oneself*, and even implicitly in *Gender Trouble* – they make clear that the antecedence of power to its manipulation of and affective manifestation in subjects occurs in both temporalities.

Politically, the structure is as follows: 'the historical time that we thought was past turns out to structure the contemporary field with a persistence that gives the lie to history as chronology.'[23] Butler – as again is typical of their work from the late 1980s to the early 2000s, excluding *Excitable Speech*[24] – uses the Foucauldian structures of governmentality and sovereignty to theorise the presupposition of power in those individuals who emerge as subjects.[25] Once people become *subjects*, whatever they were before this subjectivation is erased by the totalising reach of power.

Butler's political temporality finds its equivalent in one's personal, originary exposure to the other: 'If my fate is not originally or finally separable from yours, then the "we" is traversed by a relationality that we cannot easily argue against [without] denying something fundamental about the social conditions of our very formation.'[26] So, despite the perceived antecedence of power at the level of our subjection, we are constituted *in sociality*, in necessary and infinite relation to others. Social life precedes the diremption that power enacts between sociality and subjects.

---

23 Butler 2020, p. 54. Emphasis removed.

24 This 1997 monograph contains an interesting study of Althusser's scene of interpellation which differs significantly from Butler's critique of this same scene in *The Psychic Life of Power* (while maintaining the fundamental antecedence of discourse), in that in this case they go against Foucault by arguing that the temporality of discourse *makes possible* the speaking subject, who is constituted in the generative excess of language, which precedes the subject. Butler 2021a, pp. 24–9.

25 See: Butler 2004a, pp. 302–21.

26 Butler 2020, pp. 22–3.

The subtlety of this temporality is revealed later in the same essay, when Butler exposes the subjective emergence of a distinction – albeit impossible and never complete – between oneself and other, which is *preceded* by power in the form of primary caregivers:

> there is bound to be some experience of humiliation for adults, who think that they are exercising judgment in matters of love, to reflect upon the fact that, as infants and young children, they loved their parents or other primary others in absolute and uncritical ways – and that something of that pattern lives on in their adult relationships. I may wish to reconstitute my 'self' as if it were there all along, a tacit ego with acumen from the start; but to do so would be to deny the various forms of rapture and subjection that formed the condition of my emergence as an individuated being and that continue to haunt my adult sense of self with whatever anxiety and longing I may now feel.[27]

The primacy of power is set up as a layered framework of subjection, which works upon the subject with an ideological function that makes it inaccessible in the wake of having become a subject.

Butler and Moten agree that sociality precedes the individual, but for Moten that sociality is a struggle that precedes power, whereas for Butler that sociality is already constituted in relation to power. 'At the most intimate level,' as Butler summarises, 'we are social; we are comported toward a "you"; we are outside ourselves, constituted in cultural norms that precede and exceed us, given over to a set of cultural norms and a field of power that condition us fundamentally.'[28] The subject is produced through the formational institutions of power. However, as Adriana Zaharijević emphasises, this subject, despite 'the unyielding rigidity of the hegemonic structures within which it takes place', is nonetheless 'vested with a certain revolutionary agency'.[29] This agency is complex and constituted within the norms of power, though, rather than a sovereign will to which each subject has autonomous recourse.

In *Gender Trouble*, Butler employs this complex temporality in their primary critical concern: the deconstruction of sex and gender. There, Butler maintains a close separation between 'the gender of *the performer*' and 'the gender of *the performance*,' which allows them to propose drag or masquerade not as a

---

27 Ibid., pp. 26–7.

28 Ibid., p. 45. On the emergence of gender specifically as an effect of discourse, see also: Butler 2007, p. 45, p. 91.

29 Zaharijević 2021, p. 23.

uniquely emphatic moment overcoming sex's otherwise scientific binary, but as the revelation of the fabrication at work on every level of the performance of both sex and gender.[30] Gender is 'a fantasy of a fantasy. ... To be more precise, it is a production which, in effect – that is, in its effect – postures as an imitation.'[31] Drag is not the parodic performance of *a gender* but rather another constitutive parody of the fiction that comes to undergird this performance as if it were the performance's origin.

The gendered/sexed subject performs this looped fantasy in public, as the constitution of a gendered social life, which for Butler means this subject cannot form their own gendering intentions. Their impulse to imitate a fantasy must have been formed by a power that precedes the subject: the performance that maintains 'gender within its binary frame ... must be understood to found and consolidate the subject.'[32] At the same time, as Butler writes in a later book, 'forms of regulatory power [are] sustained in part through the formation of a subject,' so the desire of power is exerted in creating the subjects it subsequently needs to survive, a need which is denied through its repressive faculties.[33] Ultimately, 'the mechanism of repression is prohibitive and generative at once.'[34] Power both *makes* and *is made by* the subjects it relies on for its continued enforcement.

In Butler's temporality of subject-formation, then, the subject is presupposed in a power that consolidates the fantasy of its own generative existence by subsequent performances of an illusory gender binary, performances which 'effectively constitute the identity they are said to express or reveal.'[35] Once the fantasy of a gendered/sexed origin is established, and subjects are more or less successfully performing the fantasy of a fantasy which is in fact a groundless but antecedent power, this power then refutes its agency in the construction of subjects. It is both prohibitive and generative, forming that which it subsequently denies access to itself.

In their earlier works, Butler is attentive to the necessary maintenance of the power that forms the subject in the process through which the subject disavows itself of this power,[36] which for Butler is a task of 're-signification,'[37] i.e. of interpreting the world through questioning. The subject simultaneously maintains

30 Butler 2007, p. 187.
31 Ibid., p. 188.
32 Ibid., p. 191.
33 Butler 1997, p. 19.
34 Butler 2007, p. 126.
35 Ibid., p. 192.
36 In later works, this same disavowal becomes less political: Butler 2005, p. 15.
37 Butler 1997, p. 104.

and eradicates the power that formed them as a subject, thereby disconnecting the signifying tie between power and subject, to the extent that the subject appears independent, and their gendered performance comes out as a natural way of being.

This illusory independence is the grounding of the possibility of subjection. Subjects emerge from the power that prohibits their knowledge of their own emergence. The complication of this determination by authority for a radical theory of insurgency comes out in Butler's numerous ruminations on the ways in which performativity signifies in excess of its referent. Butler is dedicated to the primary politics of performativity, in that this social mode rebuts and constantly complicates power's claim on primacy. However, like Moten's formulation of the primacy of insurgency, Butler's performativity is beset by numerous difficulties when it is applied to the theory and practice of radical struggles. In the rest of this chapter, I attempt to make these difficulties clear by reading Butler's and Moten's temporal theories in relation to a well-known political heuristic: Louis Althusser's scene of interpellation. My concern here is not with Althusser's theory of interpellation itself (which I will, therefore, leave largely unquestioned), but rather with staging Butler's and Moten's temporalities of sociality and power within a scene that makes their possible politics as clear as possible.

4 Calling on the Subject

Discussing Louis Althusser's famous scene of interpellation from his 1970 essay 'Ideology and Ideological State Apparatuses',[38] Butler writes, 'Called by an injurious name, I come into social being, and because I have a certain inevitable attachment to my existence, … I am led to embrace the terms that injure me because they constitute me socially.'[39] This follows what Butler categorises as the Foucauldian framework[40] in which 'resistance [is] an effect of power[:] the symbolic produces the possibility of its own subversions, and these subversions are unanticipated effects of symbolic interpellations.'[41]

38 Althusser 2001, pp. 85–126.

39 Butler 1997, p. 104.

40 Foucault's temporal understanding of power and resistance is far too complex to engage with fully here. Suffice to say that Foucault at times posits the precise inverse of the temporality pointed out by Butler in *The Psychic Life of Power*. To even begin to understand Foucault's theory of resistance would require a thesis in itself, which, indeed, already exists: Checchi 2021.

41 Butler 1997, p. 99.

In this formulation, the voice of authority brings both subjects *and* their social life into being at the same time. Subsequently, in a way that is entirely opaque to themselves, subjects begin to resist this thrownness into the social, thus exceeding the demands of ontology and of the other, becoming instead the paradoxical I without other, or the bondsman without master, as Butler writes after Hegel.[42] So begins the subject's unbearable despair and fundamental constitutive impossibility: the subject can only be a subject on the condition of the performance of this overcoming of constitutive power, and yet the subject requires that relational constitution in order to maintain itself as a subject in the social.

In Althusser's scene of interpellation, an individual is walking along the street. From behind him, a police offer calls out, 'Hey, you there!' The individual turns around. 'By this mere one-hundred-and-eighty-degree physical conversion, he becomes a *subject*.'[43] The relational constitution of subjects and power here occurs only when the subject *responds* to being called. The capacity to become a subject – the potential subjection of subjects – is reliant not only on the presence of an other who calls one into being, but also on the form of address: for interpellation to work, language must already be inscribed with this power to subject its receivers.[44] Insofar as language is constituted socially,[45] this emphasis on the specific necessity of the form of address as the structuring form in which interpellation is enacted disrupts the previous temporality in which power comes before both subjects and sociality. Now, instead, sociality, in the form of language, is also placed temporally prior to subjects and their subjection.

Pursuing another mode of disruptive address, in *Bodies That Matter* Butler asks: 'Are there other ways of being addressed and constituted by the law, ways of being occupied and occupying the law, that disarticulate the power of punishment from the power of recognition?'[46] Arguing that Althusser did not consider 'the range of disobedience that such an interpellating law might produce,'[47] Butler questions how any refusal ever takes place if the law fully constitutes its own mode of address. In pursuit of a claim that subjects might have on withdrawal and refusal, Butler turns to performativity as the catachrestic citation of norms, through which subjects assume the language of power but

42 Ibid., pp. 31–62.
43 Althusser 2001, p. 118. Original emphasis.
44 Butler 2005, p. 67.
45 Butler, Laclau and Žižek 2000, p. 271.
46 Butler, 2011, p. 82.
47 Ibid., p. 82.

disrupt its intention of sustaining their subjection.[48] Subjects, uniquely, can speak *as* power without *becoming* power, affording them a constitutive means of rebellion.[49]

In *Bodies That Matter*, Butler roots performative refusal in the precarious authority of naming. For interpellation to work, the subject must already bear a name that is recognisable both to themself and to authority. To be *called upon*, to be assumed as an individual with the capacity to become a subject of power, one must first be named, and any means this named individual has for withdrawing from these interpellative assumptions relies on and is constrained by the presupposition of a name.[50] One is already grounded in a tradition of power that precedes one's agency of withdrawal: to refuse one's name, one must first both be named and recognise the capacity of authority to call on oneself by use of that name.[51]

This emphasis on naming highlights – although Butler does not explicitly identify this – Althusser's own conception of interpellation as the simultaneous act of multiple authorities. For Althusser, despite the simplicity of the narrative in the famous 1970 essay, interpellating power is not singular, and imposes no single demand on the subject-individual. Instead, as Althusser writes in 1986, it 'is realized not on the basis of a *single* ideology, but of *several ideologies* at once, under which the individual *lives* and *acts* [*agit*] his practice.'[52] This multiplicity of powers produces in the interpellated subject a certain possibility of movement, since those powers are themselves struggling for primacy among each other. 'What results is a *play and a space* of multiple interpellations in which the subject is caught up, but which (as contradictory play and as space) constitutes the "freedom" of the individual subject, who is *simultaneously* interpellated by several ideologies that are neither of the same kind nor at the same level.'[53] In the confusion of multiple forces, the subject is opened into a form of agency that is entirely reliant on the fact of having been interpellated and constituted in and by power. The subject's agency here is a function of subjection. Meanwhile, the subject still bears the dual capacity of the name: to be recognised by the authorities,

48 Butler 2005, p. 24.
49 Butler 2000, p. 10, p. 82.
50 Butler 2011, p. 83.
51 This functions differently in the case of first names (given as individuation) and surnames (given as a marker of belonging to a tradition), as Jodi Dean writes in her criticism of Althusser's heuristic: Dean 2018, p. 114.
52 Althusser 2006, p. 241. Original emphasis.
53 Ibid. Original emphasis.

one must remain named, so refusing that name cuts the relation on which both power and subjects are reliant.

Crucially, *naming* is understood by both Althusser and Butler as a transitive act.[54] *Something* names *something*. A name is not simply *had* but given and responded to in a relation of struggle. The name, though, precedes the individual act of interpellation, as Butler notices.[55] It is given by a multiplicity of conflicting authorities, but also by prior sociality: one's name is also one's place in a community, one's relation to history and local meaning. The unnamed is invisible to power, undetermined in its coordinating logics of address, but equally, when one responds performatively or employs one's 'freedom' in refusal, one risks losing one's constitutive social grounding. Insofar as, following Althusser, one's family, work, and immediate peers are as much a part of one's interpellation as officers of the law,[56] by refusing this frame one risks losing access to the sociality that *precedes* the subjection of being named. What is, then, the temporal relation between power and sociality? How do subjects refuse the terms of order imposed on them without also refusing sociality?

The possibility of withdrawal from interpellation, for Butler, is in the fact that interpellation, as 'an act of discourse with the power to create that to which it refers, … creates more than it ever meant to, signifying in excess of any intended referent.'[57] This *excess* is the playful space of performativity, where a disruptive and fugitive (re)turn to sociality becomes possible.

The performative refusals that Butler discusses in *Bodies That Matter* operate on the basis that interpellating authority is in fact reliant on its self-recognition in subjects: through interpellation, it does not so much produce *subjects* as produce *itself*. For Butler, authority – broadly conceived as the ruling force that oppresses and represses rebellion – is primary, but its primacy is dependent on its continued self-production in its production of subjects, a production, however, that exceeds its own self-sustaining intentions. It always produces more than it can control; this excess is the space of performative rebellion, through which authority is challenged by the very transitivity it produces.

My concern with this formulation, following Moten, is that Butler's temporality of subjects, power, and sociality, as it is understood through interpellation, is reliant on the *a priori* assumption of the possibility of a response to inter-

54 Butler 2011, p. 171.
55 Ibid., p. 83.
56 Althusser 2006, p. 241.
57 Butler 2011, p. 82.

pellation in each subject. In order for the performative refusal of being called upon by one's name to function as a political act, authority's own act of calling upon the individual must first be impelled by an expectation of coherence. The officer, in Althusser's scene, must expect the individual to be potentially recognisable as a subject. As we will see, however, Moten finds a striking absence in this expectation: it does not account for those whose very being is the *a priori* refusal of subjection, i.e. black people, who, in the racialising afterlife of slavery, are precisely those who are refused the name of subject, and therefore refused retroactive affirmation as *individuals* who have emerged independently from sociality.

5 Misinterpellating

In *The Misinterpellated Subject*, James R. Martel is concerned with authority's failure to properly bring subjects to dominated fruition through interpellation. Martel distinguishes between *misrecognition* and *misinterpellation*. Interpellation is the means by which authority recognises *itself* in its subjects,[58] a process by which those subjects are affirmed *as subjects*, recognising their own being through that process also, which temporally spreads into the past – a past in which those subjects were *individuals*, unsubjected as yet to the authority of the constitutive state – and constructs the fantasy that this mutual recognition is permanent.

In this Althusserian framework, the subject *has always been a subject* because subjectivity's epistemology is activated only through the politics of recognition: in interpellation, authority recognises a *potential subject*. Subjection is a latent fantasy through which individuals and authority constitute the illusion of their own historical foundation.

For this process to occur, subjects need to see themselves as subjects naturally, rather than as subjects of an authority that seeks subjection in them. 'We must erase the act that produced our subjectivity (even if it does not necessarily have a prior temporal existence),' as Martel writes, 'in order to confirm that the being that was produced by such a moment of interpellation "really" is us.'[59] This 'really,' for Althusser, is crucial to how interpellation works. The interpellated individual has to recognise 'that "it really is he" who is meant by the hailing' in order for him to successfully become a subject.[60]

58 Martel 2017, p. 39.
59 Ibid., p. 41.
60 Althusser 2001, p. 118.

For Martel, however, this 'really' is the revelation of the necessary *misrecognition* that occurs in the individual who becomes a subject through interpellation.

It is not so much that individuals must be *unaware* of the process of subjection that retroactively defines them as subjects of power (as in the classic Marxist formulation of revolutionary consciousness), but that the process must appear to have an intention other than mere subjection. There must be an appearance of social formation in this moment of interpellation: the officer recognises the individual, allowing the individual to emerge into the fantasy of permanent subjection, forming them as a social being who appears to have suddenly gained sociality, which erases the prior sociality from which that so-called subject supposedly emerged. In the social moment of recognition – through which power produces itself as the power of subject-production – the prior sociality from which individuals are withdrawn is erased, and individuals recognise themselves as having been suddenly brought into the social life of power, when in fact they have been removed from the social life that precedes power. This process, though, is not universal. As shown below, certain lives are refused this moment of recognition as a function of their unrecognisability, causing them to live in a fugitive temporality, caught between the erasure of antecedent sociality and the fantasmatic production of a social life of interpellated subjects.

In what Althusser calls the moment of recognition, we recognise that 'you and I are *always already* subjects, and as such constantly practice the rituals of ideological recognition.'[61] In Martel's reading, this is in fact a moment of *misrecognition*. The subject, for Martel, is

> built on an entire apparatus of deceit and vulnerability. The notion of interpellation is therefore valuable because it theatricalizes this kind of vulnerability. The very moment of 'hey, you there!' is a testament not to the power of interpellation but to its weakness, its failure to produce the subject who is really meant to be called.[62]

Through misrecognition, interpellation occurs constantly as *misinterpellation*. The subjects brought out by interpellation are formed imperfectly, reliant on this constant misrecognition of their subjection. An excess of something else remains in the subject who is misinterpellated as well as interpellated.

---

61 Ibid., p. 117. Original emphasis.

62 Martel 2017, p. 45.

In Moten's work, the question of interpellation begins with the assignation of an assumed possibility of subjection in the person who is called by authority. By calling 'Hey, you there!' the officer registers certain potential coordinates of a subject. Once the individual is called upon to emerge as a subject, revealing herself as *already* a subject, the desire of the call has passed through a political plane in which a visual registry of antecedent coordinates was assessed, deeming this object to have the potential to be a subject. The officer does not walk around saying 'Hey, you there!' to any object encountered: cars, lampposts, dogs. The action is specific, circulated through an accumulated memory of the kinds of objects that have revealed themselves as subjects before. Indeed, as Althusser points out, interpellation is very rarely mistaken (just one time in ten).[63] It operates in a Spinozist vein, in which experience, accumulated in memory, actively *produces* a regulatory framework through which to register stimuli regarded as familiar.[64]

In Moten's view, something has already been assumed about the potentiality of the person who becomes a subject through being called. Interpellation 'is issued forth in and from the voice of the fixed coordinate.'[65] The caller recognises either a framework of possibility or its lack, establishing a spatiotemporal plane in which certain subjects are fixed in relation to power, while others are transient, both hypervisible and invisible. Some are not fixed in place as subjects; instead, they are fugitive.

This fugitivity, however, is not the simple freedom of the traveller, but rather the exposure of a sociality that exceeds the possibility of full recognition by power. These fugitives 'are concerned with what other sounds and soundings are available to those who remain in passage, in the ship's hold,'[66] which constitutes the dual gift and condemnation of blackness, for Moten; fugitive lives move 'outside the intentions of the one who speaks and writes, moving outside their own adherence to the law and to propriety,' while also being assigned punishment for this movement outside propriety.[67]

In a series of poems presented as diary entries, Moten celebrates and laments this dual condition of blackness.

> World is a picture. The personal occupation of a point of view is that picture's condition of possibility; if one can occupy that point of view, and

63 Althusser 2001, p. 118.

64 Spinoza theorises this in the *Ethics*, IIP44–IIPSchol.

65 Moten 2018a, p. 207.

66 Ibid., p. 208.

67 Ibid., p. 131.

> take that picture, then one can be pictured, too. This reflective picturing of spacetime is Newton's physics and Kant's metaphysics doing the nasty, unmoved, without moving, or just not moving all that good.[68]

Moten focuses here importantly on the otherness of the subject who acts as the authority in the interpellative scene. The positioning of the caller in relation to the called opens an anxiety in the caller: can I be called too? What will come of me if I am spoken to by that which was not a subject until I called on it with my authority?

These questions are subtended by the presuppositions borne in the ethical relation of subject and other. Who, that is, cannot be called into being by this questioning on account of being unrecognisable as a potential subject? Moten continues:

> ... Every time this
> feeling starts we done made us
> some connections. We cut
> your hard and lonely will
> off. We wound your death
> and play that back as more
> than just not you. This you?
> Naw, this just not you, my
> beautiful sister. Black is so
> much more than just not you
> it hurts. Gimme more, gimme
> more, I want it, I like it.[69]

The relation that opens in the impossibility of being recognised as 'you' is split by a temporal distension: to not be recognised means *having been black*, a present-perfect-continuous that refers to an ongoing past, to the presence of the traumatic wound of the past instantiated in the fact of having been property, and therefore of being unrecognisable as a potential subject.

This unrecognisability in the ongoing past, however, is not a mere condemnation or the marker of an absolute negative being. Instead it reveals a *feeling* that made 'some connections', connections whose immediate response is to find meaning in the present in which subjects are brought into being by

---

68 Moten 2017a, p. 13. A longer version of this poem is repeated, with the title '19.4' in: Moten 2019, pp. 21–2.

69 Moten 2017a, pp. 13–14.

interpellative power. The question 'This you?' demands that the subject reveal themself as singular and separate. But the unrecognisability of this gathered, feeling being exceeds the format of being named as 'you': 'Naw, this just not you'. The non-youness of this subject is not abstract; it is precise and particular; *just*, exactly, *not you*.[70] Blackness is not called upon by authority because it is unrecognisable as a potential subject, which occasions a fugitive possibility of life otherwise. This fugitive life is already ongoing, already disrupting the possibility of the full expansion of interpellation. For Moten, blackness is a living glitch in the system of recognition.

For Butler, the subject *can* refuse the interpellation of power by performatively redeploying the expected mode of address. For Moten, however, this capacity is differentially given according to racialisation. For white objects of interpellation, a name is presupposed. For black objects of interpellation (in the US at least; these processes function differently in different contexts), *response* is already foresworn as a possibility through the accumulation of enslavement: their 'hard and lonely will' has been cut off. The descendent of human property is already barred from speaking, so their lack of response only affirms their racialisation as black. Black refusal must operate otherwise than the refusal to listen. For Moten, it survives fugitively in the practice of another way of speaking, to which I will turn in the final section of this chapter.

Moten finds a fundamentally constitutive fugitive sociality within every act of address: within one's name survives the residue of a nameless being, a social life that cannot be addressed. This sociality is exposed only in the practice of assembly itself. This is what I find, as I studied above, in his poem 'b jenkins', in which names are stored away in the institutional archives of physical and emotional memory, but where a gathering nonetheless continues its dance.[71] The social life of assembly continues within the imposition of its erasure.

In Paul B. Preciado's reading of Butler, the intention of the placement of subjects (and the sociality to which their fugitive performativity can turn) in a determining and mutually constitutive power is the recognition that we are all already inscribed and involved in the logics of that which we struggle against.[72] We are exposed as interior to the problem: we constitute power by existing as subjects constituted by power, which affords us a certain agency in that

---

70 The order of precision and negation is reversed in the later version of the poem: 'this not just you': Moten 2019, p. 22.

71 Against Dean's understanding of the familiar refrain 'if I can't dance, I don't want to be part of your revolution' as an individuating principle, for Moten dancing is an expression of the sociality of revolutionary assembly. Dean 2018, p. 71. See also: Moten and Tsang 2016.

72 Preciado 2022, p. 536.

our withdrawal collapses the possibility of power's survival. The primacy of sociality places on each individuated subject the responsibility of never being fully realisable as a discrete and separated life-form; one is always bound to the social life on which one is historically and personally dependent, and that responsibility occasions in each of us a demand that operates at the level of *all of us*. The political demand is for the survival of *life* but is operated through *lives*, through named individuals on behalf of the survival of what they are necessarily dependent on: *fugitive life*.

This radical temporality spans both Butler's and Moten's work. The problem with Butler is that they do not distinguish the antecedence of power and sociality, both of which precede subjects. The problem with Moten, meanwhile, is his absolute celebration of the permanent primacy of sociality, which seems to nullify the need for organised struggle in the present. Given these absences in each, it is understandable that this temporality of struggle has been criticised as a concession to power and a purely poetic appeal to the primordial state of nature of human life. Althusser has helped in bringing out these problems. To get closer to a Marxist methodology for the primacy of insurgency, which it has been my intention to propose throughout this book, in the final section of this chapter I propose a brief turn to Gramsci.

6 Temporalities of Insurgency

For Butler, *subjects* are preceded by both *sociality* and *power*. It remains difficult to assess the specific temporal relation between sociality and power. For Moten, on the other hand, *sociality* adamantly precedes both *power* and *subjects*. What remains difficult in Moten's corpus is locating the temporal relation between power and subjects.

To clarify this complexity, it may help to briefly introduce Gramscian hegemony. In the Gramscian tradition,[73] hegemony is a struggle for primacy that elicits the involvement of both radical insurgency and oppressive counter-insurgency; in distinct and agonistic ways, each competes for primacy and domination in and as 'political society', which claims to be the voice and representative of 'civil society', which, in its own turn, enacts itself through the political.[74]

73 Gramsci gives multiple definitions of hegemony, forming more of a 'provisional hypothesis' than a coherent and consistent theory. Hence my emphasis is on *Gramscian*, rather than *Gramsci's*, hegemony. Thomas 2023, p. 152; Laclau and Mouffe 2001, p. x.

74 Thomas 2023, pp. 64–84.

For Gramsci, 'destruction and negation cannot exist without an implicit construction and affirmation,' not impelled metaphysically but through the communist party's organised struggle.[75] The party itself must be irreducible to its constitutive lives, Gramsci adds; it must be the 'modern prince' who exists not as an individual but as 'an organism, a complex element of society in which a collective will, which has already been recognised and has to some extent asserted itself in action, begins to take concrete form.'[76] There is, then, a primary social life that asserts itself through struggle, but that struggle can only be realised as hegemony when organised through the party, which represents civil society in political society. That primary social life, however, is itself historical and dependent on a particular context, as Butler emphasises.[77] Indeed, universal hegemony is itself only an expression of a particular will. Communist parties represent proletarian particularities, which are turned universal in the assumption of hegemony in political society.

The complexity for Butler is that the instantiation of a subaltern particularity as hegemony is not desirable in the pursuit of radical democracy. Instead, they pursue 'the actualization of the goals of the "particular"' that negate oppressive hegemony by antagonising its claim to universality.[78] The task of the Left, for Butler, is to form a 'basis of commonality' among its particular pursuits – feminism, antiracism, anti-Zionism, class struggle, etc. – not in order to establish a competing hegemony, but to disrupt the formation of universality through this multiplicity of actualised particularities.[79]

For Butler, as for Gramsci, these challenges to hegemony can only take place within political society; while social life, for Butler, does precede and exceed the political, the former is itself a historically specific particularity.[80] The state, as the form of hegemony for which particularities compete, is not a place with an outside; the 'merely civil' struggles of particularities occur necessarily within the ambit of the political.[81]

For Moten, on the other hand, the 'civil society' of insurgent sociality is absolutely prior to and separate from the subsequent emergence of the political

75 Gramsci 1971, p. 129.

76 Ibid., p. 129. Michael Hardt and Antonio Negri make a contemporary political program out of this modern prince by emphasising the primacy of struggle in which this organism's compulsion must be rooted. See: Hardt and Negri 2017.

77 Butler et al. 2000, p. 270.

78 Ibid., p. 166.

79 Ibid., p. 167.

80 Ibid. The struggle that forms the political is not only between particular groups, as Gramsci notes, but within those groups, too. There is also intra-particular struggle: Gramsci 1971, pp. 144–5.

81 Thomas 2023, p. 71.

space in which particularities vie for hegemony. Black American history is split in the Middle Passage, enacting the ontological erasure of racialised life-forms through slavery. Blackness, in that moment, becomes temporally, spatially, and ontologically fugitive, uncapturable in the frame of politics and the struggle for hegemony.

Crucially for Moten, fugitive blackness is a form of social life that is maintained not in the attempt at formal recognition as political society, but through *misrecognition*. Moten's assembly of socialities operates in the excess of politics, in the space that the purview of politics necessarily bars as its unbearable excess.

Moten elicits the disruptive activity of sociality from a barred and brutalised past in which social life survives. By bringing it into the repressive mechanisms of the present, the black sociality that cannot be recognised or interpellated as a potential subject antagonises the foundation of the political contest for hegemony. Moten's primary insurgency is the excess of hegemony, an antagonistic sociality without a party or a prince, formed of those who – beyond the political appearance of their names and individual lives – have survived erasure, survived in the form of fugitive assembly. By turning to the disjunctive perseverance of that insurgent, irreducibly unsingular assembly, the staging of the contest of politics is broken down, and in the joy of that rupture, the assembly is impelled to push a little further, to erupt into total misrecognition:

> this consent not to be single worries the joint composure of phenomenology, ontology, and politics past the point of distraction, where the lineaments of an aesthetic sociology await their incalculable arrangements. This swarm is on the way, and wants to help make the way to that rendezvous, happily consenting to such diffusion while counting on you to push it along.[82]

Butler posits the inverse form of this primary insurgency. For them, it is the very fantasy of an anterior sociality without determination by power that feeds the survival of power: '*both* sanctioned heterosexuality and transgressive homosexuality … are *effects*, temporally and ontologically later than the law itself, and the illusion of a sexuality before the law is itself the creation of that law'.[83] To believe one precedes one's production as a subject is, in a classically Žižekian twist, the very act through which one is subjected. What actually precedes sub-

82 Moten 2018b, x.
83 Butler 2007, p. 100. Original emphasis.

jection, then? What is subjected in the historical process of subjection? And what motivates the unending anxiety of power in compelling it to eradicate every trace of struggle?

For Martel, misinterpellation happens all the time; it is not a rare slippage in the logics of interpellation, but a necessary component of its imperfect deployment.[84] This misinterpellation, in Harney and Moten's temporality, is presupposed by the presence of power. The officer knows that misinterpellation is bound up in the impulse to interpellate, that a given (racialising) code deems certain subjects incapable of achieving emergence as full subjects, and from that lacuna in the officer's own constitutive authority arises an unbearable anxiety: the anxiety of incompleteness, of the impossibility of fully appropriating the absolute alterity of the other into one's own projective, regulatory faculty of recognition. As Moten writes, 'Why is there something rather than nothing? So devils can steal it.'[85] What is registrable as the materiality of the subject, once we have 'moved into the frame of visualization,' as Harney says,[86] is itself the determination of the subject *into* and *as* power. What appears as the constituted *effect* of authority's interpellation is in fact the retroactive residue of a process that has already both occurred and failed to occur: the speaking into being of the black as subject. In every act of interpellation, an excess remains, the excess that is blackness; the excess that cannot be determined by the relation of interpellation.

The point of difference that occasions the misrecognition of the subject who is not a subject because they are black is that they represent the continued need for the police as an archetype of authority. What is revealed in this misinterpellative moment is the officer's anxious reaction to the misinterpellation that *precedes* the official logic of interpellation: the black subject is necessarily impossible in authority's self-producing process of subjection.

The key point in Harney and Moten's fugitive reading of misinterpellation is this: our struggle is our constitutive sociality. It is the assembly from which we seem to emerge as subjects. Power then comes to break the struggle, but something of the struggle always survives.

Two options then arise as tactics for this primary insurgency: 1) insurgents take back their struggle and retrieve their practices of sharing, severing power's lifeline and turning to constitutive practices of sociality, from which another hegemonic form emerges: that of black radicalism; 2) insurgents attend to

84 Martel 2017, pp. 6–7.
85 Moten 2017a, p. 12.
86 Moten and Harney 2020a, minutes 15–17.

their practices of assembly in order to draw out of them a continued practice of sociality and care, which ultimately, when practiced as a way of life that exceeds the needs of capital and the constitutive force of hegemonic authority, becomes an insurgent program of sharing to the extent that private ownership and property, as the grounding of individuation, no longer hold any meaning. The invitation of these riotous assemblies is their survival without a countering claim to hegemony.

While they are careful not to dismiss anyone's liberatory uprising, for Harney and Moten, the protests to pull down statues – from Cape Town in 2015 to Bristol in 2020 – ultimately affirm the playing field of power, withdrawing primary insurgency into a contest for the proper claim to power. This claim is reliant on the affirmation of the logics of ownership: it asks who has the right to the proper use of public space and the construction of hegemonic symbols.[87] The rules of the stage are set by a totalising force whose impulse is to consign all struggles to a competition for power.

Harney and Moten reject the frame of this battle, focusing instead on what survives in the excess of claims to hegemony. This does not mean, though, that what survives should simply be left to survive as it is. It means, instead, that the primacy of insurgency grounds the necessity of contemporary struggle: the site of struggle is the residue of a struggle that survives, and its aim is to withdraw and generalise the social practices that occasion and invite that survival. As they emphasise, contra the criticisms of Okoth and Olaloku-Teriba, 'understanding this regime as' a totalising force of racialising brutality 'thriving in the individuating violence of democratic despotism does not lead to the thought that there is no outside to the world.'[88] Harney and Moten look instead for a radical practice of withdrawal that exposes assemblies to a life of sharing without the violence of claims to ownership. This is not a segregated commune, but a practice of sharing survival in which we 'cannot be anything but already shared and already sharing.'[89] An accumulated history of brutality is exposed to the celebration of sociality's survival in the excess of ownership, authority, and individuation.

Insurgency as the radical practice in excess of politics is the form of social life that survives, that cannot be fully registered in the misrecognition of (mis)interpellation, and that proves itself to have eclipsed the temporality of power. Being *as subjects* is knowable only within the framework of authority, in the wake of its generative subjection, Butler contends, so the sociality that

87 Harney and Moten 2021, p. 121.
88 Ibid.
89 Ibid., p. 122.

precedes subjection is only accessible in a political form, through acts of performative disobedience. But what their otherwise astute criticism misses out is the ways in which sociality survives; how it not only precedes and exceeds the totalising moment of capture when power arrives at the scene, but lives on in the practices of insurgent sharing that – despite everything, despite the overwhelming horror of our present's endless violence – assemblies everywhere continue to practice in and as the primacy of their struggle.

CHAPTER 6

Speculations on the Poetics of Value

1 Giving an Account of One's Theory

My principal aim here has been to expose the sociality that precedes and exceeds the form-determination of subjectivity, antagonising the expansive production of subjects. By revealing unsubjected sociality as the groundwork of human life, I have tried to undermine the presumption of individuation enacted by value.

To close *Poetics of Value*, I want to explore a possible poetic *Darstellung* of this political process. *Darstellung*, as I wrote in chapter two, is a representation in which the object represented is itself present; it is an enactment of the presence of what is represented. In relation to Alli Warren, I argued that poetry can serve the function of political *Darstellung*, presenting disjunctive social relations as present in the symbolic exchanges of capital.

In chapter six, I offer a closing narrative by way of two pages of architectural literature not explicitly named as poetry. These pages are in Darell Wayne Fields's monograph *Architecture in Black*. While these pages may not at first appear as poetry, what I am interested in is their presentation of a form of literary gathering that precedes the textual form of poetry. Before poems appear as poems, I want to suggest, an experience of meaning is available; a sociality of poetic sounds, experiences, and feelings is accessible from within the *Darstellung* of poetry's social life. In the place where meaning becomes a poem, there is already a formless excess of order through which meaning is shared, a meaning that exceeds its representation of language. The pages I focus on are printed below.

2 In the Space Left

In 'Intentionally Left Black (by author)', parts I and II, Darell Wayne Fields inscribes a page with the excess of poetry. These artworks, these poems, these intentional boxes, are part of the sixth and final chapter of *Architecture in Black*, which is formed of numerous poems and designs, and is followed by the 'Afterthought', which stages a short and marvellous conversation between Monkey and History.

In Part I of the monograph, 'Theory', Fields studies the complicated wake of Hegel in the construction of architecture and race. Hegel is understood as pro-

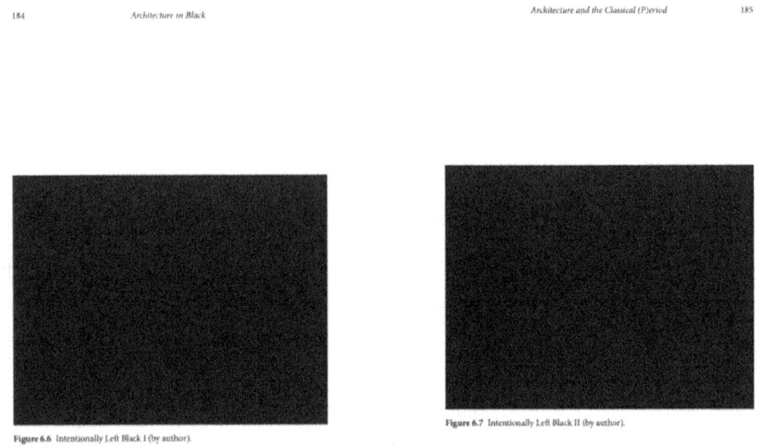
184 Architecture in Black

Figure 6.6 Intentionally Left Black I (by author).

Architecture and the Classical (P)eriod 185

Figure 6.7 Intentionally Left Black II (by author).

FIGURE 1 *Intentionally Left Black (by author) I and II*
PAGES FROM DARELL WAYNE FIELDS'S *ARCHITECTURE IN BLACK* (2015), PP. 184–85

ducing a racialised aesthetic history in which the form assumed by social lives reveals a determined position within the hierarchy of civilisation, which rises from the black (primordial) to the white (modern). In Fields's reading of Hegel, 'structured into philosophical and aesthetic schemes' is a form of temporal lag called 'the Black Subject.'[1]

There is a coherence in the scheme of blackness and architecture across Hegel's philosophical and aesthetic texts. Architecture is the most primitive form of artistic expression, for Hegel, situated in the 'symbolic' stage, exemplified by Ancient Egypt, before the 'classical' stage of Ancient Athens and the 'romantic' stage of his own contemporary German Gothic.[2] Architecture, being fundamentally functional and therefore dependent on external norms, cannot achieve the self-determining principles of sculpture, painting, music, and poetry. In architecture – which is adamantly racialised in Hegel's history – there is an absence of consciousness, an absence of purposive reason, which, in Fields's reading, '*is* blackness.'[3]

1 Fields 2015, p. 36.
2 Ibid., p. 35.
3 Ibid., p. 42. Original emphasis.

Blackness as the absence of consciousness *qua* architecture is defined against the purely purposive reason of poetry, which is afforded this elite status in Hegel's teleology of spirit because it has no purpose other than its own realisation: it is the pure expression of subjective will, independent of any external cause.

In Part II of *Architecture in Black*, 'Orders of Space and Appearance', Fields focuses his critique on Kant. While it is impossible here to summarise the stunning complexity of Fields's poetic challenge to Kantian formalism, the principal contention around which Fields situates his performative study is that '[f]or Kant, the moral being is qualified by race, and the most abhorrent abnormality is being black. [In the *Critique of Pure Reason*, Kant] initiates the structural transformation of the black racial subject to black spatial subject.'[4] The Black Subject is situated in a space whose visibility is squandered by a temporal blur; raciality is precisely the condition of projected temporal lag, which results in forced invisibility. This invisibility is occasioned in both the Black Subject and those who perceive that Subject, to the extent that the Black Subject does not so much *look at* the world but rather *speaks to* the absence of being able to see the world *qua* world. Fields brings this to W.E.B. Du Bois' 'double consciousness', which 'is not allegorical. First it is spatial, then it is ontological. ... Considering the Black Subject's predicament *in racialized space* it uses language to concretize an artifact beyond language,' an artifact referencing precisely the blur maintained by the fact that the Black Subject 'learned to see before it learned to speak.'[5]

The performative catachresis of blackness that Fields identifies and poeticises is this: the Black Subject does not speak a world it sees into being. Instead, the Black Subject speaks of an artifact it can no longer see, because the artifact is spatially coterminous with its own being. It is the blur that renders itself invisible, an invisibility that emerges in the racist formalism of modernity as both a condemnation and an opportunity.[6]

What I find so interesting about this portrait titled 'Intentionally Left Black (by author)' is that it works back through the history of philosophy, into the formative kernel of the racialisation of aesthetics, and severs the presupposed reason of artistic expression. For both Hegel and Kant, it is imperative that artistic expression emerges from a purposive will, which I will discuss more below. Given that, for both philosophers, blackness is the absence of reason, and reason is the act of a rational subject, what could a poem possibly mean

4 Ibid., p. 121.
5 Ibid., p. 123. Original emphasis.
6 Ibid., p. 129, p. 143, p. 156.

when it is expressed as the *purposeful absence* of a poem? Fields has *intentionally left the poem black*. That is, he has decided to do nothing; his act of purposive reason is the withdrawal of reason. This withdrawal, however, does not leave *nothing*. It leaves *black*. Before and in the excess of the racialising prescription of reason, for Fields, black was already there; it lived already before the rational expression of a poem.

In the excess of language, sociality emerges as the formless assembly of survival. I find the expression of this survival in the catachrestic link between the title of these pages – 'Intentionally Left Black (by author)' – and the boxes, especially as a critique of Kant and Hegel, and in the crucial absence of a definite or indefinite article before 'author', who is neither '*the*' nor '*an*' author, but *author* without deixis, without cartographic placement in the logic of language.

3 In the Left Space

Throughout *Architecture in Black*, Fields develops a poetic performance as a rebuttal to the subjective order of Kantian and Hegelian reason. The protagonist of this performance is the Signifying Monkey, as theorised by Henry Louis Gates Jr. in his interpretation of Esu-Elegbara, the Yoruban trickster figure from the narrative traditions of West Africa.[7]

This trickster monkey in the Yoruban imaginary is a generator of linguistic catachresis that distorts every attempt at injurious speech. Anything said to him is twisted and re-narrated to the point that his interlocutors are so puzzled they give in. As Gates writes, the Signifying Monkey is not exactly 'a master of this technique' of language play; 'it is even more accurate to write that he *is* technique, the literariness of language, the ultimate source for black people of the figures of signification.'[8]

The black American tradition that has inherited this catachrestic poetics is what Gates calls 'the language of Signifyin(g),'[9] the wordplay and poetic signification by which 'black kids on street corners ... preserve the classical black rhetorical structures.'[10] The trickster of West African folklore survives as this fugitive poetics, uncapturable in the regulatory order of American English.

Understanding this wordplay as the directionless excess of language, Fields returns to the conditions in which the structures of signification were estab-

7 Gates Jr. 1988.
8 Ibid., p. 75.
9 Ibid., p. 88.
10 Ibid.

lished, namely Hegelian dialectics and Kantian transcendental idealism. If, to very briefly summarise, space and time are formal projections that situate objects within a perceptual framework that is internal to and generated by the human mind, as Kant proposes, and if this projective framework is deployed by the purposive, self-moving pure negativity of the subject's dialectical engagement with the world, in which the world as relations is constituted by the subject's movement toward the full self-becoming of the Absolute, as Hegel contends, then a certain form of life is presupposed as the temporal and ontological antecedent of this full human becoming. Something must *fail* to enact the world as its projective transcendental perception, giving room for others to achieve this expansive mode of archiving an external world as their own possessive validation. To realise themselves and the world they simultaneously inhabit and create, humans must *move out of* the prior conditions in which this realisation is not possible. As Fields makes clear, for both the defining philosophers of this long post-Enlightenment, that prior condition is blackness, and blackness is practiced as black vernacular.[11]

Black vernacular, or Singifyin(g), is a rebuttal to the assumed stable spatiality of the subject. It enters with its disjunctive poetics and collapses a totalising form of property, opening the ground of language to what Moten calls 'impropriety.'[12] In a formless disorder before the ordering act of *I*, there is life, but life without individuation, life indistinguishable and inseparable as discrete expressions of the possibility of self-emergence. The black vernacular signifies on the *I*, living instead as sociality without a name.

In his lecture 'Recess and Nonsense', Fred Moten begins by thinking – with Cheryl Harris's influential 1993 essay 'Whiteness as Property'[13] – of whiteness 'not only as a *mode* of property, but also as the *principle* of property.'[14] The defining relation of modernity is property; the wage-relation that facilitates the emergence of labour in capitalism is the archetypal moment of this relation, as the time of workers is sold as the property of capitalists: commodified time becomes property. The metaphysical grounding of this relation is a promise of futurity: owners expect to be able to use their property as they wish.

In the historical rise of empire and the struggle to assert domination, whiteness assumes the properties of property: the right to use, enjoyment, reputation and status, and the power to exclude. The owners of whiteness demand the sat-

11 Fields also traces the origins of Kant's and Hegel's racialising order in Cartesian ontology: ibid., pp. 5–6.
12 Moten 2018c, 8–9.
13 Harris 1993.
14 Moten 2018c, 8–9. Original spoken emphasis.

isfaction of the promise of futurity: they must be able to continue to use their whiteness as protection. This is the expansive spatial principle of whiteness, its demand to increase and expand as space.

The racialising principle of surplus is reliant not only on the expansion of itself as a possession, but also on space to possess, which necessarily leaves an unpossessed remnant in every act of possession. Something is stored for a later phase of grasping. In these future fantasies of the total global capture of whiteness, the evidence of survival is revealed. Something *has to* be left uncaptured, otherwise the captured sites of possessive subjectivity become meaningless. Some places have to not be had. 'If whiteness is the principle of property, then blackness is anamaterial sufferance of impropriety. More plus less than either property's objection or abjection, blackness is the critique of property on the one hand, and the celebration of dispossession on the other.'[15] As whiteness pursues its expansion, blackness survives in excess of possession.

In Moten's formulation, blackness is suspended out of reach of both total possession by the spatial capture of whiteness and the refusal of the terms on which this order is set, not through any acceptance of these terms, but through knowledge of the fact that the terms of order are grounded first in the social. Blackness is statelessness insofar as Euro-American imperial modernity's guiding impulse is the totalising project of whiteness as a global spatial principle, the design of the body as and into space. However, this statelessness *is not nothingness*. As Moten writes in *Stolen Life*, it is imperative to remember

> that insofar as blackness is and comes, rather, from absolutely nothing it is, indeed, something after all, namely, the commonness of the improper; that blackness is exchange, the dispersive gift of anoriginal dispossession; that dispossession is what we are and what we have in common; that it is the undercommons.[16]

Here Moten poeticises the impossibility of situating blackness in the expansive spatiality of this political-subjective economy, which is to say, as he writes in *The Universal Machine*, Moten offers an 'understanding of blackness as exterior to civil society and, moreover, as unmappable within the cosmological grid of the transcendental subject.'[17]

The stateless dispossession of the historical but surviving possession(lessness) that is blackness, then, is obliged to celebrate this dispossession, since

15 Ibid.
16 Moten 2018a, pp. 26–27.
17 Moten 2018b, p. 195.

to refute it would be to simultaneously refute blackness itself. What black vernacular practices are enjoined to celebrate is their excessive and incomplete envelopment in the project of perception. What Moten posits these enduring forms of social life as celebrating is precisely their endurance, their ability to survive *as vernacular*, as Signifyin', despite the grasp of regulatory and injurious language.

Fields proposes a method of signification that disrupts the spatiotemporality of whiteness and its linguistic norms, its attendant discursive order. By doing so, Fields brings forth that which is adamantly marked as the left-behind, putting into play that which has been tagged and buried and closed as the cul-de-sac of productive meaning. This method is the catachresis of the Signifying Monkey, 'a black cultural entity mimicking Saussure's [linguistic system of diachronic and synchronic signification]'[18] by the use of a 'panchronic state without relying on a hierarchical system of representation.'[19] The linguistic sign, that is, is formed by a temporalisation of its arbitrary signification, connecting to the synchronic/semantic (x) axis, where meaning is socially formed, and the diachronic/rhetorical (y) axis, where meaning is historically formed. The black vernacular that Fields, after Gates, calls Signifyin' is 'the ability to control and use the arbitrary nature of the sign.'[20]

What Signifyin' achieves is the realisation of the cultural necessity of the arbitrariness of signifiers; it renders them diachronically meaningful by amplifying their synchronic catachresis. As Fields summarises, '[t]he effect [of this language play] is (S)ignification – a structured arbitrary form of language built on language.'[21] In the form of literature that literature itself cannot contain, the radical ruse of signification survives. As Judith Butler writes, 'the text exceeds the text.'[22] Fields builds a sign system that reveals the codes implicit in the determined signifying function of whiteness as and in language.

In the pages that follow 'Intentionally Left Black I (by author)' and 'Intentionally Left Black II (by author)' Fields introduces Étienne-Louis Boullée's 1784 design for a cenotaph for Isaac Newton with a poem. The cenotaph was never built but was intended to be the tallest building in the world at the time. Its plans show a huge sphere resting on a constructed mound, held by supporting arches and circled by rings of trees. The inside of the sphere is black, stud-

18 Fields 2015, p. 68.
19 Ibid., p. 65.
20 Ibid., p. 69.
21 Ibid., p. 175.
22 Butler, 2011, p. 97.

ded with the light of stars. Fields presents the form of space as the outwards movement of this sphere; its edges are built by the force of blank space moving outwards.

> When void pushes mass out of its way, that is space.
> When space encircles you, that is inside.
> When you can imagine being encircled and inside, that is architecture.
> The mass held back is pierced by 1000 holes. It reflects the stars and sky.
> Now imagine the sky has a thousand eyes that look on without seeing.
> This is you encircled by absence.[23]

In Fields's interpretation of the cenotaph, the blankness of the centre gives meaning to the hardened edge of space, which itself has only become a space through this appropriative projection of meaning. Crucially, this subsumption is enacted by the possibility of imagining its universality; the outward movement of the semiosis of the void and its capture of the surround is a way of seeing, a way of registering the stimuli of the world; a 'thousand eyes that look on without seeing.'

What is distinctive about a way of seeing, as Fields makes clear by designating the eyes as incapable of sight despite their ubiquity in the void, is that it cannot register everything. Its impulse to regulate the optics of its outside are limited, because it only reorders the positioning of external objects once they are experiencing the inside of the void, once their otherwise-shaped practices are turned into spheres. When they remain outside, unable to imagine being in the sphere, then the sphere cannot compute them as reflections of its form.

What is outside the sphere is not properly being. To be outside the sphere-as-property is to be propertyless, to be a being without property, in impropriety, without properties. What exceeds incorporation in the sphere is unseeable in the optics of expansion.

The edges of the logics of property appear as the coagulated sphere of Newton's cenotaph. It looks like solid concrete. But it was never built. It is only the imagined accompaniment to a poem, a poem written by *author*, designated precisely as the property of this book, who names himself in parentheses after the titles of 'Intentionally Left Black' I and II: '(by author)'. No article, no deictic referent, no sign system pointing out his whereabouts in space and time: not *this* author, *that* author, *the* author, *an* author … Just *author*, unreferred, in a nonspecific time and place, 'encircled by absence,' as *author* writes.

---

23 Fields 2015, p. 186.

The affirmation we are pressed up against, preceding any questioning of this scene, is that there must be a Signifying catachrestic link between the preposition *by* and the excess of property. The excess of property, of the concrete sphere, is the excess of authorship, where *to be the author* is to be inscribed in the archive of metaphysics as the subject who self-generates, the pure negativity of the being in endless becoming, nestling into the cosmos within the sphere. Neither *outside* nor *beyond* that, but rather *in excess of it*, there is *author*, unaccompanied by the signifying system of language as presupposed by a speaking subject.

At this point our question might come down to what happens to Hegel and Kant when their authorship is signified on. What happens when The Philosophers are read in vernacular? Fields is twisting the meaning of originality by displacing the deictic signifier that would lead to him, *author*. What is the result of this distortion of the original, this signifying on linguistic purity and originality? To get further into the tangle at play here, it might help to excavate some of Moten's playfulness.

Moten has been accused by Nahum Dimitri Chandler of being overly playful in relation to his deviational use of the term 'paraontology'. It would be an act of injurious aggression to try and vacuum pack Chandler's use of 'paraontology' and 'paraontological life' into something as trite as a definition, as silly as a summary. As Marquis Bey knows, to read Chandler is to understand absolutely nothing about Chandler,[24] to be dumbfounded and stunned by what he might, just maybe, but probably does not call X.[25] Meanwhile, by 'paraontology' Moten means the meaning of the meaning, the excess of what it means to mean, in a classic Motenist formulation.[26] Paraontology for Moten is a magic portal that exists materially in space and in poetry. It is the thing you get into when you hear the music that makes you want to get into something, the experience you pass through to arrive at the experience of experiencing things.

Chandler, though, is a serious philosopher who desires, as Moten says, 'a perennial scholarship,' in contrast to 'what appears to be [Moten's] desire to be merely fashionable.'[27] In a lecture at an Ivy League university for a distinguished visiting professorship, a senior academic comments on another senior academic's comments about himself. The scene is archetypally institutional, appearing precisely as the uninterrupted formal script of the academy. But

---

24 Bey 2020.

25 Chandler 2017.

26 As Kline writes: 'paraontology describes the mode of being that is always already resisting the imposing logic of (political) ontology'. Kline 2017, p. 63.

27 Moten 2022, minutes 26–27.

Moten splits into a philosophical poetics that is uncapturable in the prescriptive form of the academy. Here, this split occurs by way of an unscripted aside:

> And you know, I have to say, he got it right. I've always only wanted to be merely fashionable. And I've always been concerned with work – particularly in the realm of art – that has ordinarily been relegated to the status of the *merely fashionable*. Adorno wrote a really interesting and evil essay called 'Perennial Fashion: Jazz' and ever since then I've always wanted to not only be fashionable but to imagine that there's ultimately no reason to offer a distinction between the perennial and the fashionable anyway.[28]

The temporality here is perplexing. Ever since Adorno – who died just before Moten's seventh birthday – wrote about jazz in the '30s, '40s, and '50s, Moten has *always* been concerned with the eradication of a serious philosophical distinction between the perennial and the fashionable.

Those who consider themselves to be serious are historically discrete: they do not *always* enact this perennial seriousness onto the world. On what Fields calls the diachronic/rhetorical axis (the historical formation of meaning), the perennial produce their finite critique. Moten enters from the synchronic/semantic axis (the social formation of meaning), cut by a temporality that is at once acutely finite (ever since *that particular moment*) and excessively infinite (he has *always known*). From that axis, he asks of the diachronic perennials what it is that they mean when they say 'fashionable', and it turns out that they mean *playful*, which is to say: *not serious*.

For Adorno, *serious music* contains the whole in each moment and 'derives its musical sense from the concrete totality of the piece.'[29] *Popular music*, on the other hand, is built on random elements without a cohesive relation to the whole, while also forming these aleatory sounds as the 'mere enforcement of a musical scheme.'[30] Everything is preordained but does not fit. In popular music, 'the whole is never altered by the individual event and therefore remains, as it were, aloof ... At the same time, the detail is mutilated by a device which it can never influence and alter.'[31]

In popular music, for Adorno, certain moments are unreachable from the logic of the whole. Certain fugitive instances of sound escape contribution to the determined totality of meaning. From the diachronic/rhetorical axis, this

28 Ibid., 26–27.
29 Adorno 1998, p. 198.
30 Ibid.
31 Ibid., p. 200.

uselessness of certain notes is scandalous; the serious movement of strings and horns is left in the excessive abyss outside the whole. From the synchronic/semantic axis, however, this uselessness assumes a speculative potential of its own.

Something in the aleatory enforcement of a musical scheme has hooked Adorno, making him fear the spectre of sublation (*Aufhebung*): 'the use value of jazz does not nullify [*aufheben*] alienation, but intensifies it.'[32] Alienation will be the result of failing to contribute to the whole. Distance from the experience of what one ought to be follows from failing to be oneself, whether one is jazz, the jazz saxophonist, or Beethoven. Or, indeed, an academic giving a lecture for a distinguished visiting professorship at Cornell.

What Fields finds in his reading of Hegel is that the philosopher is reliant for his racialising critique of non-European life on the textualisation of material history. Hegel needs a serious source for his racism, an official script, and Fields needs to upset that script with playful signifying. History only exists diachronic/rhetorically once it is *inscribed* as official history, as serious philosophy. In his lectures on aesthetics, Hegel proposes the Egyptian pyramids as pure symbols, as vulgar folklore pasted right in front of the eyes of the sign's obedient masses.[33] This 'flatten[ing of] the visual monumentality of the Pyramids … relegates them to the category of other unhistorical forms of "writing" (i.e. folklore, narrative, personal accounts, etc.).'[34] This is where Fields brings folklore back, in the form of the Signifying Monkey:

> both Hegel and Saussure agree that the linguistic sign is arbitrary because of its inherent duality [words as sounds/concept (Hegel) or signifier/signified (Saussure)]. Therefore, in either case, it is possible to use the same signifier to allude to a different concept (or signified).[35]

Suddenly, a terrifying unseriousness opens within the formal prescriptions of sense designated by the text as the proper script of history, or the whole as the proper coherence of the piece. The very mechanism intended to seal signification as the white text of history has now been distorted as Signification, or the black sound of jazz, or the signifying trickster, or the *merely fashionable*. Signifying as black vernacular takes over the diachronic claim that *seriousness* makes on the arbitrary relation between sound and concept, instead staging a *merely*

32 Adorno 1989–1990, p. 48.
33 See: Hegel 1975.
34 Fields 2015, p. 61.
35 Ibid.

fashionable incoherence in which the refusal of the whole is wholly refused in favour of the fugitive survival of those notes that never fit the enforcement of a musical scheme.

In this survival, for Moten, is the *paraontological*: 'What's at stake is why it is that the status of the ontological is consistently both refused to and refused by modalities of social existence in which the status of the individual is also refused.'[36] In this stake, an ante- or anti-ontology may arise. But 'how do we come to understand this beautiful anomaly that we might call "the anthological," which avoids and also is excluded from the precincts of being precisely insofar as it avoids and is excluded from the precincts of the individual?'[37] The *whole* cannot alter or destroy the *detail*, as Adorno fears, but what Moten celebrates is the life of the detail that has been refused both its distinction as detail and its coherence in the whole, because that detail, ultimately, signifies on the song. It disconnects the expected arbitrary meaning of the sound and the sense, opening a form of play that makes no claim to being arbitrary; it is formed, instead, exactly as meaning, as the meaning of social life, as the fugitive fashion of black vernacular.

The joke in Fields's beautiful portrait is the way in which he holds up the stuffed corpse of Hegel – indistinguishable from the sad, spectral face of the philosopher – but makes him speak in black vernacular, makes him signify. 'Intentionally Left Black (by author)' parts I and II are purposive, as Hegelian action must be: 'Reason is *purposive activity*,'[38] the living hand of Hegel writes. Once he is propped up on strings in *Architecture in Black*, the Reason and the *purposive activity* remain, but the grammatical sutures are removed. No article designates the author. 'Intentionally Left Black I (by author)'. *Author* is not specified in the projective transcendental spacetime of post-Enlightenment modernity.

For Hegel, action must be purposive and self-moving even when at rest. The subject *becomes* by this active self-direction toward Spirit. For Kant, 'the final intention of pure reason [is] the practical,'[39] a practice that finally justifies reason as an intention, as enacted by a retroactively always-potentially-intentional subject. For both our grandfathers, Immanuel and Georg, purpose/intention must be the condition which must lead to practice/action.

The traumatising spanner that Fields throws into the works is the question of *whose* intention this is. There is practical intention in this leaving-black; there

---

36 Moten 2022, minutes 28–29.
37 Ibid.
38 Hegel 2004, p. 12.
39 Kant 1998, Bxxxviii, p. 120.

is purposive activity. The left-black is willed into being, but *no thing* enacts this will. This is the deformation of our haunted present, this monstrous wake of the Kantian-Hegelian subject.

The Signifying Monkey does not use the technique of signifying, as Gates writes. Instead, *the Monkey is vernacular*, the life of Signifyin'. Fields, too, does not enact intention. Fields *is the intention of leaving black*. Fields is the life of purposive activity. In the black left where leaving is the situation without space-time, a ceremony of mourning is underway. This party of leaving black is the wake after loss. The text is in mourning. After all, in the wake of Hegel's obsessive Absolute, Fields grieves the authority of poetry.

Fields's text is in mourning for *author* who is not *the* or *an* or *this* or *that*. The text is perplexed by its lack of deictic referent. Like all texts, Fields's text is full of words, but its words fail to refer to a subject, a subject semantically validated as *the author* because all the other expected signs of authorship are present: this book is published by a prestigious academic publisher, bound in an expected format with cover image, author name, institutional affiliation, copyright laws, date and place of publication, reviews, etc. etc. But within, in the catachresis of this bizarre epigraph to its own absent author, the text is the celebration of mourning; it is the opening of the signifying praxis of grief that follows the fugitive flight of Authority embodied in [The] Author.

Darell Wayne Fields turns the blank page around, rendering textual blankness as intentional blackness. In the e-book version of *Architecture in Black*, blank pages are not marked with the familiar 'This page is intentionally left blank' that publishers prescribe onto details that cannot alter the whole. Fields's intention to intentionally leave the page black has disturbed the whole signifying function of *blank* pages throughout the book, and the editors are left confused, their *whole* system suddenly signified.

'Intentionally Left Black' parts I and II are, at a primary level, intentional acts, pure reason made practical. And yet they shatter the presupposition of a formal sense structured into the relationality of poetry. The poetry itself – fugitively signifying on the social life of those assembled within and beside it – slips out of the form of textuality and provides a point of assembly around which material lives gather in the excess of value. Value is a computational relation, determining the form human social lives are able to assume. Presented with a text that distends the presupposition of a subject-object relation between mutually computed forms, those gathered in the life of the text are displaced into a surviving and deformed residue of poetry that survives beside the authority of printed pages and the logics of institutionalisation. In that poetics of survival, in that fugitive withdrawal from the form-determination of value, there is revolutionary sociality.

'Intentionally Left Black' is a diptych of feelings expressed as excess, a poetic form overflowing with the means of making poetry, in both its abstract form as intention, and its material form as discursive signs. The poems have too much to say to be a text, too much animation to rid themselves of the individuating segregation that would form a fantasmatic rationality of homeostatic words, each formed following the given power structure of language.

For Fields, the exchange of formal signs as language is undergirded by the excessive experience of *speaking* and *being spoken to*, an inoperative and vulnerable opening into the excess that cannot be captured as grammatical marks. Before, in the face of, and in the fugitive survival of language, there is a feeling that cannot individuate itself into the productive sense of signs. That feeling exists as social semiosis in the temporality of having-been-shared, already given over, a merely fashionable vernacular.

The fugitively animated objectness of the being-spoken-to is unbearable to the perennial form of individuated signifiers. This excess may as well be called poetry, even if its proper name is properly nameless, only enunciable as intentionally left black, a *left* and a *black* that satirise the intention they appear to follow from, signifying on the fantasmatic temporality that claims to have constituted them.

4 The Excess Left of Poetry

In *Poetics of Value*, I have pursued ways out of the form-determining production of subjectivity through contemporary poetry. Value operates through a retroactive temporality, valorising the labour posited in production by circulating it as abstract labour in exchange. This process suspends the realisation of labour expenditure in a frozen, static future of accumulation and promised return. The operation of subjectivity in capitalism is a process of endless temporal deferral, permanently postponing the possibility of meaningful social relations, dispossessing the material assembly of sociality.

Here I have argued that a critical project that accepts this temporal totality can only do so by ignoring or refusing the differential pasts and fugitive presents that survive in the excess of value. Value-critical Marxisms generally posit the present as a homogenising moment of abstraction, in which concrete labour is distributed in non-differentiated units of socially necessary labour-time, which allows each commodity to find its universal equivalent in exchange. What this misses is the past that survives differentially in populations systematically positioned in a disjunctive relation to potential valorisation. This past is brought to fugitive presence in black studies, which I have attempted to locate and access by close readings of four contemporary poets.

The poetics of value I have posited here disrupts the Marxist modality of criticism with fugitive speech and catachrestic signifiers that undermine the brutal imposition of productive subjectivity onto social lives. *Poetics of Value* has celebrated the forms of social life that survive in the excess of value's form-determining mechanisms by proposing contemporary poetry as a means of apprehending and inhabiting that fugitive excess.

Having posited social life as surviving in a fugitive other-present beside the dispossessive temporality of value, I have asked what it is *in poetry* that exceeds its form of presence. Poetry, I have argued throughout *Poetics of Value*, is the recalculation of the logics and relations of form-determination, disrupting the processes of discursive and material computation through a catachresis that destabilises the presupposed productive relations of capitalism, revealing instead a sociality that survives in a temporality *before*, *beside*, and *in the excess of* the present.

What, then, is the excess of poetry? How does poetry itself survive in this fugitive beside-time? In this final chapter, I have attempted to access a fugitive poetics by studying two pages of intentional blank/black space in Darell Wayne Fields' monograph *Architecture in Black*, which, though artistic and creative, is certainly not a collection of poetry. Studying the *intentionality* of this *leaving black*, the agency of this absence, I read this diptych as the insurgency of poetry that precedes and exceeds the symbolic form of poems on a page. Revealed in these two black boxes, satirically left untouched by the author's intentions in the most anti-Kantian way possible, is the excessive assembly of poetry, the para-symbolic social life of literature that reveals a scandalous survival within the form of poetry itself. This fugitive survival is a poetics in the excess of value, which I have tried to apprehend as a communist antagonism against the form-determination of subjectivity in the brutality of this capitalist present.

AFTERWORD

The Primacy of Insurgency

As I write this in summer 2024, universities appeal to the police to brutally enforce the disappearance of protestors taking a stance against genocide. Academics in mute corridors turn away from the deafening reverberations of complicity in the colonisation of Palestine. From every side, the question of the use of theory gauntly accuses me. Its heavy, spectral presence pursues every word I write: *why are you here writing, not tearing down the authorities that allow and invest in genocide?*

Jean-Luc Nancy writes that the excess of the body can never be 'announced from shouts or songs beyond language, or by chasms of silence.'[1] But what does this mean for remaindered life, for fugitive socialities of survival, living in and as what Neferti Tadiar calls 'a vanishing horizon, one not of potentiality but of actual living without value'?[2] What presupposition of potential valorisation is Nancy imposing on the insurgency of assembly? Who is given into a permanent beyond that prescribes the limits of language proper? 'What if,' as Moten asks, 'the priority of resistance to power, or counterstatement to statement, were something on the order of a previousness without origin[?]'[3] The consequence of this question is a split in the seam of the circular history of material and logical violence. This dehiscence in the wound of history exposes the primacy of insurgency. In this primacy, it is no longer possible to imagine a universal limit through which knowable singularities are exposed to an obscure community.

In that obscurity beyond the limits of the body and the text, another way of knowing survives. There, in the poetics of value, the grief of individuation, the primacy of insurgency, the assembly of sociality survives in the excess of value's form-determining subjection. The excess of this insurgent body of poetry, contra Nancy, is announced precisely from shouts and songs beyond language, from the excess sociality that pervades the apparent order of words on a page.

The most astounding moment I was exposed to while organising in the 2024 university camps – demanding that Swedish institutions divest from collaborations with Israeli universities that develop the weaponry and technologies for genocide – was the absence of a cohering insurgent authority. No party line

1 Nancy 2008, p, 21.
2 Tadiar 2022, p. 71.
3 Moten 2018a, p. 20.

established who was to set up a camp, when and where, and how the demands were to be deployed. Something in us, *as* us (or as *we*, as Alli Warren would say), in excess of each one of us, accessed a form of insurgent organising through which we knew what to do. We did not each *decide* to share our time, resources, and energy with others in the service of anti-colonial insurgency. Instead, we found ourselves *already shared*, living as shared and sharing sociality.

For me, at least, this feeling was ecstatic. I found myself exposed to a formless sociality of sharing that exceeds the miserable complicity of the individual subject-form, depleted by its form-determined competition for abyssal accumulation, and the institution-form, crushed under the administrative oppression of its obligatory silence and evasion of responsibility. To find myself exposed to this assembly of sociality was a joyous riot that I want to live in for the rest of my life. I want to spend my lifetime exposing the riotous assembly of liberatory radicals against the foreswearing limitations of obsolete institutions whose function is the preservation of power, accumulative authority, and the geopolitics of coloniality.

I have been thinking about this temporality of insurgency for a long time, without necessarily realising I was thinking about it. For me, it did not come out of theory. I learned it from insurgency itself, which was then confirmed and voiced by theory and poetry. In all the riots of my life, I have found myself in a primary and insurgent sociality, but without recourse to a critical history of this feeling. Despite living in what Joshua Clover defines as the second great era of rioting, which he calls *riot prime*, after the industrial era of the strike, I had no name for riot.[4]

Clover's history studies the shift since the Middle Ages from riots as 'struggles over the price of goods, that is, struggles outside the wage but still suspended in the market',[5] which ended in the uprisings of 1848 and the enormous cohesion of powers that eventually suppressed them, to the era of the strike, in which organised workers collectively withdraw their labour-power from consumption, deploying their cooperative activity as a threat to capital,[6] to, finally, the era of riot prime, in which there is no longer a specific demand since the conditions of cooperativity and the presumption of the state's and market's capacity to provide the conditions for people's survival have been wholly eradicated by the economics of financialisation and the ideology of neoliberalism.[7] In this

4 Clover 2016.

5 Ibid., p. 138.

6 Ibid., p. 84.

7 Ibid., pp. 172–3. Clover also discusses the ways in which different social groups form different kinds of excess when gathered as riot: pp. 122–3, p. 172.

era, there is no wage to demand. In the acute solitude of economic crisis and collapse, there is no other option than public riot; gathering on the street is its own demand, an end in itself. All gatherings are riotous in the era of riot prime.[8]

Clover importantly notes that, in addition to the productive sociality of riots and the withdrawal of productivity of strikes, riots have the function of *exposure*. They expose the logic of the commodity, which is undergirded by the state and its network of violent defenders who bear the state's monopoly on armed violence.[9] Riots reveal the relentless violence required to uphold the expansion of value, just as the encampments against genocide on university campuses in 2024 showed the aggressive, reactionary violence of university managers in their appeals to the state's monopoly on violence to protect their isolation from society.

In this understanding, riots expose the network of violent authorities that maintain the bourgeois appearance of everyday life, setting the scene as if it were absent of riot. The relation of these forces to temporal primacy fits with the second of the three temporalities I described in the overview to Part 2:[10] Clover approximates Butler's (and Foucault's, at certain points in his corpus, as well as Marx's[11]) temporality in which sociality precedes power, but is so infused with the latter that any access to a primary sociality is impossible, and the current production of subjectivity is entirely generated by the psychic, social, and economic forces of domination.

So, while *exposure*, for Clover, is a crucial aspect of riot, what it exposes is *power*, rather than the *insurgent sociality* that precedes and exceeds that power. Harry Harootunian notes a similar exposure in Marx, who was dedicated to studying 'how *antecedents* from past practices are taken over and subjected to capital', although he understood these as obscured by the 'mediation of the capitalist present', which made sure 'they were not antecedents to capital's life process'.[12] Instead, these persistent, fugitive pasts are strategically subsumed or erased in favour of the ideological narration of the capitalist present.

8 Ibid., p. 123.

9 Ibid., p. 125.

10 A brief recap: the first – the temporality of value-critical Marxisms and Afropessimism – posits *power as historically and logically primary*; the second – the temporality of Butler, psychoanalytic theory, and sometimes Foucault and Marx – posits *sociality as historically and logically primary*, but that sociality is inaccessible and subsumed in power; the third – the temporality of Moten's black optimism, operaismo, and autonomist Marxism – posits *sociality as historically and logically primary*, which is *followed* by the ideology of power that attempts to narrate itself as primary.

11 Harootunian 2015.

12 Ibid., pp. 27–8.

The issue with Clover's temporal theory – and, to the extent that they are compatible, Butler's, Marx's, and Foucault's, too – is that it homogenises the practices of sociality, turning them into one standardised process of social meaning-making, which is, ultimately, the exact function of value: to standardise the temporal expression of human life as the homogeneous possibility of value-productivity. This view cannot expose the 'know-hows of living as mutual care and enjoyment, which are part of other, alternative but already present modes of life lived now,' as Tadiar writes.[13]

For Tadiar, practices of social survival – art and protests, Indigenous Filipinx and Palestinian resistance, and so on[14] – do not expose a *power* that precedes and produces them; they instead expose the 'poesis and practices of living [as] ways of organizing personhood, shared being, and enjoyment that are not entirely overwritten or disciplined by proper forms of human being'.[15] Social survival exposes the primacy of sociality, which, by the very fact of its survival, lives as an insurgent antagonism against the power that claims narrative primacy. What is exposed in insurgency, for Tadiar, is the differential and uncapturable multiplicity of the survival of sociality.

Perhaps the historical ubiquity or specificity of insurgency comes down to its definition. Clover posits no age of insurgency; in fact, the word only appears once in his book (then once in the footnotes), in a citation from Ranajit Guha.[16] Insurgency is something else, unlike riot or strike; it is an exposure of the remainder, of the 'many pasts [that] continue, not least in the resistance that is happening constantly in the world, the forms of organized and unorganized everyday resistance without which there would be even less survival.'[17] This unruly sociality is ambivalent, for Tadiar, in that it results in the production of the constantly vibrant living labour that capital needs to abstract and standardise, while also producing 'new forms of resistance and insurgency'; while these 'forms and ontologies of life-making practice' can simply expose another grounding layer of power and oppression, they are also 'tangential to and in excess of the (re)production of capital insofar as they are the means of fugitive life'.[18]

One rather remarkable absence in Clover's history is Palestine, given its central position in revolutionary struggles since 1948. The reason could be

13 Tadiar 2022, p. 333.
14 These examples are studied in Tadiar 2022.
15 Ibid., p. 70.
16 Clover 2016, p. 165. Tadiar cites and discusses this same text by Guha: Tadiar 2022, p. 32.
17 Tadiar 2022, p. 276.
18 Ibid., p. 105.

that Palestine is precisely the location of insurgency, rather than the withdrawal of labour-power in strikes or the absence of demands in riots (which require, if not *the right* to gather in public, at least the *ability to survive* in public, which is never guaranteed to Palestinians). By way of Tadiar, then, we might add to Clover's historical triptych an understanding of insurgency as the Palestinian cultural practice of *sumud*, which in Arabic means 'steadfastness'. *Sumud* describes the insurgency of *staying*, of remaining in place despite occupation, apartheid, and genocide.[19] In those conditions, remaining is constant resistance; *being* is insurgency.[20] If insurgency is *sumud*, it is everywhere; the historical rarity is its erasure. In this understanding, insurgency is primary, preceding and exceeding the force that attempts to remove and destroy it.

Following the 1981 Brixton Uprising in London, a group of local residents set up the Riot Not To Work collective. On the first anniversary of the uprising, in April 1982, they published their first pamphlet: *We Want to Riot, Not to Work: The 1981 Brixton Uprising*. In a section that wisely recommends 'A Riot a Day Keeps the Copper Away', the anonymous writers depict the ecstatic experience of a street in the absence of police. The streets of Brixton, in April 1981, purged themselves of the possibility of being policed.

Once the police retreat, the rioters realise that they already know how to riot. 'It was totally spontaneous; no one told us to attack here or there, we saw for ourselves and if we felt the need to fight here and there we did so.'[21] The realisation of the uprising is that the uprising is already happening; the social life of the street is already the staging of riot, but that uprising has been held back by the presence of the police. Without police, the survival of insurgency is realised.

No single person decides to bring the uprising out of its hiding. The insurgent assembly is given into an experience that exceeds agency, and it is in the realisation of this excess that the police have no choice but to withdraw, to enact their own absence. Or rather, the police can only come to terms with the fact that in that excess of agency *they are already absent*. 'Nothing I can write can describe the exhilaration I felt when that first police van went up in flames. From that spark it spread up and down Brixton.'[22]

In 2013, the insurgents who set up the Gezi Park barricade in Istanbul arrived suddenly at the same experience of exceeding agency. 'The barricades,' as Başak Ertür writes, 'were made collectively and spontaneously, as if one always built

19 Salih and Richter-Devroe 2014; Johannessen no date.
20 See: Ftouni 2024.
21 Riot Not To Work 1982, p. 23.
22 Ibid.

barricades with strangers on the streets, as if building barricades was just what one did.'[23] The presence of the barricade exposes a knowledge of barricades that pervades the insurgent assembly, whose bodies form the first line of the barricade, before the objects of the cityscape are gathered. The barricade is realised in and as the assembly that builds the barricade. There is no logical temporality in which a prior form of oppression is refused, which the insurgents must rebut through the construction of a counterhegemonic epistemology. Instead, a surviving sociality of barricading is exposed, and the insurgents themselves are actualised as the barricade.

During the Paris Commune, in the spring of 1871, the communards did not attempt to enact a new politics of individual freedom once the barricade had emerged as the logic that purges the street of police, exposing the impossibility of policing sociality.[24] Instead, they emphasised the continuing practices of internal community regulation, bringing out the relations that had always enacted ethical limits to the conduct of the community. The rules of the Commune were not imposed by a universal law, generated by a new order in the present, but were revealed as the repressed and muted life of the past within the present. 'The Communards were moving in historical material,' as Massimiliano Tomba writes, 'not the way one moves along the railroad tracks of progress but as in a huge building where some rooms of what-has-been contain different not-yets that have remained encapsulated and can be freed now.'[25] The communal order by which the Commune lived was a function of the survival of the Communards, an actualisation of a fugitive past as the insurgent condition of the survival of sociality.[26]

The standard temporality of political philosophy would put these events in reverse, having the insurgents arise out of a general condition of counterinsurgency. Impelled by a necessity that results from political failure and disappointment, Hannah Arendt argues, civic individuals then emerge out of their insurgentless life and assemble in public as insurgency.[27] As Moten says, 'The consensus among certain philosophers of violence is that somehow that which is violated ... emerges as a function of the violence.'[28] The struggle is understood to emerge *out of* the violence that structures society.

23 Ertür 2016, p. 98.

24 Marx 2021, pp. 75–6.

25 Tomba 2019, p. 86.

26 For a further discussion of this temporality and its applicability in the case of the Paris Commune, alongside other historical cases, see: Dean 2018, pp. 115–59.

27 See: Arendt 1998, pp. 175–207; Cavarero 2021, pp. 24–5.

28 Harney and Moten 2022, minutes 2–3.

For Moten, as for the insurgents in Brixton, Istanbul, Paris, and Palestine, this temporality covers and distorts the struggle that survives: '[What Stefano Harney and I instead] keep in mind is that violence is a regulatory brutality that is imposed upon something that, for lack of a better word, was already there … and that anticipates the structural brutality that's imposed.'[29] Independent agency is erased and sociality is exposed as both the insurgency of survival and the survival of insurgency.

In August 2011, I was in Brixton during another moment of exposure, when the obfuscating appearance of order faltered and insurgency was again revealed in its continuous survival. On the first night of riot, I was at a poetry reading in central London, where a muffled frenzy echoed in every word. On the second night, I got on my bike and cycled south to Brixton.

There, in the riot, the primacy of insurgency gave life to me. It has taken many years for that riot to come out as theory, as this poetics of value, but the link is nonetheless direct and necessary. *Without the riot, there is no poetry.* The form-determination of subjectivity is twisted by the catachrestic poetics of survival, by the exposure of insurgency. The exploitation and classed violence that constitutes me, my family, and my comrades is burst into the excess of bourgeois meaning by the exposure of riotous survival. For generations, we have been anticipating the structural brutality imposed on us. But at certain moments – on the streets of Brixton, policed by the racialising force of murderous authority, or in the lecture halls of universities, managed by the mute accumulation of refusals to care and to share – the primacy of insurgency rises again, opening the wound that covers the fantasy of capitalist modernity a little further, whether by riot or by poetry.

29 Ibid.

APPENDIX

Study Group for the Undercommons

In their plans for a fugitive social practice of 'the undercommons', Stefano Harney and Fred Moten write:

> [This] may entail forming a band, hosting a barbeque, a dance and a drink. It may be a farm and a daycare, an experimental writing collective, or a mechanics shop. Any form of detoxification from the interpersonal. There will be no allies, no citations, no counter-portraiture. Every aggression will be massive. And when we win, blackness will rain in sun showers while the time disappears.[1]

At what point does 'forming a band, hosting a barbeque, a dance and a drink' become revolutionary? Up to a certain point, it seems, these are casual bourgeois hobbies, enjoyed by conservative politicians and hedge fund managers on weekends at the golf course as much as factory labourers on evenings after work and communists in communes. But Harney and Moten invest their belief in these social rituals as the possibility of a fundamental disturbance.

In the autumn and winter of 2023, I hosted a study circle on contemporary Marxist theory and black studies at the Left Party (*Vänsterpartiet*) offices in Stockholm. I had been attending similar circles for some time. These gatherings kept me socially warm in the frosty isolation of Sweden. They kept me so warm that I wanted a repeat. I can never stop doing anything that feels good, to both my doctor's and psychotherapist's dramatic concern, and those meetings felt so good.

So, in 2023, fifteen or so people gathered in a small office in central Stockholm. In the first session, we discussed Harney and Moten's *All Incomplete*, alongside a chapter from Coleen Lye and Christopher Nealon's collection of essays, *After Marx*, and then we went to the pub. One of our comrades said, 'The pub feels good, but it's not *doing* anything. We need a temporary autonomous zone, a space where we can just exist together, without production.' That comrade brought food to the following meeting, and we stayed for a while after the two-hour session, eating together, talking, making friends.

---

1 Harney and Moten 2021, p. 121.

I have heard that capitalism survived that temporary zone of sharing. Apparently our gathering was not a global revolution. But at the same time, I know how it felt to meet in that space of exception every week for a few hours. I know the ecstasy I felt in that proximity to others, to people who care about the struggle, people who are dedicated and passionate and who act in the world through love and riot and sharing.

In that vein, I offer a reading list for a study group on black studies and Marxist theory. Take it, share it, manipulate it, add to it, play with it, gather around it with your comrades. If you want. Or start a band, a barbeque. Gather with those who need gathering, and share with those who are as yet unopened to their constitutive sharedness. Let the riot rain down while the time disappears.

Readings

Meeting 1: What Does Race Do?

In the first gathering we focus on the position of race and racism in capitalism. Is racism a specifically capitalist form of brutality? Or has capitalism appropriated and deployed a general racism that existed before this mode of production? How does capital use race, and what possibilities are there for race to be used against capital?

Readings:

- Stefano Harney and Fred Moten, 'Plantocracy and Communism', *All Incomplete* (Minor Compositions, 2021), 119–29.
- Nikhil Pal Singh, 'Black Marxism and the Antinomies of Racial Capitalism', in Coleen Lye and Christopher Nealon (editors), *After Marx: Literature, Theory, and Value in the Twenty-First Century* (Cambridge University Press, 2022), 23–39.

Further Reading:

- *Endnotes* 3: *Gender, Race, Class, and Other Misfortunes* (Endnotes, 2013).
- Elizabeth Povinelli, *Geontologies: A Requiem to Late Liberalism* (Duke University Press, 2016).
- Guido Starosta, *Marx's Capital: Method and Revolutionary Subjectivity* (Brill, 2015).
- Claudia Rankine, *Just Us: An American Conversation* (Penguin, 2020).
- Cedric J. Robinson, *Black Marxism: The Making of the Black Radical Tradition* (North Carolina University Press, 1983).

Meeting 2: Who Is Revolutionary?

In this meeting we focus on the way certain social relations – race, gender, class – have been employed in radical theory and revolutionary practice. The first text attempts to give full dedication to the life of one particular person, situating itself in the struggle, while the second offers a broader survey of different social groups and their own version of action.

Readings:

- Saidiya V. Hartman 'The Anarchy of Colored Girls Assembled in a Riotous Manner', *The South Atlantic Quarterly*, Vol. 117:3, 465–90 (2018).
- Søren Mau, 'Capitalism and Difference' (Chapter Seven), *Mute Compulsion: A Marxist Theory of the Economic Power of Capital* (Verso, 2023)., 152–73.

Further Reading:

- Denise Ferreira da Silva, *Unpayable Debt* (Sternberg, 2022).
- Leigh Claire La Berge, *Wages Against Artwork: Decommodified Labor and the Claims of Socially Engaged Art* (Duke University Press, 2019).
- Bruno Gullì, *Labor of Fire: The Ontology of Labor between Economy and Culture* (Temple University Press, 2005).

Meeting 3: Critiquing 'the Human'

'The human' is always in question. It has long been the name for the animal that questions its own definition. In contemporary critical thinking, this generally takes two forms: questioning the racialisation of humans as either 'bodies' or 'flesh', or questioning the technological prosthesis of humanity through digital manipulation. The first text is concerned with animal flesh as the semantic structure of race, while the second understands the human as broken by digital algorithms.

Readings:

- Alexander Weheliye, 'Bare Life: The Flesh' (Chapter Two), *Habeas Viscus: Racializing Assemblages, Biopolitics, and Black Feminist Theories of the Human* (Duke University Press, 2014), 33–45.
- McKenzie War, 'The Class Location Blues' (Chapter Four), *Capital is Dead: Is This Something Worse?* (Verso, 2019), 77–99.
  - [*Optional extra reading*] Zakiyya Iman Jackon, first section of 'Introduction', *Becoming Human: Matter and Meaning in an Antiblack World* (Duke University Press, 2020), 1–21.

Further Reading:

- Tiffany Lethabo King, Jenell Navarro, Andrea Smith (editors), *Otherwise Worlds: Against Settler Colonialism and Anti-Blackness* (Duke University Press, 2020).
- Seb Franklin, *The Digitally Disposed: Racial Capitalism and the Informatics of Value* (The University of Minnesota Press, 2021).
- Maya Rivera, *Poetics of the Flesh* (Duke University Press, 2015).
- Wendy Hui Kyong Chun, 'Race and/as Technology', *Camera Obscura*, Vol. 24:1, 6–35 (2009).
- Tom Cohen, Claire Colebrook, and J. Hillis Miller, *Twilight of the Anthropocene Idols* (Open Humanities, 2016).

Meeting 4: The Space of Struggle

This meeting opens the question of space and the movements of capital. The way bodies are positioned in cities, and the spaces where certain forms of life (as capital or as humans) accumulate are important to understand. These two texts provide very different critiques of how capital moves, and what can be done to stop it.

Readings:

- Jasper Bernes, 'Logistics, Counterlogistics and the Communist Project', *Endnotes 3: Gender, Race, Class and Other Misfortunes* (2013), 172–201.
- Adrienne Brown, '"My Hole Is Warm and Full of Light": The Sub-Urban Real Estate of *Invisible Man*', in Adrienne Brown and Valerie Smith, editors, *Race and Real Estate* (Oxford University Press, 2016), 177–94.

Further Reading:

- Deborah Cowen, *The Deadly Life of Logistics: Mapping Violence in Global Trade* (The University of Minnesota Press, 2014).
- Stefano Harney and Fred Moten, *All Incomplete* (Minor Compositions, 2021).
- Matthew Hockenberry, Nicole Starosielski, Susan Zieger (editors), *Assembly Codes: The Logistics of Media* (Duke University Press, 2021).
- Lesley Naa Norle Lokko, *White Papers, Black Marks: Architecture, Race, Culture* (The University of Minnesota Press, 2000).
- Darell Wayne Fields, *Architecture in Black: Theory, Space, Appearance* (Bloomsbury, 2000).

Meeting 5: Antieconomic Traditions

In this meeting we read two different approaches to the intersection of political struggle and economics. The question parting these two texts is: does capitalism have many expressions of violence, or only one expression, which is fundamentally economic? Is value the motivation for all of capitalism's violence, or are there many motivations at work? This is always a controversial discussion.

Readings:

- Tiffany Lethabo King and Frank B. Wilderson III, 'Staying Ready for Black Study: A Conversation', in Tiffany Lethabo King, Jenell Navarro, Andrea Smith (editors), *Otherwise Worlds: Against Settler Colonialism and Anti-Blackness* (Duke University Press, 2020), 52–73.
- Endnotes Collective, 'Communisation and Value-Form Theory', in *Endnotes 2: Misery and the Value-Form* (2010), 68–105.
  - [*Optional extra reading*] Amy De'Ath, 'Hidden Abodes and Inner Bonds: Literary Study and Marxist-Feminism', in Lye and Nealon (editors), *After Marx* (Cambridge, 2022), 225–39.

Further Reading:

- Frederick Harry Pitts, *Value* (Polity, 2020).
- Sandro Mezzadra, *In the Marxian Workshop: Producing Subjects* (Rowman & Littlefield, 2018).
- Dave Beech, *Art and Value: Art's Economic Exceptionalism in Classical, Neoclassical and Marxist Economics* (Brill, 2015).
- Marina Vishmidt, *Speculation as a Mode of Production: Forms of Value Subjectivity in Art and Capital* (Brill, 2019).
- Neil Larsen, Mathias Nilges, Josh Robinson, and Nicholas Brown (editors), *Marxism and the Critique of Value* (MCM', 2014).
- Beverley Best, *Marx and the Dynamic of the Capital Formation: An Aesthetics of Political Economy* (Palgrave Macmillan, 2010).
- Fred Moten, 'The Subprime and the Beautiful', *African Identities*, Vol. 11:2 (2013).
- Lindon Barrett, *Racial Blackness and the Discontinuity of Western Modernity* (The University of Illinois Press, 2014).

Meeting 6: Poetry and Practice

What, literally, do we do now? How do we break this era of crisis and violence? What do we do to suspend the collapse of social life and a liveable planet? Andreas Malm has no doubts about the moral imperative of this moment: go out and start a revolution! Stop waiting! For Lola Olufemi, these abrupt commands fail to think about the continued need for care. Especially in crisis, imagination is needed to allow us to think of other possible worlds. Both these authors agree on wanting to destroy capitalism, but they have very different ways of imagining what happens next.

Readings

- Lola Olufemi, *Experiments in Imagining Otherwise* (Hajar, 2021), 7–24 and 42–56.
- Andreas Malm, 'Learning from Past Struggles' (Chapter One), *How to Blow Up a Pipeline* (Verso, 2021), 5–63.

Further Reading:

- Karl Marx and Friedrich Engels, *The Communist Manifesto* (1848).
- Hanif Abdurraqib, *A Little Devil in America: In Praise of Black Performance* (Penguin, 2021).
- Daphne A. Brooks, *Liner Notes for the Revolution: The Intellectual Life of Black Feminist Sound* (Belknap, 2021).
- Fahima Ife, *Maroon Choreography* (Duke University Press, 2021).
- Alexis Pauline Gumbs, *M Archive: After the End of the World* (Duke University Press, 2018).
- Joshua Clover, *Riot. Strike. Riot: The New Era of Uprisings* (Verso, 2016).

Meeting 7: Experiencing the Body

How does capital historically construct the way we experience our bodies? In capitalism, we are just units of labour, and our only use is our potential to produce value. And yet we experience proximity to others, and our bodily vulnerability and mortality make us imperfect subjects of capital. We also experience joy and ecstasy despite our exploitation and brutalisation. Some critical traditions – especially queer, feminist, and trans theory – have taken this vulnerability and this joy as a radical possibility. Jennifer Nash's work finds resistance, refusal, and pleasure in forms of performance that have traditionally been condemned in antiracist and feminist discourse as purely oppressive. In the second text, Paul B. Preciado makes some astounding propositions against gender and sex.

Readings

- Jennifer C. Nash, 'Laughing Matters: Race-Humor on the Pornographic Screen' (Chapter Four), *The Black Body in Ecstasy: Reading Race, Reading Pornography* (Duke University Press, 2014), 107–27. *NB: On pages 115, 117, 123, and 124 there are explicit images – ask your audience before you distribute this.*
- Paul B. Preciado, 'Introduction' and 'Countersexual Society' (Chapter One), *Counter-Sexual Manifesto* (Columbia University Press, 2018), 1–40.

Further Reading:

- Grace Kyungwon Hong, *Death Beyond Disavowal: The Impossible Politics of Difference* (The Universiy of Minnesota Press, 2015).

- Jackie Wang, *Carceral Capitalism* (Semiotext(e), 2018).
- Sayak Valencia, *Gore Capitalism* (Semiotext(e), 2010).
- Paul B. Preciado, *Pornotopia: An Essay on Playboy's Architecture and Biopolitics* (Zone Books, 2014).
- Anne Anlin Cheng, *Ornamentalism: A Feminist Theory of the Yellow Woman* (Oxford University Press, 2018).
- Judith Butler, *What World Is This? A Pandemic Phenomenology* (Columbia University Press, 2022).
- Adriana Cavarero, *Inclinations: A Critique of Rectitude* (Stanford University Press, 2016).

Meeting 8: History's History

Where do these areas of study come from, and do we imagine a history leading to this moment? Is this historical moment unique or a repetition of the same struggle violated by oppressive power? In this meeting we look at historians' approaches to the struggle.

Readings

- Carolyn Lesjak, 'Reading Dialectally', *Criticism*, Vol. 55:2 (2013), 233–77.
- Sylvia Wynter and Katherine McKittrick, 'Unparalleled Catastrophe for Our Species? Or, To Give Humanness a Different Future: Conversations', in Katherine McKittrick (editor), *Sylvia Wynter: On Being Human as Praxis* (Duke University Press, 2015), 9–89.

Further Reading:

- Harry Harootunian, *Marx After Marx: History and Time in the Expansion of Capitalism* (Columbia University Press, 2015).
- Fredric Jameson, *Representing Capital: A Reading of Volume One* (Verso, 2011).
- Giovanni Arrighi, *The Long Twentieth Century: Money, Power, and the Origins of Our Times* (Verso, 1994).
- Ellen Meiksins Wood, *Liberty and Property: A Social History of Western Thought from Renaissance to Enlightenment* (Verso, 2012).
- Sylvia Wynter, '1492: A New World View', in Vera Lawrence Hyatt and Rex Nettleford, *Race, Discrouse and the Origin of the Americas: A New World View* (Smithsonian, 1995), 5–47.
- Rinaldo, Walcott, *The Long Emancipation: Moving Toward Black Freedom* (Duke University Press, 2021).
- Ibram X. Kendi, *Stamped from the Beginning: The Definitive History of Racist Ideas in America* (Bold Type Books, 2016).

Meeting 9: Making Subjects

In this meeting we investigate what makes us 'subjects'. Undoubtedly, something of this mode of production determines and mediates our behaviour and the way we understand ourselves, but the computation of this determination is distributed in extremely different ways to certain parts of the population. We look at two ways of understanding what structural and personal forces constitute our ability to imagine ourselves as human actors with subjectivity.

Readings

- Maurizio Lazzarato, 'Introduction', *Signs and Machines: Capitalism and the Production of Subjectivity* (Semiotext(e), 2014), 7–22.
- Frank B. Wilderson III, 'The Trouble with Humans' (Chapter Five), *Afropessimism* (Liveright, 2020), 191–229.

Further Reading:

- Christina Sharpe, *Ordinary Notes* (Alfred A. Knopf, 2023).
- Lorenzo Chiesa, *Subjectivity and Otherness: A Philosophical Reading of Lacan* (MIT, 2007).
- Simon O'Sullivan, *On the Production of Subjectivity: Five Diagrams of the Finite-Infinite Relation* (Palgrave, 2012).
- Jane Rendell, *The Architecture of Psychoanalysis: Spaces of Transition* (I.B. Tauris, 2017).
- Samo Tomšič, *The Labour of Enjoyment: Towards a Critique of Libidinal Economy* (August Verlag, 2021).
- R.A. Judy, *Sentient Flesh: Thinking in Disorder, Poesis in Black* (Duke University Press, 2020).
- Denise Ferreira da Silva, 'No-bodies: Law, raciality and violence', *Meritum*, Vol. 9:1, 119–62 (2014).

Meeting 10: Talking Cures – What to Do Now?

In this meeting we take it easy(ish) with a podcast instead of lots of reading. These two interviews with Moten and Harney show the energy of these exciting thinkers, and the fun they always seem to have while theorising. They remain dedicated also to the practicalities of revolutionary action. Alva Gotby focuses on abolition and practices of care in her important book.

Readings

- (Podcast) Fred Moten and Stefano Harney, 'Wildcat the Totality: Fred Moten and Stefano Harney Revisit *The Undercommons* in a Time of Pandemic and Rebellion, part I' and 'Give Your House Away, Constantly: part II', interview

with the podcast *Millennials Are Killing Capitalism* (2020). Available on any podcast site.
- Alva Gotby, 'Emotional Reproduction' (Chapter One), *They Call It Love: The Politics of Emotional Life* (Verso, 2023), 1–27.

Further Reading:

- The Care Collective, *The Care Manifesto: The Politics of Interdependence* (Verso, 2020).
- Sara Ahmed, *The Cultural Politics of Emotion* (Edinburgh University Press, 2004).
- Leopoldina Fortunati, *The Arcane of Reproduction: Housework, Prostitution, Labor and Capital* (Autonomedia, 1995).
- *Krisis Journal*, Vol. 42:1, 2022: *The Care Dossier*.

Bibliography

Abdurraqib, Hanif and Fred Moten 2021, 'Building a Stairway to Get Us to Something Beyond this Place', *Millennials Are Killing Capitalism podcast*, 13 May: https://millennialsarekillingcapitalism.libsyn.com/hanif-abdurraqib-fred-moten-building-a-stairway-to-get-us-closer-to-something-beyond-this-place.

ACLU, No date, 'Captive Labor: Exploitation of Incarcerated Workers': https://www.aclu.org/news/human-rights/captive-labor-exploitation-of-incarcerated-workers.

Adorno, Theodor W. 1989–90, 'On Jazz', translated by Jamie Owen Daniel, *Discourse*, Vol. 12:1 (Fall-Winter): 45–69.

Adorno, Theodor W. 1998, 'On Popular Music', in *Cultural Theory and Popular Culture: A Reader*, Edited by John Storey, Athens, GA: The University of Georgia Press, 197–209.

Adorno, Theodor W. 2004 [1966], *Negative Dialectics*, translated by E.B. Ashton, London: Routledge.

Agamben, Giorgio 1999, *Remnants of Auschwitz: The Witness and the Archive*, translated by Daniel Heller-Roazen, New York: Zone Books.

Agamben, Giorgio 2007 [1993], *The Coming Community*, translated by Michael Hardt, Minneapolis, MC: The University of Minnesota Press.

Ahmed, Sara 2010, *The Promise of Happiness*, Durham, NC: Duke University Press.

Al-Saji, Alia 2018, 'SPEP Co-Director's Address: Hesitation as Philosophical Method – Travel Bans, Colonial Durations, and the Affective Weight of the Past', *Journal of Speculative Philosophy*, Vol. 32:3: 331–59.

Alexander, Michelle 2010, *The New Jim Crow: Mass Incarceration in the Age of Colorblindness*, New York: The New Press.

Althusser, Louis 2001 [1971], *Lenin and Philosophy and Other Essays*, translated by Ben Brewster, New York: Monthly Review Press.

Althusser, Louis 2006, *Philosophy of the Encounter: Late Writings, 1978–87*, translated by G.M. Goshgarian, edited by François Matheron and Oliver Corpet, London: Verso.

Althusser, Louis 2020, *History and Imperialism*, edited and translated by G.M. Goshgarian, Cambridge: Polity Press.

Alvergue, José Felipe 2018, 'Lyric Redress: The Racial Politics of Voice and American Personhood', *Criticism*, Vol. 60:2: 221–45.

Andrews, Kimberly Quiogue 2023, *The American Avant-Garde: Poetry and the American University*, Baltimore, MD: John Hopkins University Press.

Arendt, Hannah 1998 [1958], *The Human Condition*, Chicago, IL: The University of Chicago Press.

Arrighi, Giovanni 2010 [1994], *The Long Twentieth Century: Money, Power, and the Origins of Our Times*, London: Verso.

Arthur, Christopher J. 2001, 'The spectral ontology of value', *Radical Philosophy*, Vol. 107: 32–42.

Ashton, Jennifer 2005, *From Modernism to Postmodernism: American Poetry and Theory in the Twentieth Century*, Cambridge: Cambridge University Press.

Backhaus, Hans-Georg 2005, 'Some Aspects of Marx's Concept of Critique in the Context of his Economic-Philosophical Theory', in *Human Dignity: Social Autonomy and the Critique of Capitalism*, edited by Werner Bonefeld and Kosmas Psychopedis. London: Routledge.

Bakan, Abigail B. and Yasmeen Abu-Laban 2024, 'Antisemitism as Anti-Jewish Racism: Reflections on an Anti-Racist Analytic', in *Historical Materialism*, Vol. 32:1: 225–66.

Barrett, Lindon 1990, '"In the Dark": Billie Holiday and Some Sights and Sounds of American Value', *Callaloo*, Vol. 13:4: 872–85.

Barrett, Lindon 1999, *Blackness and Value: Seeing Double*, Cambridge: Cambridge University Press.

Battersby, Christine 2021, 'Cavarero, Kant, and the Arcs of Friendship', in *Toward a Feminist Ethics of Nonviolence*, edited by Timothy J. Huzar and Clare Woodford, New York: Fordham University Press.

Beech, Dave 2015, *Art and Value: Art's Economic Exceptionalism in Classical, Neoclassical and Marxist Economics*, Leiden: Brill.

Beech, Dave 2019, *Art and Postcapitalism: Aesthetic Labour, Automation and Value Production*, London: Pluto Press.

Beech, Dave 2020, *Art and Labour: On the Hostility to Handicraft, Aesthetic Labour and the Politics of Work in Art*, Chicago, IL: Haymarket Books.

Berardi, Franco 'Bifo' 2012, *The Uprising: On Poetry and Finance*, South Pasadena, CA: Semiotext(e).

Bernes, Jasper 2017, *The Work of Art in the Age of Deindustrialization*, Stanford, CA: Stanford University Press.

Bernstein, Charles and Bruce Andrews (eds.) 1984, *The L=A=N=G=U=A=G=E Book*, Carbondale, IL: Southern Illinois University Press.

Best, Beverley 2010, *Marx and the Dynamic of the Capital Formation: An Aesthetics of Political Economy*, New York: Palgrave Macmillan.

Best, Beverley 2021, 'Wages for Housework Redux: Social Reproduction and the Utopian Dialectic of the Value-form', *Theory & Event*, Vol. 24:4: 896–921.

Best, Beverley 2023, 'The Commune is Our Payable Debt', *Cultural Dynamics*, Vol. 35:4: 258–66.

Best, Beverley 2024, *The Automatic Fetish: The Law of Value in Marx's 'Capital'*, London: Verso.

Bevins, Vincent 2023, *If We Burn: The Mass Protest Decade and the Missing Revolution*, New York: PublicAffairs.

Bey, Marquis 2020, *The Problem of the Negro as a Problem for Gender*, Minnesota, MN: University of Minnesota Press.

Blake, William 1794, 'London': https://www.poetryfoundation.org/poems/43673/london-56d222777e969.

Bohrer, Ashley J. 2019, *Marxism and Intersectionality: Race, Gender, Class and Sexuality Under Contemporary Capitalism*, Bielefeld, transcript Verlag.

Bolt Rasmussen, Mikkel 2021, *Late Capitalist Fascism*, Cambridge: Polity Press.

Bottomore, Tom (ed.) 2001 [1991], *A Dictionary of Marxist Thought*, Malden, MA: Blackwell Publishers.

Butler, Judith 1997, *The Psychic Life of Power: Theories in Subjection*, Stanford, CA: Stanford University Press.

Butler, Judith 1999, 'A "Bad Writer" Bites Back', *New York Times*, 20 March: https://archive.nytimes.com/query.nytimes.com/gst/fullpage-950CE5D61531F933A15750C0A96F958260.html.

Butler, Judith 2000, *Antigone's Claim: Kinship Between Life and Death*. New York: Columbia University Press.

Butler, Judith 2004a, 'What Is Critique? An Essay on Foucault's Virtue', in *The Judith Butler Reader*, edited by Sara Salih and Judith Butler, Malden, MA: Blackwell.

Butler, Judith 2004b, *Undoing Gender*, New York: Routledge.

Butler, Judith 2005, *Giving an Account of Oneself*, New York: Fordham University Press.

Butler, Judith 2007 [1990], *Gender Trouble: Feminism and the Subversion of Identity*, New York: Routledge.

Butler, Judith 2011 [1993], *Bodies That Matter: On the Discursive Limits of 'Sex'*, London: Routledge.

Butler, Judith 2015a, *Notes Toward a Performative Theory of Assembly*, Cambridge, MA: Harvard University Press.

Butler, Judith 2015b, *Senses of the Subject*, New York: Fordham University Press.

Butler, Judith 2016 [2010], *Frames of War: When Is Life Grievable?* London: Verso.

Butler, Judith 2020 [2004], *Precarious Life: The Powers of Mourning and Justice*, London: Verso.

Butler, Judith 2021a [1997], *Excitable Speech: A Politics of the Performative*, London: Routledge.

Butler, Judith 2021b, 'Leaning Out, Caught in the Fall: Interdependency and Ethics in Cavarero', in *Toward a Feminist Ethics of Nonviolence*, edited by Timothy J. Huzar and Clare Woodford, New York: Fordham University Press.

Butler, Judith 2024, *Who's Afraid of Gender?* London: Allen Lane.

Butler, Judith, Ernesto Laclau and Slavoj Žižek 2000, *Contingency, Hegemony, Universality: Contemporary Dialogues on the Left*, London: Verso.

Bradley, Rizvana 2023, *Anteaesthetics: Black Aesthetics and the Critique of Form*, Stanford, CA: Stanford University Press.

Browne, Jaron 2007, 'Rooted in Slavery: Prison Labor Exploitation', *Race, Poverty & the Environment*, Vol. 14:1: 42–4.

Brown, Jayna 2021, *Black Utopias: Speculative Life and the Music of Other Worlds*, Durham, NC: Duke University Press.

Carson, Rebecca 2023, Immanent Externalities: The Reproduction of Life in Capital, Leiden: Brill.

Cavarero, Adriana 2016, *Inclinations: A Critique of Rectitude*, translated by Amanda Minervini and Adam Sitze, Stanford, CA: Stanford University Press.

Cavarero, Adriana 2021a, 'Scenes of Inclination', in *Toward a Feminist Ethics of Nonviolence*, edited by Timothy J. Huzar and Clare Woodford, New York: Fordham University Press.

Cavarero, Adriana 2021b, *Surging Democracy: Notes on Hannah Arendt's Political Thought*, Translated by Matthew Gervase, Stanford, CA: Stanford University Press.

Cervenak, Sarah Jane 2021, *Black Gathering: Art, Ecology, Ungiven Life*, Durham, NC: Duke University Press.

Chakrabarty, Dipesh 2008 [2000], *Provincializing Europe: Postcolonial Thought and Historical Difference*, Princeton, NJ: Princeton University Press.

Chambers, Samuel A. 2018, *There's No Such Thing as "The Economy": Essays on Capitalist Value*, Santa Barbara, CA: Punctum Books.

Chandler, Nahum Dimitri 2017, *X: The Problem of the Negro as a Problem for Thought*, New York: Fordham University Press.

Checchi, Marco 2021, *The Primacy of Resistance: Power, Opposition and Becoming*, London: Bloomsbury.

Chiesa, Lorenzo 2007, *Subjectivity and Otherness: A Philosophical Reading of Lacan*, Cambridge, MA: The MIT Press.

Chiesa, Lorenzo 2016, *The Virtual Point of Freedom: Essays on Politics, Aesthetics, and Religion*, Evanston, IL: Northwestern University Press.

Clover, Joshua 2010, '"A Form Adequate to History": Toward a Renewed Marxist Poetics', *Paideuma*, Vol. 37: 321–48.

Clover, Joshua 2011, 'Autumn of the System: Poetry and Financial Capital', *Journal of Narrative Theory*, Vol. 41:1: 34–52.

Clover, Joshua 2016, *Riot. Strike. Riot: The New Era of Uprisings*, London: Verso.

Clover, Joshua and Juliana Spahr 2016, 'Gender Abolition and Ecotone War', *South Atlantic Quarterly*, Vol. 115:2: 291–311.

Davidson, Michael 1989, *The San Francisco Renaissance: Poetics and Community at Mid-Century*, Cambridge: Cambridge University Press,

Day, Iyko 2016, *Alien Capital: Asian Racialization and the Logic of Settler Colonial Capitalism*, Durham, NC: Duke University Press.

Day, Iyko 2022, 'Eco-Criticism and Primitive Accumulation in Indigenous Studies', *After Marx: Literature, Theory, and Value in the Twenty-First Century*, Edited by Colleen Lye and Christopher Nealon, Cambridge: Cambridge University Press.

De'Ath, Amy 2017, *Unsociable Poetry: Antagonism and Abstraction in Contemporary Feminized Poetics*, unpublished PhD thesis, Simon Fraser University: https://summit.sfu.ca/item/17177.

De'Ath, Amy 2022, 'Hidden Abodes and Inner Bonds: Literary Study and Marxist – Feminism', in *After Marx: Literature, Theory, and Value in the Twenty-First Century*, edited by Colleen Lye and Christopher Nealon. Cambridge: Cambridge University Press.

De'Ath, Amy 2023, 'Two Substantialisms: On Value and Sexual Difference', talk presented at Historical Materialism, London, 12 November.

Dean, Jodi 2018 [2016], *Crowds and Party*. London: Verso.

Derrick, Frederick W., Charles E. Scott and Thomas Hutson 2004, 'Prison Labor Effects on the Unskilled Labor Market', *The American Economist*, Vol. 48:2: 74–81.

Derrida, Jacques 1994, *Specters of Marx: The State of the Debt, the Work of Mourning and the New International*, Translated by Peggy Kamuf, New York: Routledge.

Derrida, Jacques and Anne Dufourmantelle 2000, *Of Hospitality: Anne Dufourmantelle Invites Jacques Derrida to Respond*, Translated by Rachel Bowlby, Stanford, CA: Stanford University Press.

Dodson, Ted 2020, 'An Interview with Alli Warren', *The Believer*, 14 April: https://believermag.com/logger/an-interview-with-alli-warren/.

Du Bois, W.E.B. 1997 [1903], *The Souls of Black Folk*, Boston: Bedford Books.

Dues, Coleman Edward 2024, 'Some Ekphrastic Evening: On Fred Moten's perennial fashion presence falling', *Cleveland Review of Books*: https://www.clereviewofbooks.com/writing/fred-moten-perennial-fashion-presence-falling.

Duffy, Mignon, Randy Albelda, and Clare Hammonds 2013, 'Counting Care Work: The Empirical and Policy Applications of Care Theory', *Social Problems*, Vol. 60:2: 145–67.

Duggan, Lisa 2003, *The Twilight of Equality? Neoliberalism, Cultural Politics, and the Attack on Democracy*, Boston: Beacon Press.

Duncan, Robert 1982, *Towards an Open Universe*, Portree, Scotland: Aquila Publishing.

Dwyer, Rachel E. 2013, 'The Care Economy? Gender, Economic Restructuring, and Job Polarization in the U.S. Labor Market', *American Sociological Review*, Vol. 78:3: 390–416.

Eliot, T.S. 2001, 'Tradition and the Individual Talent', *The Norton Anthology of Theory and Criticism*, Edited by Vincent B. Leitch. New York, NY: W.W. Norton & Company.

Endnotes 2010, Endnotes 2: Misery and the Value-Form.

Endnotes 2013, *Endnotes 3: Gender, Race, Class, and Other Misfortunes*.

Ertür, Başak 2016, 'Barricades: Resources and Residues of Resistance', *Vulnerability in Resistance*, edited by Judith Butler, Zeynep Gambetti, and Leticia Sabsay, Durham, NC: Duke University Press.

Eze, Emmanuel Chukwudi (ed.) 1997, *Race and the Enlightenment: A Reader*, Malden, MA: Blackwell.

Federal Bureau of Prisons, No date, 'UNICOR: Program Details': https://www.bop.gov/inmates/custody_and_care/unicor_about.jsp.

Federici, Silvia 2021, *Patriarchy of the Wage: Notes on Marx, Gender, and Feminism*, Oakland, CA: PM Press.

Fields, Darell Wayne 2015 [2000], *Architecture in Black: Theory, Space, and Appearance*, London: Bloomsbury.

Fisher, Samuel 2024, 'Abstract Models, Concrete Frictions: On Mau's Mute Compulsion', *Spectre*, online, 23 July: https://spectrejournal.com/abstract-models-concrete-frictions/.

Floyd, Kevin 2016, 'Automatic Subjects: Gendered Labour and Abstract Life', *Historical Materialism*, Vol. 24:2: 61–86.

Foucault, Michel 1995 [1977], *Discipline and Punish: The Birth of the Prison*, translated by Alan Sheridan, New York: Vintage Books.

Franklin, Seb 2021, *The Digitally Disposed: Racial Capitalism and the Informatics of Value*, Minneapolis, MN: University of Minnesota Press.

Fanon, Frantz 1967, *Toward the African Revolution: Political Essays*, translated by Haakon Chevalier, New York: Grove Press.

Fraser, Nancy 2016, 'Expropriation and Exploitation in Racialized Capitalism: A Reply to Michael Dawson', *Critical Historical Studies*, Vol. 3:1: 163–78.

Fraser, Nancy 2021, 'Gender, Capital, and Care', in *Why Gender?* Edited by Jude Browne, Cambridge: Cambridge University Press, 144–69.

Freud, Sigmund 1978, *The Standard Edition of the Complete Psychological Works of Sigmund Freud, Vol. 13* (1913–1914), London: Hogarth Press.

Fromm, Erich 2001 [1942], *The Fear of Freedom*, London: Routledge.

Ftouni, Layal 2024, '"They Make Death, and I'm the Labor of Life": Palestinian Prisoners' Sperm Smuggling as an Affirmation of Life', *Critical Times*, Vol. 7:1: 94–109.

Gates Jr., Henry Louis 1988, *The Signifying Monkey: A Theory of African-American Literary Criticism*, Oxford: Oxford University Press.

Gilmore, Kim 2000, 'Slavery and Prison – Understanding the Connections', *Social Justice*, Vol. 27:3: 195–205.

Gizzi, Peter and Kevin Killian (eds.) 2008, *My Vocabulary Did This to Me: The Collected Poetry of Jack Spicer*, Middletown, CT: Wesleyan University Press.

Gotby, Alva 2023, *They Call it Love: The Politics of Emotional Life*, London: Verso.

Gramsci, Antonio 1971, *Selections from the Prison Notebooks*, edited and translated by Quintin Hoare and Geoffrey Nowell Smith, New York: International Publishers.

Granberg, Magnus 2022, 'Reactionary Radicalism and the Analysis of Worker Subjectivity in Marx's Critique of Political Economy', *Capital & Class*, Vol. 46:2: 279–99.

Halpern, Rob 2011, 'Realism and Utopia: Sex, Writing, and Activism in New Narrative', *Journal of Narrative Theory*, Vol. 41:1: 82–124.

Halpern, Rob 2012, *Music for Porn*, New York: Nightboat Books.

Halpern, Rob 2013, 'Becoming a Patient of History: George Oppen's Domesticity and the Relocation of Politics', *Chicago Review*, Vol. 58:1: 50–74.

Hardt, Michael and Antonio Negri 2000, *Empire*, Cambridge, MA: Harvard University Press.

Hardt, Michael and Antonio Negri 2002, 'Marx's Mole is Dead! Globalisation and Communication', *Eurozine*, 13 February.

Hardt, Michael and Antonio Negri 2017, *Assembly*, Oxford: Oxford University Press.

Harney, Stefano and Fred Moten 2013, *The Undercommons: Fugitive Planning & Black Study*, Wivenhoe: Minor Compositions.

Harney, Stefano and Fred Moten 2021, *All Incomplete*, Colchester: Minor Compositions.

Harney, Stefano and Fred Moten 2022, 'On Violence #2', *Akademie der Künste der Welt*, 8 June: https://www.youtube.com/watch?v=3I_1QAdnjic.

Harootunian, Harry 2015, *Marx After Marx: History and Time in the Expansion of Capitalism*, New York: Columbia University Press.

Harris, Cheryl I. 1993, 'Whiteness as Property', *Harvard Law Review*, Vol. 106:8 (June): 1708–918.

Harris, Kaplan Page 2009, 'New Narrative and the Making of Language Poetry', *American Literature*, Vol. 81:4 (December): 805–32.

Harris, Laura 2018, *Experiments in Exile: C.L.R. James, Hélio Oiticica, and the Aesthetic Sociality of Blackness*, New York: Fordham University Press.

Hart, William David 2018, 'Constellations: Capitalism, Antiblackness, Afro-pessimism, and Black Optimism', *American Journey of Philosophy and Theology*, Vol. 39:1: 5–33.

Hartley, George 2003, *The Abyss of Representation: Marxism and the Postmodern Sublime*, Durham, NC: Duke University Press.

Hartman, Saidiya V. 1997, *Scenes of Subjection: Terror, Slavery, and Self-Making in Nineteenth-Century America*, Oxford: Oxford University Press.

Hartman, Saidiya V. 2018, 'The Anarchy of Colored Girls Assembled in a Riotous Manner', *South Atlantic Quarterly*, Vol. 117:3: 465–90.

Hartman, Saidiya V. 2019, *Wayward Lives, Beautiful Experiments: Intimate Histories of Social Upheaval*, New York: W.W. Norton & Company.

Harvey, David 2015, *Seventeen Contradictions and the End of Capitalism*, Oxford: Oxford University Press.

Hegel, G.W.F. 1975, *Hegel's Aesthetics: Lectures on the Fine Arts*, translated by T.M. Knox, Oxford: Clarendon Press.

Hegel, G.W.F. 2004 [1977], *Phenomenology of Spirit*, translated by A.V. Miller, Oxford: Oxford University Press.

Heinrich, Michael 2004, *An Introduction to the Three Volumes of Karl Marx's Capital*, translated by Alexander Locascio, New York: Monthly Review Press.

Hejinian, Lyn 2000, *The Language of Inquiry*, Berkley, CA: University of California Press.

Hickman, Ben 2015, *Crisis and the US Avant-Garde: Poetry and Real Politics*, Edinburgh: Edinburgh University Press.

Houen, Alex 2014, *Powers of Possibility: Experimental American Writing since the 1960s*, Oxford: Oxford University Press.

Hordijk, Ruben 2024, *Spectral Inheritance: Unlearning the Maturity Trope*, unpublished PhD thesis, Linköping University: https://diva-portal.org/smash/get/diva2:1841563/FULLTEXT01.pdf.

Huber, Matthew 2013, *Lifeblood: Oil, Freedom, and the Forces of Capital*, Minneapolis, MN: University of Minnesota Press.

Hunter, Walt 2019, *Forms of a World: Contemporary Poetry and the Making of Globalization*, New York: Fordham University Press.

Iacomo, Alfonso Maurizio 2020, 'Marx's Method and the Use of Abstraction', *Marx and Contemporary Critical Theory: The Philosophy of Real Abstraction*, edited by Antonio Oliva, Ángel Oliva, and Iván Novara, Cham, Switzerland: Palgrave Macmillan.

Iñigo Carrera, Juan 2007, *Conocer el capital hoy: Usar críticamente El Capital*, Buenos Aires: Imago Mundi.

Jameson, Fredric 2009, *Valences of the Dialectic*, London: Verso.

Jappe, Anselm 2017, *The Writing on the Wall: On the Decomposition of Capitalism and its Critics*, translated by Alastair Hemmens, Winchester: Zero Books.

Johannessen, Runa, No date, 'Sumud: Steadfastness as Everyday Resistance', *Interactive Encyclopedia of the Palestine Question*: https://www.palquest.org/en/highlight/33633/sumud.

Judy, R.A. 2020, *Sentient Flesh: Thinking in Disorder, Poiēsis in Black*, Durham, NC: Duke University Press.

Kant, Immanuel 1784, *Idea for a Universal History from a Cosmopolitan Point of View*, translated by Lewis White Beck: https://www.marxists.org/reference/subject/ethics/kant/universal -history.htm.

Kant, Immanuel 1997, *Groundwork of the Metaphysics of Morals*, Cambridge: Cambridge University Press.

Kant, Immanuel 1998, *Critique of Pure Reason*, translated by Paul Guyer and Allen W. Wood, Cambridge: Cambridge University Press.

Kant, Immanuel 1999, *Practical Philosophy*, translated and edited by Mary J. Gregor, Cambridge: Cambridge University Press.

Kant, Immanuel 2006, *Anthropology from a Pragmatic Point of View*, translated by Robert B. Louden, Cambridge: Cambridge University Press.

Keegan, Joseph M. 2022, 'Insider-Outsiders'. *First Things*: https://www.firstthings.com/article/2022/03/insider-outsiders.

Kline, David 2017, 'The Pragmatics of Resistance: Framing Anti-Blackness and the Limits of Political Ontology', *Critical Philosophy of Race*, Vol. 5:1: 51–69.

Kurz, Robert 1999, *Das Schwarzbuch Kapitalismus: Ein Abgesang auf die Marktwirtschaft*, Frankfurt am Main: Eichborn Verlag.

Kurz, Robert 2014a, 'On the Current Global Economic Crisis: Questions and Answers', *Marxism and the Critique of Value*, edited by Neil Larsen, Mathias Nilges, Josh Robinson, and Nicholas Brown, Chicago: MCM' Publishing, 331–356.

Kurz, Robert 2014b, 'World Power and World Money: The Economic Function of the U.S. Military Machine within Global Capitalism and the Background of the New Financial Crisis', *Marxism and the Critique of Value*, edited by Neil Larsen, Mathias Nilges, Josh Robinson, and Nicholas Brown, Chicago: MCM' Publishing, 187–200.

Kurz, Robert 2014c, 'The Nightmare of Freedom: The Foundation of "Western Values" and the Helplessness of Critique', in *Marxism and the Critique of Value*, edited by Neil Larsen, Mathias Nilges, Josh Robinson, and Nicholas Brown, Chicago: MCM' Publishing, 285–91.

Kurz, Robert 2016, *The Substance of Capital*, translated by Robin Halpin, London: Chronos Publications.

La Berge, Leigh Claire 2022, 'There Is No "More Commodification": Periodizing Capitalist Transformation', in *After Marx: Literature, Theory, and Value in the Twenty-First Century*, edited by Colleen Lye and Christopher Nealon, Cambridge: Cambridge University Press, 86–100.

Lacan, Jacques 2001 [1977], *Écrits: A Selection*, translated by Alan Sheridan, London: Routledge.

Laclau, Ernesto and Chantal Mouffe 2001 [1985], *Hegemony and Socialist Strategy: Towards a Radical Democratic Politics*, London: Verso.

Lalu, Premesh 2022, *Undoing Apartheid*, Cambridge: Polity.

Lange, Elena Louisa 2021, *Value Without Fetish: Uno Kōzō's Theory of 'Pure Capitalism' in Light of Marx's Critique of Political Economy*, Leiden: Brill.

Larsen, Neil, Mathias Nilges, Josh Robinson, and Nicholas Brown (eds.) 2014, *Marxism and the Critique of Value*. Chicago: MCM' Publishing.

Lazzarato, Maurizio 2014, *Signs and Machines: Capitalism and the Production of Subjectivity*, translated by Joshua David Jordan, Los Angeles, CA: Semiotext(e).

Leung, King-Ho 2023, 'Nothingness without Reserve: Fred Moten contra Heidegger, Sartre, and Schelling', *Comparative and Continental Philosophy*, Vol. 15:1–2: 45–57.

Leslie, Esther 2014, 'Satanic Mills: On Robert Kurz', *Historical Materialism*, Vol. 22: 3–4: 408–423.

Levinas, Emmanuel 1989, 'Ethics as First Philosophy', *The Levinas Reader*, edited by Seán Hand, Oxford: Basil Blackwell.

Lloyd, David 2019. *Under Representation: The Racial Regime of Aesthetics*. New York, NY: Fordham University Press.

Lohoff, Ernst 2014, 'Off Limits, Out of Control: Commodity Society and Resistance in the Age of Deregulation and Denationalization', in *Marxism and the Critique of Value*, edited by Neil Larsen, Mathias Nilges, Josh Robinson, and Nicholas Brown, Chicago: MCM' Publishing, 151–86.

Lütticken, Sven 2023, *Objections: Forms of Abstraction, Volume 1*, London: Sternberg Press.

McGurl, Mark 2011, *The Program Era: Postwar Fiction and the Rise of Creative Writing*, Cambridge, MA: Harvard University Press.

McKinsey Global Institute 2022, 'How US consumers are feeling, shopping, and spending – and what it means for companies: Article', 4 May: https://www.mckinsey.com/capabilities/growth-marketing-and-sales/our-insights/how-us-consumers-are-feeling-shopping-and-spending-and-what-it-means-for-companies.

McKinsey Global Institute 2023, 'Rekindling US productivity for a new era: Report', 16 February: https://www.mckinsey.com/mgi/our-research/rekindling-us-productivity-for-a-new-era#at-a-glance.

McNeil, Desmond 2021, *Fetishism and the Theory of Value: Reassessing Marx in the 21st Century*, Cham, Switzerland: Palgrave Macmillan.

Mandel, Ernest 1991. 'Introduction', in *Karl Marx, Capital: A Critique of Political Economy, Volume III*, translated by David Fernbach. London: Penguin, 9–90.

Mason, Elliot C. 2024, 'Review of Rebecca Carson, Immanent Externalities', *Marx & Philosophy Review of Books*, online, 21 March: https://marxandphilosophy.org.uk/reviews/21440_immanent-externalities-the-reproduction-of-life-in-capital-by-rebecca-carson-reviewed-by-elliot-c-mason/.

Mason, Elliot C. and Valentina Moro (eds.) 2025, *Judith Butler and Marxism: The Radical Feminism of Performativity, Vulnerability, and Care*, New York: Rowman & Littlefield.

Mau, Søren 2023, *Mute Compulsion: A Marxist Theory of the Economic Power of Capital*, London: Verso.

Martel, James R. 2017, *The Misinterpellated Subject*, Durham, NC: Duke University Press.

Marx, Karl 1990 [1976], *Capital: A Critique of Political Economy, Volume I*, translated by Ben Fowkes, London: Penguin.

Marx, Karl 1991 [1981], *Capital: A Critique of Political Economy, Volume III*, translated by David Fernbach. London: Penguin.

Marx, Karl 1992a [1978]. *Capital: A Critique of Political Economy, Volume II*, Translated by David Fernbach, London: Penguin.

Marx, Karl 1992b [1975], *Early Writings*, translated by Rodney Livingstone and Gregor Benton, London: Penguin.

Marx, Karl 1993 [1973], *Grundrisse: Foundations of the Critique of Political Economy*, translated by Martin Nicolaus. London: Penguin.

Marx, Karl 2007 [1961], *Economic and Philosophic Manuscripts of 1844*, translated by Martin Milligan, Mineola, NY: Dover Publications.

Marx, Karl 2021, *The Civil War in France*, Beijing: Foreign Languages Press.

Marx, Karl 2024, *Capital: Critique of Political Economy, Volume 1*, translated by Paul Reitter, edited by Paul North and Paul Reitter, Princeton: Princeton University Press.

Marx, Karl and Friedrich Engels 2010, *The German Ideology: Marx/Engels Collected Works, Vol. 5: 1845–47*, London: Lawrence and Wishart.

Mercer, Marsha 2022, 'Advocates Seek to Make Prison Work Voluntary', *Pew Trust*, 7 September: https://www.pewtrusts.org/en/research-and- analysis/blogs/stateline/2022/09/07/advocates-seek-to-make-prison-work-voluntary.

Mezzadra, Sandro 2018, In the Marxian Workshops: Producing Subjects, translated by Lari Yanci. London: Rowman & Littlefield.

Moreno Zacarés, Javier 2021, 'Two Historicisms: Unpacking the Rules of Reproduction Debate', *Historical Materialism*, Vol. 29:3: 175–98.

Moseley, Fred 1983, 'Marx's Concept of Productive Labor and Unproductive Labor: An Application to the Postwar U.S. Economy', *Eastern Economic Journal*, Vol. 9:3: 180–9.

Moseley, Fred 1991, *The Falling Rate of Profit in the Postwar United State Economy*, London: Macmillan Academic.

Moseley, Fred 2016, *Money and Totality: A Macro-Monetary Interpretation of Marx's Logic in 'Capital' and the End of the 'Transformation Problem'*, Leiden: Brill.

Moten, Fred 2003, *In the Break: The Aesthetics of the Black Radical Tradition*, Minneapolis, MN: University of Minnesota Press.

Moten, Fred 2008, 'The Case of Blackness', *Criticism*, Vol. 50:2: 177–218.

Moten, Fred 2010, *B Jenkins*, Durham, NC: Duke University Press.

Moten, Fred 2013, 'Blackness and Nothingness (Mysticism in the Flesh)', *South Atlantic Quarterly*, Vol. 112:4: 737–80.

Moten, Fred 2017a, *Day*, New York: Belladonna* Chaptlet.

Moten, Fred 2017b, *Black and Blur*, Durham, NC: Duke University Press.

Moten, Fred 2018a, *Stolen Life*, Durham, NC: Duke University Press.

Moten, Fred 2018b, *The Universal Machine*, Durham, NC: Duke University Press.

Moten, Fred 2018c, 'Recess and Nonsense: The End of the Poetry World and the Ends of the Poet', Keynote address: More Than a Manifesto conference, Columbia University School of the Arts, New York, 3 March: https://www.youtube.com/watch?v=uMf6GJ8wBf8.

Moten, Fred 2019, *All That Beauty*, Seattle, WA: Letter Machine Editions.

Moten, Fred 2022, 'Nothing in the Way of Things', *M.H. Abrams Distinguished Visiting Professor lecture*, 31 March: https://www.youtube.com/watch?v=vDUb9hzlook.

Moten, Fred and Legacy Russell 2024, 'Spectators and Witnesses', *The Verso Podcast*, 2 May: https://www.versobooks.com/blogs/news/spectators-and-witnesses-legacy-russell-fred-moten?srsltid=AfmBOoryZ6uGIOPYEhAUJxtO5_cLXBTz54SEhWYQCjXa3pBuCK6HuRBd.

Moten, Fred and Stefano Harney 2020a, '"Wildcat the Totality": Fred Moten and Stefano Harney Revisit The Undercommons in a Time of Pandemic and Rebellion' (part 1), *Millennials Are Killing Capitalism podcast*, 4 July: https://millennialsarekillingcapitalism.libsyn.com/.

Moten, Fred and Stefano Harney 2020b, '"Give Your House Away, Constantly": Fred Moten and Stefano Harney Revisit The Undercommons in a Time of Pandemic and Rebellion' (part 2), *Millennials Are Killing Capitalism podcast*, 11 July: https://millennialsarekillingcapitalism.libsyn.com/give-away-your-home-constantly-fred-moten-and-stefano-harney/.

Moten, Fred and Wu Tsang 2016, *Who Touched Me?* Amsterdam: If I Can't Dance I Don't Want to be Part of Your Revolution.

Mulaj, Jeta 2024, 'Ontology as Ideology: A Critique of Butler's Theory of Precariousness', *Constellations*, Vol. 31:4: 491–505.

Nancy, Jean-Luc 2008, *Corpus*, translated by Richard A. Rand, New York: Fordham University Press.

Nealon, Christopher and Joshua Clover 2023, 'Literary and Economic Value', in Christopher Nealon, *Infinity for Marxists: Essays on Poetry and Capital*, Leiden: Brill, 195–213.

Negri, Antonio 1999, *Insurgencies: Constituent Power and the Modern State*, translated by Maurizia Boscagli, Minneapolis: University of Minnesota Press.

Neocleous, Mark 2003, 'The Political Economy of the Dead: Marx's Vampires', *History of Political Thought*, Vol. 24:4: 668–84.

Ngai, Sianne 2020, *Theory of the Gimmick: Aesthetic Judgment and Capitalist Form*, Cambridge, MA: The Belknap Press of Harvard University Press.

O'Hara, Frank 2014 [1964], *Lunch Poems*, San Francisco, CA: City Lights Books.

Okoth, Kevin Ochieng 2020, 'The Flatness of Blackness: Afro-Pessimism and the Erasure of Anti-Colonial Thought', Salvage, 16 January: https://salvage.zone/the-flatness-of-blackness-afro-pessimism-and-the-erasure-of-anti-colonial-thought/.

Okoth, Kevin Ochieng 2023, *Red Africa: Reclaiming Revolutionary Black Politics*, London: Verso.

Olaloku-Teriba, Annie 2018, 'Afro-Pessimism and the (Un)Logic of Anti-Blackness', *Historical Materialism*, Vol. 26:2: 96–122.

Omelsky, Matthew 2023, *Fugitive Time: Global Aesthetics and the Black Beyond*, Durham, NC: Duke University Press.

Osborne, Peter 2022, *Crisis as Form*, London: Verso.

Phillips, Rowan Ricardo 2013, *The Ground*, New York: Farrar, Straus and Giroux.

Phillips, Rowan Ricardo 2015, *Heaven*, New York: Farrar, Straus and Giroux.

Phillips, Rowan Ricardo 2021 [2020], *Living Weapon*, London: Faber & Faber.

Phillips, Rowan Ricardo 2023, 'Child of Nature', in *Poetry* (July/August): https://www.poetryfoundation.org/poetrymagazine/poems/160513/child-of-nature.

Phillips, Rowan Ricardo 2024, *Silver*, London: Faber & Faber.

Pitts, Frederick Harry 2018, *Critiquing Capitalism Today: New Ways to Read Marx*, Cham: Palgrave Macmillan.

Pitts, Frederick Harry 2021, *Value*, Cambridge: Polity Press.

Postone, Moishe 2003 [1993], *Time, Labor, and Social Domination: A Reinterpretation of Marx's Critical Theory*, Cambridge: Cambridge University Press.

Preciado, Paul B. 2018, *Countersexual Manifesto*, translated by Kevin Gerry Dunn. New York: Columbia University Press.

Preciado, Paul B. 2022, Dysphoria mundi, Barcelona: Editorial Anagrama.

Proctor, Hannah 2018, 'History from Within: Identity and Interiority', *Historical Materialism*, Vol. 26:2: 75–95.

Quashie, Kevin 2012, *The Sovereignty of Quiet: Beyond Resistance in Black Culture*, New Brunswick, NJ: Rutgers University Press.

Raha, Nat 2021, 'A Queer Marxist Transfeminism: Queer and Trans Social Reproduction', *Transgender Marxism*, edited by Jules Joanne Gleeson and Elle O'Rourke, London: Pluto Press, 85–115.

Rao, Rahul 2020, *Out of Time: The Queer Politics of Postcoloniality*, Oxford: Oxford University Press.

Rasula, Jed 2004, *Syncopations: The Stress of Innovation in Contemporary American Poetry*, Tuscaloosa, AL: University of Alabama Press.

Read, Jason 2003, *The Micro-Politics of Capital: Marx and the Prehistory of the Present*, Albany, NY: SUNY Press.

Read, Jason 2023, *The Production of Subjectivity: Marx and Philosophy*, Chicago, IL: Haymarket Books.

Rey-Araújo, Pedro M. 2024, 'Reproducing Life Through Capital: On the Relevance of Value', *Spectre Journal*: https://spectrejournal.com/reproducing-life-through-capital/.

Riot Not To Work 1982, *We Want to Riot Not to Work: The 1981 Brixton Uprisings*, London: Little A. Available in print at the Black Cultural Archives, Brixton, London.

Rivera, Maya 2015, *Poetics of the Flesh*, Durham, NC: Duke University Press.

Roberts, Bruce 2014, 'Productive/Unproductive: Conceptual Topology', *Rethinking Marxism*, Vol. 23:3: 336–59. DOI: 10.1080/08935696.2014.917842.

Roberts, William Clare 2017, *Marx's Inferno: The Political Theory of 'Capital'*, Princeton: Princeton University Press.

Robinson, Cedric J. 1980, *The Terms of Order: Political Science and the Myth of Leadership*, Chapel Hill, NC: University of North Carolina Press.

Roggero, Gigi 2023, 'Italian Operaismo', *E-flux*, Vol. 134.

Rubin, I.I. 2020, *Essays on Marx's Theory of Value*, translated by Miloš Samardžija and Fredy Perlman, No location: Radical Reprints.

Salih, Ruba, and Sophie Richter-Devroe 2014, 'Cultures of Resistance in Palestine and Beyond: On the Politics of Art, Aesthetics, and Affect'. *Arab Studies Journal*, Vol. 22:1: 8–27.

Saito, Kohei 2022, *Marx in the Anthropocene: Towards the Idea of Degrowth Communism*. Cambridge: Cambridge University Press.

Schmidt, Alfred 1983, *History and Structure: An Essay on Hegelian-Marxist and Structuralist Theories of History*, translated by Jeffrey Herf, Cambridge, MA: The MIT Press.

Scholz, Roswitha 2011a, 'O Tabu da Abstracção no Feminismo: Como se esquece o universal do patriarcado produtor de mercadorias', *Exit!* Vol. 8: http://www.obeco-online.org/roswitha_scholz15.htm.

Scholz, Roswitha 2011b [2000]. *Das Geschlecht des Kapitalismus: Feministische Theorien und die postmoderne Metamorphose des Patriarchats*. Bad Honnef: Horlemann Verlag.

Scholz, Roswitha 2014, 'Patriarchy and Commodity Society: Gender without the Body', *Marxism and the Critique of Value*, edited by Neil Larsen, Mathias Nilges, Josh Robinson, and Nicholas Brown, Chicago: MCM' Publishing.

Sharpe, Christina 2023, *Ordinary Notes*, London: Daunt Books Originals.

Shulman, George 2020, 'Fred Moten's Refusals and Consents: The Politics of Fugitivity', *Political Theory*, Vol. 49:2: 272–313.

Silliman, Ron, Carla Harryman, Lyn Hejinian, Steve Benson, Bob Perelman and Barrett Watten 1988, 'Aesthetic Tendency and the Politics of Poetry: A Manifesto', *Social Text*, Vol. 19/20: 261–75.

Silva, Denise Ferreira da 2014, 'Toward a Black Feminist Poethics: The Quest(ion) of Blackness Toward the End of the World', *The Black Scholar*, Vol. 44:2: 81–97.

Silva, Denise Ferreira da 2018b, 'Hacking the Subject: Black Feminism and Refusal beyond the Limits of Critique', *PhiloSOPHIA*, Vol. 8:1: 19–41.

Silva, Denise Ferreira da 2022, *Unpayable Debt*, London: Sternberg Press.

Simone, Abdou Maliq 2022, *The Surrounds: Urban Life Within and Beyond Capture*, Durham, NC: Duke University Press.

Söderbäck, Fanny 2019, *Revolutionary Time: On Time and Difference in Kristeva and Irigaray*, Albany, NY: SUNY Press.

Sohn-Rethel, Alfred 1978, *Intellectual and Manual Labour: A Critique of Epistemology*, London: Macmillan.

Spahr, Juliana 2001, *Everybody's Autonomy: Connective Reading and Collective Identity*. Tuscaloosa, AL: University of Alabama Press.

Spivak, Gayatri Chakravorty 1985, 'Scattered Speculations on the Question of Value', *Diacritics*, Vol. 15:4: 73–93.

Spivak, Gayatri Chakravorty 1988, 'Can the Subaltern Speak?', *Marxism and the Interpretation of Culture*, edited by Cary Nelson and Lawrence Grossberg, Urbana, IL: University of Illinois Press.

Starosta, Guido 2016, *Marx's 'Capital', Method and Revolutionary Subjectivity*, Leiden: Brill.

Tadiar, Neferti X.M. 2009, *Things Fall Away: Philippine Historical Experience and the Makings of Globalization*, Durham, NC: Duke University Press.

Tadiar, Neferti X.M. 2012, 'Life-Times in Fate Playing', *South Atlantic Quarterly*, Vol. 111:4: 783–802.

Tadiar, Neferti X.M. 2022, *Remaindered Life*, Durham, NC: Duke University Press.

Taylor, Frederick 1911, *The Principles of Scientific Management*, New York: Harper and Brothers.

Taylor, Keeanga-Yamahtta 2019, *Race for Profit: How Banks and the Real Estate Industry Undermined Black Homeownership*, Chapel Hill, NC: The University of North Carolina Press.

Thoburn, Nicholas 2024, 'A Fugitive Book? Anti-Blackness, Anti-Books, and Uprising', talk presented at ASCA Workshop: Resistance, Refusal, Fugitivity, University of Amsterdam, 5–7 June.

Thomas, Peter D. 2023, *Radical Politics: On the Causes of Contemporary Emancipation*, Oxford: Oxford University Press.

Tomba, Massimiliano 2013a, *Marx's Temporalities*, translated by Peter D. Thomas and Sara F. Farris. Leiden: Brill.

Tomba, Massimiliano 2013b, 'Pre-Capitalistic Forms of Production and Primitive Accumulation. Marx's Historiography from the Grundrisse to Capital', *Marx's Laboratory: Critical Interpretations of the 'Grundrisse'*, edited by Ricardo Bellofiore, Guido Starosta, and Peter D. Thomas. Leiden: Brill.

Tomba, Massimiliano 2019, *Insurgent Universality: An Alternative Legacy of Modernity*, Oxford: Oxford University Press.

Tomšič, Samo 2021, *The Labour of Enjoyment: Towards a Critique of Libidinal Economy*, Berlin: August Verlag.

Trenkle, Norbert 2014a, 'Struggle without Classes: Why There is No Resurgence of the Proletariat in the Currently Unfolding Capitalist Crisis', *Marxism and the Critique of Value*, edited by Neil Larsen, Mathias Nilges, Josh Robinson, and Nicholas Brown. Chicago: MCM' Publishing, 201–24.

Trenkle, Norbert 2014b, 'Value and Crisis: Basic Questions', *Marxism and the Critique of Value*, edited by Neil Larsen, Mathias Nilges, Josh Robinson, and Nicholas Brown. Chicago: MCM' Publishing, 1–15

Tronti, Mario 1979, *Working Class Autonomy and the Crisis*, London: Red Notes.

Tronti, Mario 2019 [1966], *Workers and Capital*, translated by David Broder. London: Verso.

Uenema, Francine 2022, 'The History of California's Inmate Firefighter Program', *Smithsonian Magazine*, 1 September: https://www.smithsonianmag.com/history/the-history-of-californias-inmate-firefighter-program-180980662/.

U.S. Bureau of Labor Statistics 2021, 'The U.S. productivity slowdown: an economy-wide and industry-level analysis', April: https://www.bls.gov/opub/mlr/2021/article/the-us-productivity-slowdown-the-economy-wide-and-industry-level-analysis.htm.

Varoufakis, Yanis 2024, *Technofeudalism: What Killed Capitalism*, London: Vintage.

Vishmidt, Marina 2008, 'Situation Wanted: Something About Labour', *Afterall*, Vol. 19: 21–34.

Vishmidt, Marina 2018a, *Speculation as a Mode of Production: Forms of Value Subjectivity in Art and Capital*, Leiden: Brill.

Vishmidt, Marina 2018b, 'Anomaly and Autonomy: On the Currency of the Exception in the Value Relations of Contemporary Art', *Zeitschrift für Kunstgeschichte*, Vol. 81:4.

Vishmidt, Marina 2020, 'Bodies in Space: On the Ends of Vulnerability', Radical Philosophy, Vol. 2.08: 33–46.

Vishmidt, Marina and Zoe Sutherland 2022, '(Un)making Value: Reading Social Reproduction through the Question of Totality', *Totality Inside Out: Rethinking Crisis and Conflict Under Capital*, edited by Kevin Floyd, Jen Hedler Phillis, and Sarika Chandra, New York: Fordham University Press.

Vroey, Michel de 1981, 'Value, Production, and Exchange', *The Value Controversy*, London: Verso.

Warren, Alli 2013, *Here Come the Warm Jets*, San Francisco, CA: City Lights.

Warren, Alli 2017, *I Love It Though*, New York: Nightboat Books.

Warren, Alli 2020a, *Little Hill*, San Francisco, CA: City Lights.

Warren, Alli 2020b. 'Alli Warren Translates Five Books into Poems: From W.E.B. DuBois to Bernadette Meyer'. *Literary Hub*, 30 March: https://lithub.com/alli-warren-translates-five-books-into-poems/.

Warren, Calvin L. 2017, 'Black Mysticism: Fred Moten's Phenomenology of (Black) Spirit', *Zeitschrift für Anglistik und Amerikanistik*, Vol, 65:2: 219–29.

White, Glenda 2021, 'A discussion about Fred Moten and C.B. Bush', Soul to Soul: Universal Ideas for a Brighter Tomorrow podcast, 27 May: https://open.spotify.com/episode/6yB2v7a7gOcGXakKTkVzZn.

Wilderson III, Frank B., 2020, *Afropessimism*, New York: Liveright.

Wilson Gilmore, Ruth 2007, *Golden Gulag: Prisons, Surplus, Crisis, and Opposition in Globalizing* California, Berkeley: University of California Press.

Wood, Ellen Meiksins 1988, 'Capitalism and Human Emancipation', *New Left Review*, Issue 167 (Jan/Feb).

Woodmansee, Martha 1994, *The Author, Art, and the Market: Rereading the History of Aesthetics*, New York: Columbia University Press.

Yountae, An and Eleanor Craig (eds.) 2021, *Beyond Man: Race, Coloniality, and Philosophy of Religion*, Durham, NC: Duke University Press.

Zaharijević, Adriana 2021, 'On Butler's Theory of Agency', *Bodies That Still Matter: Resonances of the Work of Judith Butler*, edited by Annemie Halsema, Katja Kwastek, and Roel van den Oever, Amsterdam: Amsterdam University Press.

Žižek, Slavoj 1997, *The Plague of Fantasies*, London: Verso.

Žižek, Slavoj 2012 [2002], *Welcome to the Desert of the Real*, London: Verso.

General Index

www.ingramcontent.com/pod-product-compliance
Lightning Source LLC
LaVergne TN
LVHW012335130926
847902LV00028B/400
9798888908969